GATEWAY TO
SIBERIAN RESOURCES

(The BAM)

SCRIPTA SERIES IN GEOGRAPHY

Theodore Shabad • Consulting Editor

Shabad and Mote • Gateway to Siberian Resources, 1977

GATEWAY TO SIBERIAN RESOURCES

(The BAM)

THEODORE SHABAD
Columbia University

and

VICTOR L. MOTE
University of Houston

1977

Scripta Publishing Co
a division of Scripta Technica, Inc.
Washington, D.C.

A Halsted Press Book

JOHN WILEY & SONS

New York   Toronto   London   Sydney

Publishers, Scripta Publishing Co
a division of Scripta Technica, Inc.
1511 K Street, N.W., Washington, D.C. 20005

Distributed solely by Halsted Press Division,
John Wiley & Sons, Inc., New York

Library of Congress Cataloging in Publication Data:

Shabad, Theodore.
    Gateway to Siberian resources (The BAM)

    (Scripta series in geography)
    "A Halsted Press book."
    Includes bibliographies and index.
    1. Baykal-Amur Railroad. 2. Siberia, Eastern—Economic conditions.
3. Natural resources—Siberia, Eastern. I. Mote, V.L., joint author.
II. Title. III. Series.
HE3140.B34S52   385'.0957'5   77-63
ISBN 0-470-99040-6

Composition by Marie A. Maddalena, Scripta Technica, Inc.

CONTENTS

PREFACE

In 1974, the Soviet Union announced the start of construction of the Baykal-Amur Mainline, a 2,000-mile railroad serving the southeast quadrant of Siberia that will take nearly a decade to complete; it represents one of the great rail construction projects of the 20th century.

When placed in full operation about 1983, the Baykal-Amur Mainline (BAM) may have a significant impact not only on the further domestic development of the Soviet economy, but also on the Soviet Union's economic relations with the rest of the world. The region between Lake Baykal and the lower Amur River that will be opened up by the railroad has lagged in development because of the huge overland distance separating it from the populated and industrially developed European portion of the USSR. The potential resources of the BAM zone have long been viewed as complementary with the raw-material needs of countries in the Pacific basin, particularly Japan and the United States. But lack of transport access to resources has limited the role played by Soviet regions facing the Pacific Ocean. The BAM is expected to rectify the situation by providing a direct outlet for Siberian resources through Pacific ports.

In addition to its resource-export role, the Baykal-Amur Mainline is also expected to strengthen the Soviet Union's east-west transport system by providing an alternative route across the eastern portion of Siberia to the north of the Trans-Siberian Railroad. The availability of such a second rail link is likely to foster container transit shipments between Japan and Western Europe and to facilitate foreign trade connections between more westerly portions of Siberia and the Pacific basin. Such prospective trade links may include Soviet exports of crude oil from West Siberia over a combined pipeline and rail route to the Pacific, and Soviet imports of bauxite and alumina through Pacific ports for the growing Siberian aluminum industry. The BAM is also viewed by some as having strategic importance because of the hostility between the Soviet Union and China.

In magnitude of required investment and implications for regional development, the BAM clearly ranks among the leading economic development programs conducted by the Soviet planners in Siberia. These include the coal and steel oriented Urals-Kuznetsk Combine of the 1930's; the hydroelectric development of the Angara-Yenisey basin beginning in the 1950's, and the oil and gas development of West Siberia since the mid-1960's. Already visible in rough outline is the next major regional program, focused on the lignite-based thermal power development in the Kansk-Achinsk Basin of southern Siberia, which is expected to unfold in the 1980's while the full impact of the BAM project will be felt farther east.

The present volume describes and analyzes the long-term significance of the BAM against the background of Siberian resource development in general. An opening chapter, by this author, examines the sequence of Soviet economic development of Siberia with emphasis on resource-oriented industries and on the major regional development programs that have been the focus of Soviet investment in Siberia over the years. Siberia is treated here in its broadest sense as encompassing the vast northern third of Asia, between the Ural Mountains and the Pacific, and including three of the Soviet Union's official major economic regions—West Siberia, East Siberia and the Soviet Far East. For convenience, particularly in the discussion of the BAM, the eastern portion of Siberia, oriented toward the Pacific basin, is sometimes designated as Pacific Siberia. The basic chapter on the BAM, by Victor L. Mote, focuses on the physical geography of the BAM zone, the history of the project, its route and resource potential, and its likely impact on regional development and the Soviet Union's foreign trade position as well as human and environmental problems associated with the rail project. The book concludes with brief chapters by five Soviet authors that examine the BAM project from specific Soviet perspectives. Viktor V. Biryukov of the Gosplan of the USSR discusses the project from the point of view of the transport planner; N. P. Belen'kiy and V. S. Maslennikov of the State Institute of Technical-Economic Surveys and Design of Rail Transportation approach it as railroad survey and design engineers; Pavel G. Bunich of Khabarovsk as an economist; Oleg A. Kibal'chich of the Central Economic Research Institute of the Gosplan of the RSFSR as an economic geographer, and Viktor B. Sochava of the Irkutsk Institute of Geography as a physical geographer concerned with applied environmental problems. The Soviet contributions, originally published in *Soviet Geography*, have been revised and updated for this volume.

Theodore Shabad
December, 1976

Chapter 1

SIBERIAN RESOURCE DEVELOPMENT
IN THE SOVIET PERIOD

Theodore Shabad

The strategy of Siberian development has passed through several stages during the Soviet period depending on the needs of the national economy, labor policies and the changing setting of international relations.

During the Stalin period, beginning with the program of forced industrialization under the five-year plans and continuing until the mid-1950's, the basic Soviet aim was to foster an integrated development of Siberia. This strategy was based both on the then current desire to achieve a more uniform distribution of productive forces in the Soviet Union through the development of local resource-based industries and on strategic considerations calling for the construction of backup plants in key industries that would duplicate the output of establishments in the European part of the Soviet Union, but in safer interior locations far from the exposed western frontiers. This early eastward movement was fostered to a large extent by the availability of a vast forced labor pool, estimated in millions, that could be used in industrial development projects under harsh environmental conditions and could be easily maneuvered from place to place according to need.

A new phase in Siberian development began after Stalin's death in 1953 as the large-scale use of forced labor ended and the shortage of free labor in Siberia became a serious constraint on further integrated development. In addition, the depletion of fuel and energy reserves in the economically developed western regions of the country focused attention on the vast fuel and energy potential of Siberia. This resource pattern led increasingly to a geographical division of labor, in which manufacturing activities with large labor requirements were located in the European portion of the Soviet Union, where population and markets were concentrated, while power-intensive industries with large fuel and energy requirements began to be located to a greater extent in Siberia.

Within this overall pattern, Siberian industrialization has been dominated over the years by a sequence of major regional development programs that focused the

1

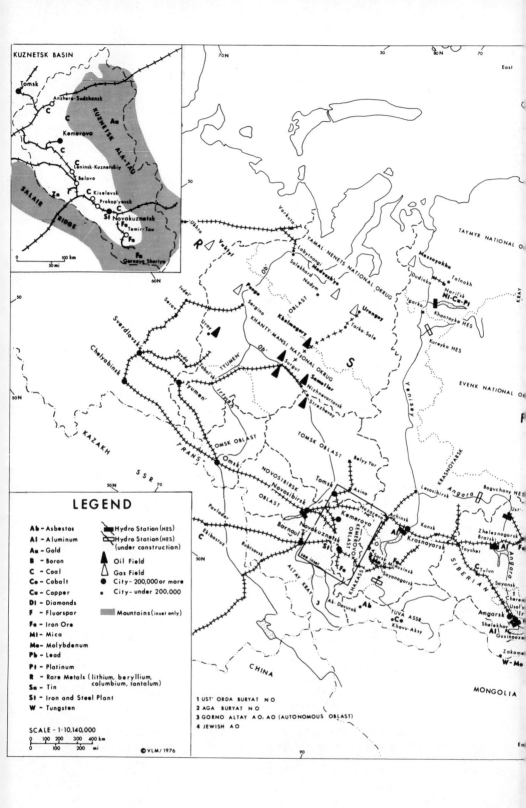

KUZNETSK BASIN

Tomsk
C
Anzhero-Sudzhensk
C
KUZNETSK ALA-TAU
Au
Kemerovo
C
Leninsk-Kuznetskiy
C
Belovo
Zn
C Kiselevsk
SALAIR RIDGE
Prokop'yevsk
St Novokuznetsk
Fe Temir-Tau
Fe
Fe Gornaya Shoriya

0   100 km
0   50 mi

LEGEND

Ab – Asbestos
Al – Aluminum
Au – Gold
B – Boron
C – Coal
Co – Cobalt
Cu – Copper
Di – Diamonds
F – Fluorspar
Fe – Iron Ore
Mi – Mica
Mo – Molybdenum
Pb – Lead
Pt – Platinum
R – Rare Metals (lithium, beryllium, columbium, tantalum)
Sn – Tin
St – Iron and Steel Plant
W – Tungsten

SCALE – 1:10,140,000

0   100 200 300 400 km
0   100   200 mi

© VLM/1976

Hydro Station (HES)
Hydro Station (HES) (under construction)
Oil Field
Gas Field
City – 200,000 or more
City – under 200,000

Mountains (inset only)

1 UST' ORDA BURYAT N O
2 AGA BURYAT N O
3 GORNO ALTAY A O; A O (AUTONOMOUS OBLAST)
4 JEWISH A O

TAYMYR NATIONAL O

Messoyakha
Dudinka   Talnakh
Igarka   Noril'sk Ni-Cu-Pt
Khantayka HES
Kureyka HES

EVENK NATIONAL O

KRAY

Vorkuta
Ukhta
Vektsy'
Ob'
YAMAL-NENETS NATIONAL OKRUG
Labytnangi Nadvoitskiy
Salekhard
Nadym
Tarko-Sale
Urengoy

R

Ivdel'
Serov
OBLAST
Sergino
Kholmogory
Uray
Ob'
KHANTY-MANSI NATIONAL OKRUG
Samotlor
Surgut
Nizhnevartovsk
Strezhevoy

S

Sverdlovsk
Chelyabinsk
Tavda
Tobol'sk
TYUMEN'
Irtysh
Tyumen'

KAZAKH
SSR
50N   70

TRANS-

OMSK OBLAST
Omsk

Balyy Yar

TOMSK OBLAST

KRASNOYARSK

Lesosibirsk   Angara   Boguchany HES
Ust'

NOVOSIBIRSK
Novosibirsk
OBLAST
Tomsk
Asino
Nazarovo Achinsk
Kansk
Tayshet
Zheleznogorsk
Bratsk

Pavlodar
Ekibastuz
Rubtsovsk
Barnaul
Novokuznetsk
Kemerovo
KEMEROVO OBLAST
St
Fe
Krasnoyarsk
Al
Tulun
C
SIBERIAN
Angara

ALTAY KRAY
Lee inset
KHAKASS

Sayanogorsk
Sorsk Mo
Minusinsk
Ust'-Kam
Cheremkhovo
Usol'ye
Angarsk
Shelekhov
Al
Gusinoozersk

3
Ak-Dovurak   Ab
TUVA ASSR
Co
Khovu-Aksy

Sayansk

Zakamensk
W-Mo

CHINA

MONGOLIA

70N   50   80N   70   East

60N

50

50N

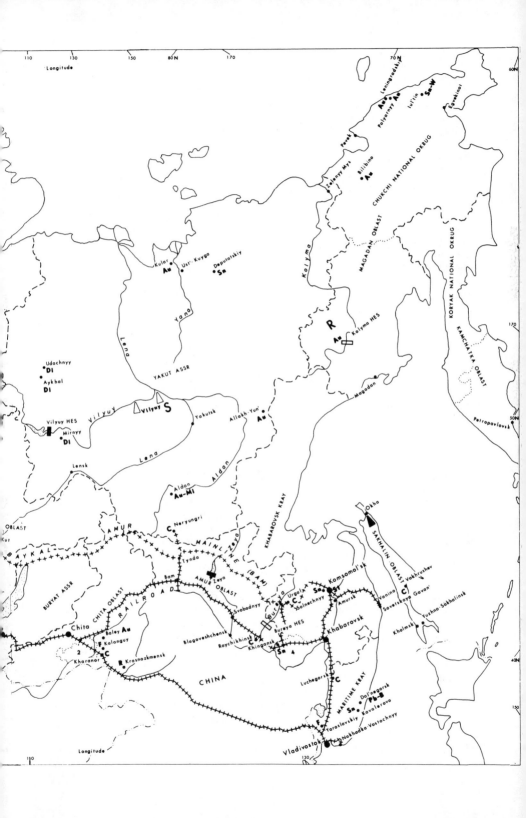

investment effort on particular portions of Siberia. *The first* such program was the Urals-Kuznetsk Combine, which combined Urals iron ore and Kuznetsk Basin coking coal in a 1,400-mile-long rail shuttle operation aimed at building up an iron and steel industry in the Urals and in West Siberia. This early effort, which involved mainly primary industries, was supplemented during World War II by an influx of manufacturing, especially metal-fabricating and machinery industries, as war-threatened plants were evacuated from exposed western regions of the Soviet Union. *The second* regional program, beginning in the early 1950's, was the development of East Siberia's vast hydroelectric potential on the Angara and Yenisey rivers, attracting power-intensive industries such as aluminum. *The third* development program, which started in the mid-1960's, was the use of the newly discovered oil and gas reserves of West Siberia, both for pipeline transmission to the fuel-short manufacturing centers of the western Soviet Union and to export markets and for building up a Siberian petrochemical industry. Finally, beginning in the mid-1970's, the Siberian development effort involved *two additional* programs: one, the use of the large lignite reserves of East Siberia's Kansk-Achinsk Basin in strip-mining operations that will feed a huge minehead power-generating complex for extra-high-voltage electricity transmission westward and, two, the Baykal-Amur Mainline project, designed in part as a transport access route that will help open up new resource areas in East Siberia and the Soviet Far East, mainly for export through the Soviet Union's Pacific ports.

The changing investment priorities in Siberian development can be discussed in terms of three distinctive periods: (1) the prewar eastward movement focused on the Urals-Kuznetsk Combine and accelerated by the eastward evacuation of manufacturing plants during World War II; (2) a downward trend in Siberian development during the early postwar period, until the mid-1950's; and (3) the new resource-based focus, shifting successively from East Siberian hydroelectric development to the oil and gas program of West Siberia, the Kansk-Achinsk lignite and power development, and to the Baykal-Amur Mainline project in the Far East.

The Eastward Movement

At the start of the industrialization drive under the first five-year plan (1928–32), the Siberian economy was still largely agrarian, with agriculture contributing about three-fourths and industry about one-fourth to the combined product of these two economic sectors. In the USSR as a whole, agriculture and industry each represented about one-half of the total product. There was relatively little modern factory industry in Siberia, and small craft industries accounted for slightly more than one-half of the total industrial production compared with one-fourth in the USSR as a whole. The share of Siberian production in Soviet industrial output was virtually unchanged from the prerevolutionary period, at 1.5 percent, although the structure of industry during the Soviet period had already begun to shift in favor of greater stress on coal mining, metal fabrication and forest-product activities. However, little investment had been allocated to the Siberian economy in the decade since the Bolshevik Revolution as most of the attention focused on rebuilding the more highly developed infrastructure and production capacity of the European regions. Still, even in that early pre-five-year plan period, 14.7 percent of the limited government investment then being allocated to the economy was channeled into Siberia, an investment share that was to remain close to the average investment allocation to Siberia throughout the Soviet period (Table 1).

4

TABLE 1

Investment of Government and Cooperative Enterprises in Siberia
(in percent of USSR total)

	1918–28	1928–32 (1st FYP)	1933–37 (2d FYP)	1938–41 (3d FYP)	1941–45 (WW II)	1946–50 (4th FYP)	1951–55* (5th FYP)
West Siberia	3.9	4.4	4.0	3.7	6.1	4.4	5.7
East Siberia	4.5	4.2	3.5	3.8	4.1	4.1	4.7
Far East	6.3	4.8	5.8	7.6	7.8	4.5	4.8
Total	14.7	13.4	13.3	15.1	18.0	13.0	15.2

Source: Narodnoye khozyaystvo SSSR v 1961 godu [The Economy of the USSR in 1961], statistical yearbook. Moscow, 1962, pp. 548–549 (investments for the period from 1918 to 1955).

	1951–55*	1956–60	1961–65	1966–70
West Siberia	6.1	6.6	6.4	6.5
East Siberia	4.5	5.2	5.5	5.1
Far East	5.1	4.4	4.4	4.7
Total	15.7	16.2	16.3	16.3

Note: *The first series is in 1955 prices, and the second in 1969 prices, accounting for the different percentages for 1951–55.

Sources: Narodnoye khozyaystvo SSSR v 1970 godu [The Economy of the USSR in 1970], statistical yearbook. Moscow, 1971, p. 478.
Narodnoye khozyastvo RSFSR v 1970 godu [The Economy of the RSFSR in 1970], statistical yearbook. Moscow, 1971, p. 320.

TABLE 2

Pig Iron, Steel and Iron-Ore Production of Siberia
(in million metric tons)

	1928	1932	1937	1940	1945	1950	1955	1960	1965	1970	1975
Pig Iron											
Kuznetsk	—	0.25	1.47	1.54	1.57	1.91	2.40	3.3	3.5	4	4.5
West-Sib	—	—	—	—	—	—	—	—	1.3	3	4.5
Total	—	0.25	1.47	1.54	1.57	1.91	2.40	3.3	4.8	7.3	9
% of USSR	—	7.6	10.1	10.3	17.8	10.0	7.2	7.1	7.3	8.5	9
Crude Steel											
Kuznetsk*	—	0.05	1.61	1.87	2.41	3.01	3.86	4.6	5.1	5.5	5.5
West-Sib	—	—	—	—	—	—	—	—	—	2.4	5.5
East Siberia	—	—	0.02	0.06	0.11	0.24	0.37	0.5	0.7	0.7	0.8
Komsomol'sk	—	—	—	—	0.06	0.17	0.25	0.4	0.8	0.8	1.1
Total	—	0.05	1.63	1.93	2.58	3.42	4.48	5.5	6.7	9.4	13
% of USSR	—	0.9	9.2	10.6	21.1	12.5	9.9	8.4	7.4	8.1	9
Iron Ore											
Kuznetsk	—	0.05	0.51	0.49	0.82	2.19	3.62	4.3	5.3	4.5	4.5
Teya	—	—	—	—	—	—	—	—	—	1.4	2
Abaza	—	—	—	—	—	—	—	1.7	2.1	2	2
Krasnokamensk	—	—	—	—	—	—	—	—	—	—	0.5
Zheleznogorsk	—	—	—	—	—	—	—	—	0.8	5.0	6.2
Total	—	0.05	0.51	0.49	0.82	2.19	3.62	6.0	8.2	12.8	15
% of USSR	—	0.5	1.8	1.6	5.2	5.5	5.0	5.7	5.3	6.5	6.4

*Includes steel production of Novosibirsk steel plant, which was founded in 1942 and produces about 1 million tons a year.

Siberia's agriculture, which had recovered rapidly from the devastation of the civil war that followed the Bolshevik Revolution, made a more significant contribution than industry to the Soviet economy during that period, accounting for 5 to 6 percent of the nation's agricultural production. In 1928, Siberia contributed 13 percent of all the marketed grain, of which three-fourths was shipped to other parts of the country; nearly half of the government's butter procurements and over one-fourth of the meat. Roughly three-fourths of the Soviet Union's butter exports originated in West Siberia, traditionally the principal butter-producing region.

When the Soviet industrialization drive began in 1928 with the first five-year plan, the early tendency of giving priority in investment to the developed European regions continued to be evident at first. Existing industrial capacity in the western regions together with a reservoir of skilled labor and research and development facilities assured a more rapid return on investment than in Siberia where infrastructure was still lacking, the transport net was undeveloped, labor was short and the mineral and raw-material potential was still largely unexplored. The share of Siberian investment in the first and second five-year plans (1928–32 and 1933–37) thus declined below the 14.7-percent level of the pre-five-year-plan period, averaging 13.3 to 13.4 percent.

The biggest single investment effort focused on the Urals-Kuznetsk Combine, which, in the simplest terms, involved the development of two new integrated iron and steel centers at Magnitogorsk, in the Urals, and Stalinsk (after 1961, Novokuznetsk), in the Kuznetsk Basin, based on Urals iron ore and Kuznetsk coking coal. The Siberian portion of the Urals-Kuznetsk project, involving basically the construction of the Stalinsk iron and steel plant and the expansion of coal production in the Kuznetsk Basin, absorbed 44 percent of all industrial investment in West Siberia during the first five-year plan, and 25 percent during the second plan period. The iron and steel plant went into operation in 1932, and by the end of the decade its four blast furnaces were producing 1.5 million tons of pig iron, or 10.3 percent of the national total (Table 2). The Stalinsk plant and its Urals counterpart at Magnitogorsk, with the same capacity, were then the Soviet Union's leading iron and steel producers.

The Kuznetsk Basin had been expanding at a rapid rate even before the start of the first five-year plan, having more than doubled its coal output from the previous high point of 1.26 million tons in 1917, during World War I, to 2.6 million at the start of the planning period in 1928. Because of large reserves, thick seams and high grades of coal, the Kuzbas was viewed over the long term as the Soviet Union's second most important coal district (after the Donets Basin of the Ukraine). Kuznetsk coal production rose by two and a half times both in the first and in the second five-year plan, and reached 22.5 million tons in 1940 (Table 3). In view of the needs of the iron and steel industry, greater attention was given to the mining of coking coals, and their share in the basin's output rose from 10 percent in 1928 to 26 percent in 1940. Both coking coals and steam coals had a wide market, extending across the Urals into the Volga valley, with the Urals alone consuming about one-fifth or more of Kuzbas output.

Although the original design of the Urals-Kuznetsk Combine envisaged the shipment of Urals iron ore from Magnitogorsk to the iron and steel plant in the Kuznetsk Basin. Siberian ores soon provided a substantial portion of the

7

TABLE 3

Coal Production in Siberia
(in million metric tons)

	1928	1932	1937	1940	1945	1950	1955	1960	1965	1970	1975
West Siberia (Kuzbas)	2.6	7.3	17.8	22.5	30.0	38.5	58.5	84.0	97.1	113	137
East Siberia	1.0	2.5	5.8	9.2	9.2	17.5	26.6	36.9	46.8	54.9	
Krasnoyarsk Kray	0.1	0.3	1	1.7	2.5	5.3	8.8	14.5	21.7	27	
Kansk-Achinsk	—	—	—	0.4	0.6	1.7	4.3	8.5	13.9	19	28
Chernogorsk	0.1	0.3	1	1.0	1.4	2.1	2.4	3.7	4.7	5.2	
Noril'sk	—	—	—	0.4	0.8	1.6	2.1	2.5	3.1	3	
Irkutsk Obl.	0.6	1.5	4	5.1	4.5	8.5	13.4	16.6	19.4	21.9	24
Cheremkhovo	0.6	1.5	4	5.0	4.2	8.0	12.9	15	17	16	14
Azey	—	—	—	—	—	—	—	1	2	6	10
Buryat ASSR	—	—	—	0.04	0.19	0.58	0.64	1.1	1.1	1.4	1.5
Gusinoozersk	—	—	—	0.04	0.15	0.52	0.55	1.0	1.0	1.3	1.4
Chita Oblast	0.3	0.6	1	2.2	1.8	2.8	3.1	3.4	4.1	4	7.5
Chita	0.3	0.6	1	1.1	1.0	1.5	1.7	1.7	1.7	1.2	1.2
Bukachacha	—	—	—	0.8	0.5	0.9	1.0	1.0	1.0	0.8	0.8
Kharanor	—	—	—	—	—	—	—	0.4	1.0	2	5.5
Tuva ASSR	—	—	—	—	—	—	0.04	0.11	0.28	0.52	0.6
Far East	1.1	2.2	4.8	7.2	7.9	13.1	17.3	21.8	28.3	31	
Raychikhinsk	—	—	1.4	2.4	2.7	4.4	6.5	8.7	12.3	12.3	13.5
Urgal	—	—	—	—	—	0.15	0.49	0.91	1.2	1.5	
Maritime Kray	1.1	1.9	3.0	3.7	3.6	5.0	5.5	6.4	7.2	9	
Sakhalin	0.01	0.28	0.32	0.5	0.6	2.3	3.7	4.6	4.6	4.7	
Magadan Obl.	—	—	—	0.1	0.6	0.9	1.0	1.1	1.5	1.9	
Yakut ASSR	—	—	0.05	0.14	0.32	0.28	0.58	0.92	1.5	1.6	
Neryungri	—	—	—	—	—	—	0.04	0.11	0.2	0.3	
Total Siberia	4.7	12.0	28.5	38.9	47.1	69.2	102.4	142.8	172.2	199.4	
% of USSR	13.2	18.6	22.3	23.4	31.5	26.5	26.3	28.0	29.8	31.9	

blast-furnace mix as iron deposits were developed in the Shor uplands, south of the basin. Local iron-ore output rose from 55,000 tons in 1932 to about 500,000 tons by the end of the decade, providing about 19 percent of the ore requirements of the Stalinsk plant, the rest being hauled over the 1,400-mile rail shuttle from Magnitogorsk (Table 2).

A major component of the Urals-Kuznetsk Combine was the coke-based chemical industry of the Kuznetsk Basin. Aside from coke production associated with the Stalinsk iron and steel plant, the first five-year plan called for expansion of a separate coke-chemical plant that had gone into operation at Kemerovo in 1924. The expansion gave rise to what was in effect a new coke-chemical complex, which went on stream in 1934, early in the second five-year plan period. It provided the basis for the manufacture of nitrogenous fertilizers, aniline dyes and other coal-tar derivatives. The nitrogenous fertilizer plant (opened in 1938) produced 223,000 tons of fertilizer (mostly ammonium sulfate) by 1940, or 6.9 percent of Soviet fertilizer output.

Sulfuric acid for the fertilizer was derived from byproduct gases of a zinc smelter inaugurated at Belovo in the Kuznetsk Basin in 1931. The zinc plant, using distillation retorts rather than the electrolytic method, was supplied with zinc concentrate from a nearby mine at Salair and used local coke as a reducing agent. It was then one of four zinc smelters in the USSR, and by 1937 yielded 18,000 tons of zinc, or 21 percent of national output. Byproduct sulfuric acid amounted to 18,300 tons in 1940, or a little more than one percent of the Soviet total. West Siberia also contributed a small portion of the Soviet Union's alkali production, with soda ash (sodium carbonate) being recovered from the soda lakes of the Kulunda Steppe in Altay Kray. The output level in 1940 was 13,000 tons, or 2.6 percent of Soviet production of soda ash.

Outside of the Urals-Kuznetsk Combine, early Siberian resource development was limited to the mining of gold and rare metals (tin, tungsten, molybdenum) as well as some nonmetals like mica and fluorspar that were not found in significant amounts in the western regions of the USSR. These mining activities were concentrated in Transbaykalia and the Far East. Early gold-mining centers included Darasun and Baley in Transbaykalia, where lode deposits were being worked, and the Aldan placer mines of southern Yakutia, which were reached by a motor road from the Trans-Siberian Railroad in 1931.

Early tin-mining operations were limited to Transbaykalia, which in 1936 contributed 95 percent of all the Soviet Union's tin concentrate. The mines were in the areas of Sherlovaya Gora and Khapcheranga. Transbaykalia also yielded 80 percent of the nation's tungsten and 70 percent of the molybdenum at that time. The Kalanguy mine provided almost all the fluorspar, with an output level of 42,000 tons in 1936, and Slyudyanka, at the southwest end of Lake Baykal had a virtual monopoly on mica production, yielding phlogopite, or magnesium mica, one of the two commercial varieties (the other is muscovite, or potassium mica).

Although the Urals-Kuznetsk Combine in West Siberia represented the largest single investment program in Siberia before World War II, the largest share of regional investment was channeled into the Far East (Table 1). This regional priority was dictated by a desire to speed the settlement of the Pacific coastal areas of the Soviet Union, to develop needed mineral resources, particularly gold, and to provide

TABLE 4

Cement Production in Siberia
(in thousand metric tons)

	1928	1932	1937	1940	1945	1950	1955	1960	1965	1970	1974
West Siberia	27	131	242	263	147	567	1194	2432	3748	5425	6388
Novosibirsk	–	–	120	138		192	493	971	2075	2276	2550
Kemerovo	27	131	122	125		375	701	1461	1673	3149	3838
East Siberia	–	–	–	–	7	250	647	2088	2808	4101	4568
Krasnoyarsk	–	–	–	–	7	250	390	906	1519	2563	2885
Irkutsk	–	–	–	–	–	–	–	715	763	941	1046
Buryat	–	–	–	–	–	–	257	467	526	597	637
Far East	18	36	164	234	101	480	668	1569	1827	2118	2527
Maritime	18	36	164	234	101	436	486	905	1156	1388	1422
Khabarovsk	–	–	–	–	–	44	135	600	595	645	800
Sakhalin	–	–	–	–	–	–	47	64	76	85	93
Yakut	–	–	–	–	–	–	–	–	–	–	212
Total Siberia	45	167	406	497	255	1297	2509	6089	8383	11644	13483
% of USSR	2.4	4.8	7.4	8.8	13.8	12.7	11.2	13.4	11.6	12.2	11.7

the Far East with an integrated economy that would eliminate costly hauls of essential commodities all the way from the western regions of the USSR across Siberia. Early investment was directed into the oilfields of northern Sakhalin, which by 1940 yielded half a million tons of crude oil, or 1.6 percent of total Soviet production. A refinery opened at Khabarovsk in 1935. Much of the Far Eastern investment went into the construction of the new heavy-industry center of Komsomol'sk on the lower Amur River. The city, carved out of the tayga in 1932, was selected as the site for an integrated iron and steel plant, to be based on coking coal from the Urgal mine in the Bureya basin and iron ore from the Kimkan site, to the south on the Trans-Siberian. Subsequently it developed that neither the coal nor the ore was suitable for use in an iron and steel plant, and the project was reduced to a small steel plant using long-haul pig iron and scrap. The plant went into operation in 1942, during the war, and after slow expansion reached a crude steel output of 1.1 million tons in 1975. It meets only about one-fourth of the Far East's steel needs. Komsomol'sk also acquired a small oil refinery in 1942, supplied with crude oil from Sakhalin by a pipeline across the Tatar Strait. As in the case of steel, regional oil production also meets only a portion of needs. In the mid-1970's, when Sakhalin was producing oil at the rate of 2.5 million tons a year, Far Eastern consumption was about 10 million, and the balance had to be hauled by rail from the West Siberian fields.

Investment in the Soviet Far East intensified during the third five-year plan on the eve of World War II as Moscow perceived a growing military threat from Japan and took steps to strengthen the defense potential of the region. At the same time, an apparent increase in the supply of forced labor resulting from the purges of 1936–38 led to a spurt in the development of an important new gold-mining district in the upper Kolyma valley north of the new port city of Magadan. In the three and a half years from 1938 to mid-1941, when the German invasion of the Soviet Union interrupted the third five-year plan, the share of investment in the Far East (7.6 percent of the national total) was roughly equal to the investment in West and East Siberia combined (Table 1). The investment effort became evident both in the Far East's share of capital stock (plants and equipment) added to the economy and in the rate of growth of industry. In 1940, the Far East accounted for almost one-tenth (9.5 percent) of capital stock additions compared with 8.8 percent for the rest of Siberia. Industrial output in 1940 was double the 1937 level in the Far East, 30 percent higher in East Siberia and 50 percent higher in West Siberia. The output rise was particularly marked in the Magadan-Kolyma region, where it increased almost fivefold during this period. The Kolyma district had succeeded the Aldan district in gold production in 1934, and output soared particularly after the completion of a 350-mile truck road from Magadan to the goldfields, reaching a peak in 1940. During the war and in the early postwar period, gold production in the Kolyma district declined as the richest surface placers were depleted and the gold tenor dropped. Gold output reached a low point in 1956 (55 percent of the 1940 level), and then began to rise again as floating dredges began to replace the small-scale hand methods of the forced laborers of the Stalin era.

Industrial development of Siberia during the prewar period focused mainly on primary, resource-oriented industries, as exemplified by the coal and steel of the Urals-Kuznetsk Combine and mineral resources not found elsewhere in the Soviet Union. Although a number of defense-oriented industries like aircraft and shipbuilding were fostered in the Far East, metal-fabrication and machinery manufacture played a relatively small role in early Siberian industrialization. In

11

TABLE 5

Roundwood Production in Siberia
(in million cubic meters)

	1940	1945	1950	1955	1960	1965	1970	1974
West Siberia	8.6	5.4	11.4	17.2	17.0	20.8	22.8	25.5
Altay	2.2	0.9	1.3	2.3	2.3	2.5	2.0	2.3
Kemerovo	2.0	2.0	3.2	3.7	2.8	3.4	3.0	2.9
Novosibirsk	1.0	0.5	0.9	1.3	1.1	1.4	0.9	1.0
Omsk	0.5	0.3	0.9	1.2	1.3	1.3	1.2	1.3
Tomsk	1.9	1.0	2.6	4.8	5.1	6.3	6.6	6.8
Tyumen'	1.0	0.8	2.5	4.0	4.3	5.9	9.1	11.2
Khanty-Mansi	0.2	0.2	0.5	1.0	1.4	3.8	7.1	9.3
East Siberia	9.9	3.6	16.3	24.4	35.5	44.5	52.1	55.9
Krasnoyarsk	4.2	1.8	6.5	9.0	13.3	17.2	20.8	20.7
Irkutsk	2.8	1.0	5.9	9.9	15.4	19.8	23.4	27.1
Chita	1.5	0.4	1.2	1.9	2.4	2.9	3.4	3.3
Buryat	1.4	0.4	2.6	3.3	4.0	4.3	4.2	4.4
Tuva	–	0.02	0.06	0.25	0.34	0.31	0.3	0.4
Far East	8.2	2.9	9.2	11.9	14.8	16.7	22.8	25.3
Maritime	1.8	0.6	1.6	2.0	2.7	3.4	4.6	4.7
Khabarovsk	3.1	0.9	2.8	3.6	5.3	5.9	9.9	12.4
Amur	1.1	0.4	1.3	1.8	2.2	2.6	2.8	2.9
Kamchatka	0.3	0.1	0.2	0.4	0.4	0.4	0.6	0.5
Magadan	1.3	0.5	0.6	0.3	0.3	0.3	0.4	0.3
Sakhalin	0.2	0.1	2.0	2.8	2.2	3.1	3.1	3.3
Yakut	0.4	0.3	0.8	1.0	1.7	1.1	1.4	1.2
Total Siberia	26.7	11.9	36.9	53.5	67.3	82.0	97.7	106.7
% of USSR	22.6	19.3	22.9	25.2	25.7	30.0	32.7	35.1

1937, for example, this sector of the economy accounted for only 17 percent of the total value of industrial production compared with 30 percent in the Soviet Union as a whole. A key indicator of metal fabrication is the manufacture of machine tools, and in this category the Siberian contribution was 2.4 percent of national output in 1940. Early machine-manufacturing centers were the large cities situated at the points where the Trans-Siberian Railroad crossed Siberia's great northward flowing rivers: Omsk, on the Irtysh River, with a specialization in agricultural equipment for the surrounding farm belt; Novosibirsk on the Ob'; Krasnoyarsk on the Yenisey; Irkutsk on the Angara; Khabarovsk and the new city of Komsomol'sk on the Amur River.

An indicator of construction activity is the production of cement, which rose rapidly during the prewar period as Siberian industrial development proceeded (Table 4). In West Siberia, a new cement plant (the Chernorechenskiy plant) was inaugurated in 1934 at Iskitim, south of Novosibirsk, supplementing the older Yashkino plant in the Kuznetsk Basin. In the Far East, the Spassk plant was expanded. As a result, cement production in Siberia rose elevenfold during the prewar five-year plans, reaching nearly 500,000 tons in 1940, or 8.8 percent of Soviet production.

The forest products industry, a traditional activity in Siberia, also expanded during the prewar period to supply building timber to industrial projects, ship wood to the Central Asian republics and Kazakhstan over the newly built Turkestan-Siberia Railroad, and export timber through the northern Siberian port of Igarka, on the lower Yenisey. The share of sawtimber in total wood production increased because of the growing needs of the construction industry, but firewood still represented one-half of the total wood production in 1940. In that year Siberia contributed 26.7 million cubic meters of sawtimber, or 22.6 percent of the Soviet total (Table 5). Most logging activities were restricted to the immediate vicinity of the Trans-Siberian mainline; more northerly forests still lacked access railroads. There was little processing of forest products; most of the timber was shipped in the form of roundwood or was subjected to primary processing, yielding sawnwood for the construction industry, pitprops for mines, and railroad ties.

The eastward movement that had been initiated during the prewar five-year plans was accelerated during World War II, and assumed a new aspect as the original resource-oriented industries were supplemented by an onrush of manufacturing plants evacuated from centers in European USSR that were threatened by the German advance. West Siberia was the principal beneficiary of this evacuation program, being situated nearest to the war zone. Out of 1,523 manufacturing plants that were dismantled in the western regions in the second half of 1941, 244 were moved to West Siberia and 78 to East Siberia, with apparently no plant evacuation to the Far East. Most of the dismantled plants were shipped to the Urals, the Volga valley, Kazakhstan and Central Asia. The emphasis on West Siberia during the wartime emergency was also evident in the allocation of new investment. Mean annual investment in West Siberia rose by more than 20 percent during the war years compared with the immediate prewar period, while declining by 20 in East Siberia and by 10 percent in the Far East.

The principal destinations of evacuated manufacturing plants were Novosibirsk and Omsk, which became virtual boomtowns during the war (Table 6). The population of Novosibirsk grew by 480,000 during the intercensal period of 1939–1959, and that of Omsk grew by 300,000. The rapid expansion of manufacturing in the two cities was reflected in the growth of industrial output, which rose by 5.4 times from 1940 to 1945 in the city of Novosibirsk, and by 4.2 times in Omsk Oblast, where Omsk was the only significant manufacturing city. In all of West Siberia, the value of industrial production increased by 2.7 times during the five-year period, and the spurt was particularly pronounced in the metal-fabricating and machinery manufacturing industries. As the plants evacuated from the western regions were installed in their new sites and put back into makeshift operation, the value of output of the metal-fabricating and machine-building sector rose by 7.9 times over the 1940 level in 1942 and by 11 times in 1943. Many of the evacuated plants were devoted to defense production, turning out warplanes, tanks, tractors, motorcycles and other military material. Since relatively few defense plants were in operation in West Siberia before the war, the rise in defense industry production was particularly marked. The value of production in this sector rose 27 times over the 1940 level in 1942 and 34 times in 1943. The contribution made by West Siberia to the war effort is evident from the fact that one aircraft plant produced one-fourth of the 60,000 fighter planes turned out by Soviet industry during the war.

13

TABLE 6

Population Growth of Selected Siberian Cities
(in thousands)

	1926 Census	1939 Census	1956 Estimate	1959 Census	1970 Census	1976 Estimate
West Siberia						
Tyumen' Oblast						
Tyumen'	50	79	125	150	269	335
Tobol'sk	19	32		36	49	51
Ishim	14	31		48	56	62
Omsk Oblast						
Omsk	162	289	505	581	821	1002
Novosibirsk Oblast						
Novosibirsk	120	404	731	885	1161	1286
Altay Kray						
Barnaul	74	148	255	303	439	514
Biysk	46	80	112	146	186	209
Rubtsovsk	16	38		111	145	171
Kemerovo Oblast						
Novokuznetsk	4	166	347	382	499	530
Kemerovo	22	137	240	289	385	446
Prokop'yevsk	11	107	260	282	274	267
Leninsk-Kuznetskiy	20	83	119	132	128	131
Kiselevsk		44	116	128	127	125
Anzhero-Sudzhensk	30	69	116	116	106	104
Belovo		43		100	108	111
Mezhdurechensk				55	82	89
Tomsk Oblast						
Tomsk	92	145	224	249	338	413
East Siberia						
Krasnoyarsk Kray						
Krasnoyarsk	72	190	328	412	648	758
Noril'sk		14		118	135	168
Abakan	3	37		56	90	120
Achinsk	18	32		50	97	114
Kansk	19	42		74	95	97
Chernogorsk	1.4	17		51	60	69
Minusinsk	21	31		38	41	45
Lesosibirsk						30
Sayanogorsk						22
Irkutsk Oblast						
Irkutsk	99	250	314	366	451	519
Angarsk				135	203	231
Bratsk				43	155	195
Usol'ye	8	20		48	87	100
Cheremkhovo	9	56	124	122	99	88
Zima	8	28		39	42	50
Ust'-Ilimsk					21	30

14

TABLE 6 (continued)

Population Growth of Selected Siberian Cities
(in thousands)

	1926 Census	1939 Census	1956 Estimate	1959 Census	1970 Census	1976 Estimate
East Siberia (contd.)						
Buryat ASSR						
Ulan-Ude	29	126	158	174	254	302
Chita Oblast						
Chita	62	121	162	172	241	290
Far East						
Yakut ASSR						
Yakutsk	11	53		74	108	143
Amur Oblast						
Blagoveshchensk	61	59		95	128	171
Maritime Kray						
Vladivostok	108	206	265	291	441	526
Nakhodka				64	104	127
Ussuriysk	35	72	101	104	128	145
Khabarovsk Kray						
Khabarovsk	50	207	280	323	436	513
Komsomol'sk		71	169	177	218	246
Amursk				4	24	32
Sovetskaya Gavan'		12		26	28	31
Vanino				12	15	
Sakhalin Oblast						
Yuzhno-Sakhalinsk		39		86	106	131
Kamchatka Oblast						
Petropavlovsk	2	35		86	154	202
Magadan Oblast						
Magadan		27		62	92	112

Although the accent in industrial development during the war period was on manufacturing, particularly in the defense industry, resource-based primary industries also continued to grow. Their contribution to the Soviet economy was particularly pronounced because the German occupation of the highly developed western regions had put most of the nation's heavy industry out of action, including 68 percent of the pig-iron capacity, 58 of the steel capacity and 63 percent of the coal. The prewar development of the coal and steel industry of the Urals-Kuznetsk Combine played a significant role in sustaining the war effort. In 1942, when the output of the Soviet iron and steel industry declined to its wartime low, the Kuznetsk plant contributed one-third of the nation's pig iron and one-fourth of the crude steel. In an effort to ease the load on the transport system, more iron ore was mined in the Shor uplands, south of the Kuznetsk Basin, thus reducing the amount of ore that needed to be shipped from the Urals. Local ore production rose by 67 percent, from 490,000 tons in 1940 to 820,000 tons in 1945; as a result, its share in the Kuznetsk blast-furnace mix increased from 19 to 32 percent. The metallurgical industry of the Kuznetsk Basin was diversified by the addition in 1943 of an aluminum reduction plant (evacuated from Volkhov, near Leningrad) and of a ferroalloys plant (with equipment evacuated from Zaporozh'ye in the Ukraine). The rapid development of metal-fabrication furnished a source of scrap that could be used in new steel-smelting capacity associated with machinery manufacture. The largest such steel plant went into operation in 1942 in Novosibirsk.

With the Donets Basin of the Ukraine under German occupation, the Kuznetsk Basin became the biggest coal producer for the wartime Soviet economy. In 1942, when the total coal output reached a low point of 76 million tons (45 percent of the 1940 level), the Kuzbas contributed 21.7 million tons, or 29 percent. The basin was particularly crucial as a source of coking coal for the iron and steel industry of the Kuznetsk Basin and the Urals; in 1945, it contributed 44 percent of the Soviet Union's coking coal output (12.9 million tons out of a total of 29.4 million).

Among the new manufacturing industries introduced into Siberia during the wartime emergency were key agricultural equipment plants, including facilities for the manufacture of tractors and tractor-drawn plows at Rubtsovsk, in Altay Kray, and a combine harvester plant at Krasnoyarsk. The Rubtsovsk tractor plant, installed with equipment evacuated from Khar'kov in the Ukraine, turned out its first tractor in August 1942, and produced 2,900 at the end of the war in 1945. In recent years it has been producing about 35,000 units a year, or roughly 7 percent of the national total, both for agricultural use and for the logging industry. The tractor-plow plant had been evacuated from Odessa at the outbreak of war in June 1941 and was removed to Rostov-on-Don; but when Rostov itself was threatened by the German advance, it was moved to Rubtsovsk, and was back in production in late 1941. It now accounts for 38 percent of Soviet production of tractor-drawn plows. The Krasnoyarsk grain-harvester plant, based on equipment evacuated from Zaporozh'ye and Lyubertsy (near Moscow) produced all of the Soviet Union's combined harvesters at the end of the War (a total of 300) and still accounts for about one-fourth of national production (Table 15).

The city of Krasnoyarsk was one of the main beneficiaries of the evacuation program during the war, and gross industrial output in Krasnoyarsk Kray increased by 75 percent from 1940 to 1945. Some machinery plants were also evacuated to Irkutsk, where industrial output rose by 20 percent during the wartime period, but no evacuated plants moved east of Lake Baykal. In Transbaykalia, industrial output declined during the war, by as much as one-third of the 1940 level in the case of Chita Oblast. The eastern regions of Siberia continued to contribute a number of key metals, such as tin, tungsten, molybdenum, used in the special alloy steels needed by the defense industries. Also in that category was the production of nickel, which began in 1942 at Noril'sk with equipment evacuated from a nickel smelter under construction at the outbreak of war at Monchegorsk on the Kola Peninsula. Noril'sk was totally isolated from the rest of the country except during the brief icefree shipping season of three to four months along the Northern Sea Route off the Siberian coast and along the Yenisey River. The rest of the year, nickel was airlifted to defense plants from the far northern smelter. A cobalt plant, producing another key steel alloy, went into operation at Noril'sk in September 1945, after the war had ended. The Noril'sk deposit, similar to the complex nickel-copper sulfide deposit of the Sudbury district of Ontario, also yielded copper, gold, silver, tellurium and selenium as well as platinum-group metals, which were recovered as byproducts of nickel processing. The development of the Noril'sk complex began in the mid-1930s and a narrow-gauge railroad was completed in

16

1937 from the metals deposit to the port of Dudinka, on the lower Yenisey, but the project was accelerated during the wartime emergency.

In a number of defense-oriented industries, Siberia's contribution to the Soviet economy reached a high point that was not to be equaled again during the immediate postwar period. In 1945, Siberia accounted for 31.5 percent of the Soviet Union's coal, a share that was not again matched until the early 1970s. Almost all the increase in wartime coal production was recorded by the crucial Kuznetsk Basin, where output rose from 22.5 million tons in 1940 to 30 million in 1945. In East Siberia and the Far East, coal mining declined in some areas (as in the Cheremkhovo Basin of Irkutsk Oblast) or rose only slightly (as in the Raychikhinsk district of Amur Oblast) partly because of a shortage of labor (Table 3). The high levels of iron and steel production relative to total Soviet output have not been equaled since the war; in fact the Siberian share in the mid-1970's—about 9 percent—was still slightly below the 10 percent of the Soviet steel industry that Siberia contributed in 1940, in the heyday of the Urals-Kuznetsk Combine. The wartime labor shortage also affected the forest-products industries, with logging volumes in Siberia down to 45 percent of the 1940 level by the end of the war.

The Postwar Retrenchment

The pronounced eastward movement that began during the prewar period and was accelerated during World War II was reversed during the early postwar era as the share of investment in the Siberian economy declined and its rate of growth fell below the national average. The reversal was particularly pronounced in such wartime boomtowns as Novosibirsk and Omsk as some of the evacuated industries and their labor force were returned to their original locations in the European part of the USSR. Total industrial output during the first postwar five-year plan (1946—1950) declined by 4 to 5 percent in both Novosibirsk and Omsk. Industrial growth immediately after the war was also slowed by the need for reconverting from a war-oriented defense economy to civilian needs. Moreover the bulk of new investment was channeled into the war-devasted western regions, and the Siberian share declined from 18 percent of all investment in the national economy to 13 percent during the 1946—1950 period (Table 1). The reduced investment allocation was distributed more or less evenly among the three Siberian regions, with West Siberia receiving 4.4 percent of the national total, East Siberia 4.1 percent and the Far East 4.5 percent.

The first postwar five-year plan provided for few major construction projects in Siberia as the focus remained on the reconstruction of the western regions. Among the few Siberian projects on which construction was under way during this period was a new coke-based chemical plant at Kemerovo in the Kuznetsk Basin, a chemical fiber plant at Barnaul in Altay Kray, and oil refineries at Omsk and at Angarsk (near Irkutsk), using crude oil transported by pipeline from the Volga-Urals fields. However, these projects did not go into operation until the 1955—1960 period so that they had no impact on Siberian economic performance during the late 1940's and in the 1950's. No new machinery industries of any significance were built in Siberia.

In most industrial sectors, Siberian growth thus remained below the national average. This was true particularly for iron and steel, coal mining, machinery as well as chemicals, which were still largely based on coal-tar derivatives. All these

17

industries were characteristic of West Siberia, which accordingly recorded the lowest rate of growth during the early postwar period. Industrial production in all of Siberia rose 27 percent by 1950 from the 1945 level compared with a national growth rate of 89 percent; the rise of industrial output in West Siberia was 16 percent compared with 55 percent in East Siberia and 45 percent in the Far East.

Only in the nonferrous metals industry and in forest products did the rate of growth in Siberia exceed the national average even during this period. Siberia continued to account for most of the Soviet Union's production of precious and rare metals (gold, platinum), tin, tungsten as well as nonmetals like fluorspar and mica. In the gold industry, the depletion of surface placers in old mining districts like Aldan and the upper Kolyma valley led to the development of buried placers and lode deposits requiring a higher degree of mechanization and concentration compared with the old small-scale hand methods. The trend toward less reliance on manual labor was also speeded by the abolition of forced labor on the mass scale in the mid-1950's. The shift to the new technology took place both in the old goldfields and led to greater activity in new areas, such as Yakutia's Allakh-Yun district, in the Dzhugdzhur Mountains, and the Chukchi National Okrug, in northeasternmost Siberia. The production of platinum-group metals, notably palladium and platinum, expanded in the Noril'sk complex, where mining shifted partly from early open-pit operations to deep mines. A large copper smelter, inaugurated in 1950, replaced a smaller copper plant dating from the war period.

Tin mining shifted increasingly toward the Far East from the early production centers in Transbaykalia. A wartime tin development, started during World War II around Kavalerovo, in Maritime Kray, was substantially expanded in the 1950's; similarly, production increased at the Khingansk tin mine in the Jewish Autonomous Oblast of Khabarovsk Kray. The need for tin, often associated with tungsten, had also led to development of tin operations in the extreme northeast of Siberia, both in Magadan Oblast (at Omsukchan) and in Chukchi National Okrug (in the Pevek area and at Iultin'). A similarly remote location was the tin mine of Deputatskiy, in northern Yakutia. Many of these mining centers could be reached only by seasonal winter roads and by air. However, in the mid-1950's a large tin lode deposit was discovered at Solnechnyy, 40 miles west of Komsomol'sk, and subsequent development centered on this more accessible location.

In the old Aldan goldfields, declining gold production began to be overshadowed by the development of phlogopite (magnesium) mica, superseding the older and largely depleted deposit of Slyudyanka, while the other mica variety, muscovite, or potassium mica, was mined in the Mama-Chuya district, in the northeast portion of Irkutsk Oblast. Fluorspar, originally concentrated in Transbaykalia, was supplied by an additional mining complex, developed in the 1950's at Yaroslavskiy near Ussuriysk, in Maritime Kray. And in the old Transbaykal mining district of Chita Oblast, the emphasis shifted in the 1950's to new space-age and nuclear-age metals like lithium, beryllium, tantalum, columbium, associated with granite pegmatite dikes found in the area.

The forest products industry rebounded dramatically from its wartime decline. By 1950, Siberia's contribution of sawtimber was again up to the prewar level—23 percent—and continued to increase steadily. Most significantly, the increase in logging operations stemmed from more northerly areas that had been virtually untouched in the past. This northward movement of the logging industry was made possible by the construction of feeder railroads northward from the Trans-Siberian mainline, beginning in the 1950's. Most affected by the spatial expansion of the industry were Tyumen' and Tomsk oblasts in West Siberia; Krasnoyarsk Kray and Irkutsk Oblast in East Siberia; and Khabarovsk Kray in the Far East. These five major civil divisions accounted for 49 percent of Siberian roundwood production in 1940. In the mid-1950's, when the northward movement was still in its early stages, their share was 58 percent, and by the mid-1970's it had risen to 76 percent (Table 5).

In Tyumen' Oblast, improved access to timber reserves was first fostered in 1949 by the completion of a spur from the Pechora railroad across the northern Urals to Labytnangi, on the lower Ob' River opposite Salekhard. This northern spur was to be extended eastward from Salekhard toward Igarka, the timber port on the lower Yenisey, and work proceeded on this Arctic project with the use of forced labor in the early 1950's. However, the project was abandoned in 1953 after Stalin's death as lacking an economic rationale, and has not been renewed despite the recent development of gigantic gas fields in the area. The short spur completed to the Ob' did, however, have an economic purpose in making possible the transfer of logs floated down the Ob' River to the railroad for shipment to market areas in European Russia.

Farther south, work got under way in the late 1950's on a 230-mile line from Ivdel', a railhead in the northern Urals, to Sergino, on the Ob' River. The new railroad opened up a vast new forest region of high-grade timber, estimated at 2 billion cubic meters of reserves. Although the Ivdel'-Ob' line had been designed mainly as a logging railroad, it played a more diversified function because of the development of the West Siberian gas fields around Igrim, which was being pressed about the same time. Logging operations expanded along the new line through the 1960's, even before the railroad was officially inaugurated, in 1969. A second logging railroad was completed at the same time from the railhead of Tavda northward for a distance of 120 miles to the Konda River at Mezhdurechenskiy. This line, too, was to play a broader role in connection with the development of the nearby Shaim oilfield, with its center in the town of Uray. Both rail lines opened up forest areas in the southwest portion of Khanty-Mansi National Okrug, an ethnic area within Tyumen' Oblast, and the impact of the new access routes was most evident in the increase of logging production for the Khanty-Mansi okrug. It became West Siberia's principal roundwood producer, increasing its output from 1.4 million cubic meters, before the construction of the railroads, to 9.2 million by the mid-1970's, when it accounted for more than 80 percent of Tyumen' Oblast sawtimber production (Table 5).

In Tomsk Oblast, the logging industry was fostered by the construction of a rail spur from Tomsk to Asino on the Chulym River, a major logging stream, and its extension by the mid-1970's from Asino northward for 110 miles to Belyy Yar, on the Ket' River, another logging river. In this case, the rail line served not only for the shipment of roundwood, but for the development of a wood-processing industry centered on Asino, exceeding 30,000 in population by the mid-1970's. Logging operations centered on the Asino complex accounted for a major portion of the increase in Tomsk Oblast roundwood production, from 2.6 million cubic meters in 1950 to 6.8 million in 1974 (Table 5).

19

The logging industry in East Siberia achieved a higher level of development than in West Siberia because of larger reserves (one-half of the Soviet total), better growing conditions (less swampy terrain than in West Siberia), earlier construction of access railroads and greater amount of local wood-processing (mostly pulp).

In Krasnoyarsk Kray, third largest commercial timber producer (after neighboring Irkutsk Oblast and European Russia's main logging region, Arkhangel'sk Oblast), the development of northern forests was fostered by feeder railroads from Achinsk northward to Lesosibirsk and from Nizhnyaya Poyma (Reshoty station) northward toward the Boguchany area, site of a future hydroelectric station on the Angara River. Construction on the 170-mile railroad north from Achinsk began in the 1950's and reached its destination in 1963, with official inauguration of the line in 1967. The arrival of the railroad intensified the development of a wood-processing complex at Maklakovo, south of Yeniseysk, that began after World War II. A new sawmill went into operation in 1969; development of a new timber port on the Yenisey River began in 1971, and, in February 1975, the town of Maklakovo was merged with nearby settlements to form the new wood-processing city of Lesosibirsk, with a population of about 50,000.

Construction on the railroad northward from Nizhnyaya Poyma also began in the mid-1950's, opening up logging areas between the Trans-Siberian and the lower Angara River. Advancing northward along the boundary between Krasnoyarsk Kray and Irkutsk Oblast, the line successively reached a series of tributaries of the Angara River—the Biryusa in the mid-1960's and the Chuna in the early 1970's. It is expected to reach the site of the Boguchany hydro project in the early 1980's.

The expansion of the logging industry after World War II resulted in more than a tripling of roundwood shipments in Krasnoyarsk Kray, from 6.5 million cubic meters in 1950 to about 21 million in the mid-1970's. But even this rapid rate of growth was exceeded in neighboring Irkutsk Oblast, which surpassed Arkhangel'sk Oblast in 1967—1968 to become the Soviet Union's leading logging region. In Irkutsk Oblast roundwood shipments more than quadrupled, from close to 6 million cubic meters in 1950 to more than 27 million in the mid-1970's.

In Irkutsk Oblast, the principal access route into the high-grade timberlands of the Middle Angara valley and its tributaries was the westernmost segment of the future Baykal-Amur Mainline, from the Trans-Siberian junction of Tayshet eastward toward Bratsk and Ust'-Kut. The development of the region began in the Biryusa valley around Tayshet, where the wood-processing center of Biryusinsk arose, and then moved eastward in the late 1940's and early 1950's to the Chuna River valley. There a trio of logging and wood-processing centers—Lesogorsk, Oktyabr'skiy and Chunskiy—arose in the mid-1950's, reaching a combined population of about 40,000 by the mid-1970's. Finally, in the 1960's the great timber complex of Bratsk went into operation, converting about 6 million cubic meters of wood into one million tons of pulp as well as containerboard, fiberboard and sawnwood by the mid-1970's.

In the Far East, the logging industry developed in particular in Khabarovsk Kray, whose share in the regional output of roundwood rose from 30 percent in 1950 to 50 percent in the mid-1970's. Much of the expansion was for export, particularly to Japan. The opening up of new logging districts took place both along mainline railroads, such as the Trans-Siberian, its northern spur to Komsomol'sk and the connection between Komsomol'sk and Sovetskaya Gavan' (completed in 1945), as well as along special logging railroads, including the Obor line running east from Khor, south of Khabarovsk; the Komsomol'sk-Duki line (which was in effect a segment of the BAM), and a line running from Selikhino (on the Komsomol'sk-Sovetskaya Gavan' railroad') northeast along the right bank of the Amur to Chernyy Mys.

Until the mid-1960's, the development of the wood-processing industry in Siberia lagged behind the growth of the logging industry, and much of the product was shipped out as roundwood with little processing. In view of the great distances separating the Siberian logging districts from the markets in the western regions costs were high, particularly for roundwood shipments from Eastern Siberia to the western portion of the USSR. Only the logging districts of Khanty-Mansi National Okrug (Tyumen' Oblast) were within relatively easy reach of the western markets. Pulp production was traditionally concentrated in the European North and in the Urals, on the periphery of the European market, as was the production of paper and paperboard. In the 1950's, when Siberia accounted for about one-fourth of Soviet roundwood output and a somewhat smaller percentage of sawnwood, it produced 7 to 8 percent of the nation's pulp, paper and paperboard, most of it in the mills of southern Sakhalin Oblast that had been inherited from the Japanese (Table 7). A reversal in the Siberian contribution to the Soviet pulp and paper industry began in 1960 with the opening of the Krasnoyarsk pulp and paper mill, but it gained particular impetus in the mid-1960's with the inauguration of the huge Bratsk woodpulp complex as well as the smaller processing centers at Baykal'sk (Irkutsk Oblast) and Amursk (Khabarovsk Kray) (Table 7). As a result of these developments, the Siberian contribution to the Soviet Union's pulp production rose from less than 10 percent in 1965 to about one-fourth of the national output by the mid-1970's. The largest producer by far is the Bratsk mill, with a 1975 capacity of one million tons of woodpulp. The trend is to be maintained with the construction of the 500,000-ton pulp mill at Ust'-Ilimsk, another hydroelectric site on the Angara River, below Bratsk, scheduled to go on stream in 1978. This upsurge of Siberian production of pulp, which is the chief raw material for the manufacture of paper and paperboard, has disrupted a close spatial correspondence that long existed between the production of pulp and the production of paper and paperboard. The production of pulp is affected by the economies of scale, in the sense that pulp plants must produce a specific minimum output to be profitable. In addition they require large amounts of cheap electric power, heat and water. All these factors have attracted them to the Siberian locations, particularly hydroelectric sites like Bratsk and Ust'-Ilimsk, situated in areas with large forest resources. Shipment of pulp rather than roundwood from Siberia to the European markets has also resulted in considerable transport savings. Much of the pulp is also used in the manufacture of tire cord and viscose rayon fabric.

Some of the Siberian pulp mills are associated with paperboard manufacture and with paper-making, but in general the eastward shift in pulp production has not been matched by an equivalent shift in the paper and paperboard industries. Except for the several Sakhalin paper mills inherited from the Japanese, paper is being made in significant amounts only by the medium size pulp and paper mill opened in 1960 at Krasnoyarsk. Newsprint accounts for one-fourth of the Soviet Union's paper production, and no Siberian mills are in the class of the big Soviet newsprint producers of Solikamsk (Perm' Oblast), Pravdinsk (Gor'kiy Oblast) and Kondopoga (Karelian ASSR), favorably situated relatively to the big newsprint markets of

TABLE 7

Siberian Production of Woodpulp, Paper and Paperboard
(in thousands of metric tons)

	1950	1955	1960	1965	1970	1974
			Woodpulp			
East Siberia	–	–	18	82	667	
Krasnoyarsk Kray	–	–	18	81	146	
Irkutsk Oblast	–	–	–	1.4	521	
Far East	47	134	195	232	374	
Khabarovsk Kray	–	–	–	–	110	
Sakhalin Oblast	47	134	195	232	264	
Total Siberia	47	134	213	314	1041	1330*
% of USSR	4.2	7.7	9.3	9.7	20.4	21.9*
			Paper			
West Siberia	1.2	1.2	1.4	1.9	2.5	1.2
East Siberia	–	–	10	94	121	133
Krasnoyarsk Kray	–	–	10	94	108	120
Irkutsk Oblast	–	–	–	–	13	13
Far East	60	123	159	167	195	220
Khabarovsk Kray	2.3	4.6	7.5	8.7	8.9	9.0
Amur Oblast	–	–	–	–	3.7	4.2
Sakhalin Oblast	57	118	151	158	183	207
Total Siberia	61	124	170	263	319	355
% of USSR	5.2	6.7	7.3	8.1	7.6	7.0
			Paperboard			
West Siberia				11	16	54
Kemerovo Oblast				11	16	18
East Siberia	0.9	0.9	3.4	12	252	341
Krasnoyarsk Kray	–	–	2.4	11	68	151
Irkutsk Oblast	0.9	0.9	1.0	1.3	185	190
Far East	12	36	68	107	121	131
Khabarovsk Kray	–	6.5	10	24	36	41
Sakhalin Oblast	12	29	58	83	85	90
Total Siberia	13	37	71	129	390	526
% of USSR	4.3	6.6	8.0	8.9	15.5	16.7

*1973

Moscow, Leningrad and other major cities of Central Russia. In the mid-1970's, Siberia still accounted for only 7 percent of the Soviet Union's paper manufacture, with about two-thirds coming from Sakhalin and one-third from Krasnoyarsk.

Siberia makes a more significant contribution to the Soviet Union's paperboard production, particularly in the manufacture of containerboard, which has accounted for most of the recent increase in Soviet paperboard output. The two leading Siberian containerboard producers are Krasnoyarsk (where production began in 1969) and Bratsk (in 1967), each with a designed capacity of a quarter million tons. The start of these two units raised Siberia's share in paperboard from 9 percent (mostly Sakhalin mills) in 1965 to about 17 percent in the mid-1970's. A pulp and paperboard mill at Selenginsk, near Lake Baykal, under construction since the late 1950's, was still not fully in operation by 1976 because of problems with waste-treatment facilities designed to protect Lake Baykal against pollution.

Recent Resource-Based Development

Aside from nonferrous metals and forest-product industries, the Siberian contribution to the Soviet economy has focused increasingly in the last two decades on resource-based development, particularly in the field of energy. In the mid-1950's began the long-planned development of the huge hydroelectric potential of the Angara and Yenisey rivers, attracting power-intensive industries like aluminum, the above-mentioned pulp mills and some chemical industries like the power-intensive chlorine-caustic soda cycle. This was followed, beginning in the mid-1960's, by the development of the vast oil and natural gas reserves of West Siberia, which by the mid-1970's were contributing 30 percent of Soviet crude oil and 13 percent of the natural gas. These activities, in turn, were beginning to attract an increasing share of the petrochemical sector of Soviet industry. Finally, in the mid-1970's, began the development of the large lignite resources of the Kansk-Achinsk basin of southern Siberia, with the start of construction of a series of major thermal stations to be fired with lignite from adjacent strip mines, with the electricity to be transmitted westward to the European regions over extra-high-voltage transmission lines.

This shift of priorities in Siberian development strategy, from an earlier effort to endow Siberia with an integrated economy and settlement, derived from several factors. An earlier eastward movement of population, fostered in part by the use of forced labor under Stalin and a policy of compulsory work assignments, ceased in the mid-1950's when forced labor as a mass institution was abolished and constraints on the movement of workers were lifted. Because of the relatively better living conditions in western and, especially, southwestern regions of the Soviet Union, more people began to leave Siberia than arrived there.

A number of devices were used to draw workers to the harsher physical environment and less attractive conditions of Siberia, for example, wage increments, longer vacations and other benefits. But as economic costs become increasingly an important factor in Soviet decision-making, planners realized that the costs of maintaining workers in Siberia did not justify the notion of settling Siberia for settlement's sake. An influx of population was encouraged only to the extent that workers were needed to operate resource-oriented industries, power-intensive activities and other sectors of the economy in which Siberia continued to make a major contribution to the Soviet economy.

23

The reorientation of Siberian development priorities was also motivated by the growing raw-material and energy needs of the European part of the USSR. The planners were increasingly faced with the dichotomy shaped by the historical development and economic evolution of Russia, in which 75 to 80 percent of the population and economic activity continue to be concentrated in the European part of the country while similar proportions of natural resources such as energy, key raw materials and water resources are found in Siberia. As long as the Soviet economy had moderate resource needs, the European resources were adequate. But as development proceeded, the limited European resources became gradually depleted and planners were forced to draw on the more abundant and more distant Siberian resources. The transfer of resources from east to west, particularly in the field of energy, was facilitated by modern technology, such as the use of pipelines for oil and gas transportation and extra-high-voltage transmission lines for the long-distance transfer of large blocks of electricity.

Thus the trend in recent years has been to limit Siberian development to those activities that operate most effectively in the eastern regions—the extraction and primary processing of raw materials and energy resources, energy-intensive activities and manufacturing industries that are oriented toward the Siberian resource base and have limited labor requirements.

The principal signal alerting Soviet economic planners to the Siberian population problem has been the net out-migration. This trend, which involved principally departures from Siberian urban places, was associated with an intensive rural-urban migration within Siberia, leading to increasing depopulation of the countryside. These migration patterns were aggravated by a steady decline in the rate of natural increase, which declined by more than one-half between 1950 and the early 1970's: in West Siberia from 20 to 7 per 1000; in East Siberia from 24 to 10, and in the Far East from 28 to 11 per 1000. In some years, net out-migration actually exceeded natural increase.

Because of the opposite directions of migration during the intercensal period 1939—1959 (a pronounced eastward movement, intensified during the war, followed by an ebbing or even countermovement of migration streams in the late 1940's and in the 1950's), the situation cannot be precisely documented for the period before the 1959 census. A westward migration in the middle and late 1950's may also have been balanced to some extent by the eastward movement associated with the cultivation of the so-called virgin lands, beginning in 1954. These new wheat areas were situated largely in northern Kazakhstan, but also extended into adjacent portions of Siberia, notably Omsk Oblast. Novosibirsk Oblast and Altay Kray, where the combined wheat area doubled in the four-year period 1954—57. At any rate, within the entire 20-year intercensal period, Siberia's population increased by 5.9 million, from 16.7 million in 1939 to 22.6 million in 1959, and the region's share in the total Soviet population (within postwar boundaries) rose from 8.9 to 10.8 percent. The intensive growth of cities (Table 6) had raised the urbanization level in Siberia substantially above the national average (in Siberia 55 percent of the population was urban in 1959 compared to 51.8 percent in the European part of the RSFSR). Urban population had more than doubled, 5.7 million in 1939 to 12.4 million in 1959, and rural population had declined from 11.0 to 10.1 million, which was a slower rate of rural depopulation than in the western regions of the USSR.

TABLE 8

Siberian Urban-Rural Population Distribution and
Migration (1959–1970)
(in thousands)

	Siberia as a Whole			West Siberia		
	Total	Urban	Rural	Total	Urban	Rural
1959 census	22558	12403	10155	11251	5724	5527
Natural increase	+3574	+1939	+1635	+1645	+826	+819
Net migration	−779	+1833	−2612	−787	+881	−1668
1970 census	25353	16175	9178	12109	7431	4678

	East Siberia			Far East		
	Total	Urban	Rural	Total	Urban	Rural
1959 census	6473	3414	3059	4834	3265	1569
Natural increase	+1125	+580	+545	+804	+533	+271
Net migration	−135	+618	−753	+143	+334	−191
1970 census	7463	4612	2851	5781	4132	1649

Source: Soviet Geography: Review and Translation, September 1975,
pp. 469, 471, 472.

This picture was dramatically reversed during the intercensal period 1959–1970 as the rate of urbanization slowed, rural-urban migration increased, and the net movement of people was out of Siberia. The population growth of Siberia fell below the national rate. Total population in Siberia increased from 22.6 million in 1959 to 25.4 million in 1970, or by 12.4 percent, compared with a national growth rate of 15.7 percent. Accordingly, Siberia's share in the Soviet Union's population declined slightly, from 10.8 percent in 1959 to 10.5 percent in 1970. It has since remained roughly at that level. The slowdown was reflected particularly in cities as the Siberian urbanization rate—63.7 percent—more closely approached the level of European Russia—62 percent. At the same time, the rate of decline of rural population in Siberia exceeded that of European Russia.

But it was in the migration patterns that the Siberian population problem became most clearly evident. In the intercensal period 1959–1970, all of Siberia lost 779,000 people through net out-migration, or 22 percent of the region's natural increase (Table 8). The general tendency was for rural residents to migrate to cities (a net rural outflow of 2.6 million) and for urban residents to move outside of the region.

Within this overall trend, patterns varied by major economic regions. The net out-migration was most pronounced in the case of West Siberia, which recorded a net outflow of 787,000 during the intercensal period. This represented 48 percent of natural increase. The net out-migration was much smaller in East Siberia, where the outflow of 135,000 represented only 12 percent of natural increase. And in the Far East, where the physical environment in the southern portion is less hostile than in Siberia and government policy has fostered in-migration, there was a net

25

TABLE 9

Population of Siberian Administrative Divisions (1939–1975)
(in thousands)

	1939 census	1959 census	1970 census	1976 estimate
West Siberia	8,928	11,251	12,109	12,503
Tyumen' Oblast proper	850	906	1,055	1,085
Khanty-Mansi National Okrug	93	124	271	425
Yamal-Nenets National Okrug	48	62	80	126
Omsk Oblast	1,390	1,645	1,824	1,898
Novosibirsk Oblast	1,861	2,299	2,505	2,559
Altay Kray proper	2,225	2,525	2,502	2,474
Gorno-Altay Autonomous Oblast	162	157	168	169
Kemerovo Oblast	1,654	2,786	2,918	2,932
Tomsk Oblast	643	747	786	835
East Siberia	4,771	6,473	7,463	7,905
Krasnoyarsk Kray proper	1,659	2,160	2,465	2,549
Khakass Autonomous Oblast	275	411	446	474
Taymyr National Okrug	15	33	38	43
Evenki National Okrug	10	11	13	14
Tuva ASSR*	–	172	231	253
Irkutsk Oblast	1,303	1,976	2,313	2,492
Buryat ASSR	546	673	812	865
Chita Oblast	963	1,037	1,145	1,215
Far East		4,834	5,781	6,579
Amur Oblast	634	717	793	901
Yakut ASSR	414	487	664	779
Khabarovsk Kray	657	1,142	1,346	1,514
Maritime Kray	888	1,381	1,721	1,933
Sakhalin Oblast*	100	649	616	662
Kamchatka Oblast proper	86	193	257	323
Koryak National Okrug	23	28	31	34
Magadan Oblast proper	151	189	251	308
Chukchi National Okrug	22	47	101	125

*Tuva was not in USSR in 1939; Sakhalin included only the northern part in 1939.

in-migration during the 1959–1970 period. Similarly, rural depopulation was most pronounced in West Siberia, where the net outflow from rural areas was double the natural population increase; in East Siberia, net rural out-migration exceeded natural increase by only 38 percent, and in the Far East, rural out-migration was actually less than natural increase, so that the Far East gained population in rural areas (Table 8).

The slowdown in the population growth of much of Siberia is clearly evident from Table 9. Highly industrialized areas like Kemerovo Oblast, after having boomed in the preceding intercensal period 1939–1959 (a 68 percent increase), virtually ceased to grow in recent years. Areas with a high rural component like Altay Kray, after having grown only slightly during the previous period (13 percent between 1939 and 1959), have been declining in population since 1959. The only significant population growth in the 1960's and 1970's has taken place in the new oil and gas regions of the northern portions of Tyumen' Oblast–Khanty-Mansi National Okrug, where population more than doubled from 1959 to 1970, and rose again by 44 percent in the first half of the 1970's, and in the gas-producing Yamal-Nenets National Okrug farther north, where the development got under way only in the 1970's.

In East Siberia, the greatest population growth between 1939 and 1959 was recorded in Krasnoyarsk Kray, including its dependent Khakass Autonomous Oblast to the south and the far northern Taymyr National Okrug, which appeared to benefit from the development of the Noril'sk complex (although Noril'sk proper is administratively part of Krasnoyarsk Kray proper, and not the national okrug); a high population growth was also evident in Irkutsk Oblast (52 percent from 1939 to 1959). Population growth rates declined in almost all parts of East Siberia during the 1960's and 1970's as rural-urban migration intensified together with westward migration from East Siberian cities. Growth rates were highest in ethnic areas like Tuva ASSR and Buryat ASSR, where rates of natural increase tend to be above the Russian ethnic level.

In the Soviet Far East, population growth was particularly high during the 1939–1959 period in the well settled southern portion, including Khabarovsk Kray and Maritime Kray, less so in largely rural Amur Oblast. This trend has continued since 1959. A major migration stream into southern Sakhalin in the late 1940's and in the 1950's (after its annexation from Japan) was reversed during the 1960's, resulting in a population decline between 1959 and 1970. The highest rate of growth was evident in the 1960's in Chukchi National Okrug as gold-mining operations were extended from Magadan Oblast proper toward the northeast.

Hydroelectric development

Until the start of the great hydroelectric development on the Angara and Yenisey rivers of south central Siberia in the 1950's, Siberia had derived almost all of its electric power from coal-fired thermal power stations. The largest concentration of generating capacity was located in the industrial Kuznetsk Basin. The largest station at that time was the South Kuzbas power plant, which had gone into operation in April 1951 and had an installed capacity of 546 megawatts. Thermal power development in the Kuznetsk Basin continued even as the first hydroelectric stations went into operation. The Tom'-Usa power plant, also in the southern portion of the basin, opened in November 1958, achieving a total capacity

27

of 1300 megawatts, and the Belovo station began producing power in June 1964, achieving a total capacity of 1200 megawatts. The Kuznetsk stations and a number of large heat and power plants in the manufacturing cities of West Siberia (Omsk, Novosibirsk, Barnaul) accounted for West Siberia's leading position in Siberian power production. In the early 1950's, before the start of the first big hydro stations, Siberia generated 11 to 12 percent of Soviet power production, and more than one-half was contributed by thermal electric stations in West Siberia.

As a forerunner of the future development of a set of large lignite-fired minehead stations in the Kansk-Achinsk Basin, construction also began in 1955 on the Nazarovo thermal electric plant adjoining a strip mine in Krasnoyarsk Kray. The Nazarovo station began generating electricity in 1961 with a 150-megawatt unit and achieved a rated capacity of 1400 megawatts in 1968. It played a key role as a power supply source for the industries of Krasnoyarsk in the early 1960's pending the construction of a high-voltage transmission system based on the hydroelectric development in Irkutsk Oblast.

The program of hydroelectric development on the Angara and Yenisey rivers that got under way in the 1950's was the first major Siberian regional program since the Urals-Kuznetsk Combine of the 1930's. Unlike the combine, which was based on West Siberia's Kuznetsk Basin, the hydroelectric program was focused on East Siberia. It involved not only the construction of large power dams and associated generating capacities, but also a series of major power users, such as aluminum, some power intensive chemicals, and woodpulp production. The new development focus was evident in the increasing share of investment that was channeled into East Siberia in the 1950's and early 1960's (see Table 1) while the share of investment going to West Siberia and the Far East either held steady or declined. The new development program was also reflected in the rates of industrial growth in Irkutsk Oblast and Krasnoyarsk Kray, which were among the highest in Siberia in the 1950's and early 1960's. As the large power dams were completed, East Siberia quickly assumed a leading role in Soviet electricity production, particularly in hydroelectricity. In the early 1960's, East Siberia passed West Siberia's power output, and by the mid-1970's was contributing about one-tenth of all Soviet electricity production (Table 10), including close to 40 percent of all the hydroelectricity.

The early developments in the 1950's were still relatively small and did not suggest the magnitude of the big power dams that were to follow. One of the early stations was the Novosibirsk hydroelectric plant, on the Ob' River, south of the manufacturing city of Novosibirsk. Its designed capacity of 400 megawatts was less than the capacity of the Dnieper dam at Zaporozh'ye in the Ukraine. The Novosibirsk plant, which went into construction in 1950 and reached its full designed capacity in 1959, served peak-load purposes, with the base load being supplied by coal-fired power stations in the Kuznetsk Basin.

In the Angara-Yenisey region, too, the first major station, at Irkutsk, was relatively modest, with a designed capacity of 662 megawatts, or virtually identical with the older Dnieper station. The Irkutsk plant, situated on the Angara River just above Irkutsk was built concurrently with the Novosibirsk project, reaching its designed capacity in 1958. It was the first of the Siberian hydro stations to be associated with an aluminum reduction plant, inaugurated in 1962 at Shelekhov, about 10 miles southwest of Irkutsk. The Irkutsk aluminum plant, with a capacity

28

TABLE 10

Electric Power Production in Siberia
(billion kilowatt-hours)

	1940	1945	1950	1955	1960	1965	1970	1974
West Siberia	1.8	4.0	5.9	11.7	23	35	44	63
Hydro stations					1.6	1.7	2.1	
East Siberia	0.65	1.1	2.3	4.8	16	43	74	96
Irkutsk Oblast						28.3	36.3	
Hydro stations					3.7	18.3	42.4	
Far East	0.68	1.0	2.1	3.5	5.3	9.3	14	21
Hydro stations							0.6	
Total Siberia	3.2	6.1	10.3	20.0	44	87	132	180
% of USSR	6.6	14	11	12	15	17.2	17.9	18.4
Total Siberian hydro					5.3	20	45.1	
% of USSR hydro					10.4	24.5	36.3	

of about 200,000 tons of aluminum metal a year, set the pattern for the great Siberian aluminum plants in relying on long-haul alumina from the Urals and later Pavlodar (Kazakhstan) for raw material sources.

It was only in the mid-1950's that the construction of large-scale stations on the Angara and Yenisey rivers began. The river-basin development had its antecedents in the 1930's when the hydroelectric potential of the Angara and the Yenisey was studied by Soviet planners in conjunction with the introduction of power-intensive industries, but neither the Soviet Union's technological capacity of that period nor its investment resources were adequate to the task; moreover the war intervened.

The first great Siberian power project was the Bratsk dam, where construction began in 1954. Bratsk had been reached by the rail branch from Tayshet in late 1947, before plans for the construction of the hydroproject had been made, and the decision to go ahead with the dam required shifting a 125-mile segment of the rail line northward so that it would cross the Angara River on the proposed dam. The bypass went into operation in July 1961, three months before the first 225-megawatt unit went on stream in the Bratsk station. In record time, within a span of two years, 16 units were installed (the last in December 1963) for a combined capacity of 3,600 megawatts. Two more units of 250 megawatts each were added in 1966, bringing the total to 4,050 megawatts (Table 11). Because of poor construction coordination, much of the power potential of the Bratsk station was wasted in the early years. The Bratsk aluminum plant, with a designed capacity of 500,000 tons of aluminum metal, did not begin production until 1966 even though it had been envisaged as the principal consumer of Bratsk power. It reached about one-half of its designed capacity by 1970, and was completed only in 1976. In its first years of operation the Bratsk dam was generating only about 25 to 30 percent of its potential in the absence of local power users, transmitting most of its output over two 220-kilovolt lines running 360 miles to Irkutsk. In 1963 the two

TABLE 11

Major Hydroelectric Stations of Siberia

Name	Location	River	Designed Capacity (megawatt)	Number of generating units (megawatt)	Construction dates Start	First unit	Last unit
Novosibirsk	Novosibirsk	Ob'	400.4	7 × 57.2	1950	1957	1959
Irkutsk	Irkutsk	Angara	662.4	8 × 82.8	1950	1956	1958
Bratsk	Bratsk	Angara	4050	16 × 225* 2 × 250	1954	1961	1966
Krasnoyarsk	Divnogorsk	Yenisey	6000	12 × 500	1956	1967	1971
Ust'-Ilim	Ust'-Ilimsk	Angara	4320	18 × 240	1962	1974	(1978)
Sayan	Sayanogorsk	Yenisey	6400	10 × 640	1963	(1978)	
Boguchany	Koda	Angara	4000	12 × 340	1976	(1983)	
Vilyuy	Chernyshevskiy	Vilyuy	308	4 × 77	1960	1967	1969
Vilyuy	(second stage)	Vilyuy	340	4 × 85	1972	1975	
Zeya	Zeya	Zeya	1290	6 × 215	1964	1975	
Bureya	Talakan	Bureya	2000	7 × 285	1976	(1983)	
Kolyma	Sinegor'ye	Kolyma	750		1970	(1980)	
Khantayka	Snezhnogorsk	Khantayka	441	7 × 63	1963	1970	1972
Kureyka	Svetlogorsk	Kureyka	500		1975	(1981)	

*The 225-megawatt units at Bratsk were being upgraded to 250 megawatts during the five-year plan 1976—80, raising the installed capacity to 4,500 megawatts.

lines to Irkutsk were raised to 500 kilovolt, increasing the combined transmission capacity to 1,300 megawatts, and a new 500-kilovolt power line was completed from Bratsk 390 miles westward to Krasnoyarsk, with a transmission capacity of 700 megawatts. At that point, utilization of the Bratsk power-generating potential rose to 50–60 percent, as 2,000 megawatts of the installed 3,600 megawatts found an outlet. A second 500-kilovolt line to Krasnoyarsk was added in 1966. The completion of the central Siberian 500-kilovolt power transmission grid between Irkutsk and Krasnoyarsk—subsequently extended to the Kuznetsk Basin—and the start of operations at the Bratsk aluminum plant in 1966 and at the Bratsk woodpulp mill the following year improved the utilization of the hydro station's generating capacity. Over the years, an average of 40 percent has been consumed locally, 40 has been transmitted to the Irkutsk area, and 20 percent has moved westward toward Krasnoyarsk.

In 1962, after the completion of the Bratsk dam, the construction team moved northward to the next Angara River hydro site, at Ust'-Ilimsk, where a 4,320-megawatt station was to be constructed. The new town of Ust'-Ilimsk, which had a population of about 40,000 in the mid-1970's, was reached by a railroad in 1971, and the first of 18 generating units of 240 megawatts each went into operation in December 1974. The new station has been connected to the Siberian 500-kilovolt transmission grid, and is feeding its electric power into the system pending the completion of power-consuming industries at Ust'-Ilimsk. A large diversified timber-processing complex is under construction, and has been designed to process 6.5 million cubic meters of wood into 500,000 tons of pulp, 1.2 million cubic meters of sawnwood, railroad ties, chipboard and other wood products. The mill is being built with the help of East European countries, which will receive pulp in payback.

Site preparation for the next Angara power project, near Boguchany, began in the winter of 1975–76 as trucks lumbering over a 200-mile winter road bulldozed through the frozen forest delivered the first supplies and equipment from Bratsk. Additional material moved downstream on the Angara during the brief shipping season. The station had originally been planned at the Mura rapids, 30 miles above Boguchany, but a dam at that site would have flooded a large area with valuable timber stands as well as potential, though low-grade bauxite deposits in the Chadobets River valley. An alternative site was therefore selected in the late 1960's just below the mouth of the Koda River, 30 miles farther upstream. Construction on the Boguchany project is expected to extend well into the 1980's.

On the Yenisey River, in the meantime, work on the Krasnoyarsk hydro station began in 1956 at Divnogorsk, 20 miles west of Krasnoyarsk, and the first of twelve 500-megawatt generating units went into operation in 1967; full capacity of 6,000 megawatts was achieved in 1971. The principal consumer of the cheap power generated by the station was the Krasnoyarsk aluminum plant, which had begun production in 1964 and used Nazarovo thermal power and electricity transmitted from the Bratsk hydro station for three years, until the arrival of power from the Krasnoyarsk station. At Krasnoyarsk, too, the completion of aluminum-making capacity was not synchronized with the availability of electric power. By 1970, when much of the Krasnoyarsk generating capacity was already installed, the Krasnoyarsk aluminum plant was only one-third complete; it did not achieve its full capacity of about 400,000 tons until the mid-1970's. Unlike other Siberian aluminum plants, which are dependent on long-haul alumina, the Krasnoyarsk plant

31

was intended to use nepheline-based alumina from the nearby Achinsk plant. But technological problems delayed the start of operations at Achinsk until 1970, and continued to plague the alumina plant afterward; by 1975, it was still operating 40 percent below the designed capacity of 800,000 tons of alumina a year. In contrast to the hydroelectric development on the Angara River, which is not significant as a waterway, provision had to be made on the Yenisey for continued shipping. A ship elevator, overcoming the level difference of more than 300 feet, went into operation at the Krasnoyarsk dam in 1975.

In the mid-1960's, construction work shifted south to the next great Yenisey dam, the Sayan-Shushenskoye complex, named for the Sayan Mountains through which the Yenisey carved a channel and for the nearby village of Shuchenskoye, where Lenin was exiled in 1897–1900. The construction site at the village of Mayna was reached by a railroad in 1968, a temporary 110-kilovolt power supply line was completed in 1972, and the new city of Sayanogorsk was founded at the site in 1975; at the time of founding it had a population of 25,000, with its ultimate population projected at 200,000. The first of a designed total of twelve 640-megawatt units is scheduled to go into operation in 1978 followed by the first potlines of a 500,000-ton aluminum plant at Sayanogorsk. This aluminum plant will receive alumina shipped over a rail distance of 3,000 miles from the seaboard alumina plant at Nikolayev on the Black Sea based on imported Guinean bauxite. Because of a relatively mild climate, the Sayan complex offers an unusually favorable environment for settlement for Siberia, and the big hydroelectric project is expected to become the heart of a diversified industrial district, including not only power-intensive activities like aluminum, special electric steels and ferroalloys, but also a wide range of manufacturing. A freight-car building plant went into operation in 1976 at Abakan to manufacture container flat cars for the burgeoning Trans-Siberian container rail traffic; a container manufacturing plant is also under construction. There are plans for a large electrical equipment manufacturing complex near Minusinsk.

Over the long term, further hydroelectric development is expected to proceed downstream along the Yenisey River, where four other huge projects have long been projected near the mouths of the Angara, the Podkamennaya (Stony) Tunguska, the Nizhnyaya (Lower) Tunguska, and in the Igarka area. The next project, following completion of the Sayan station, is likely to be the so-called Middle Yenisey complex near the mouth of the Angara River, with a tentative generating potential of 6,500 megawatts. Site studies were reported under way in the mid-1970's.

Outside of the big hydro projects of the Angara-Yenisey region, more modest stations are in operation or under construction in other parts of Siberia as additional sources of local power supply.

In the Soviet Far East, hydroelectric development began about a decade after the big East Siberian stations, with the first project getting under way in the mid-1960's on the Zeya River in Amur Oblast. The 1,290-megawatt Zeya project, just above the town of Zeya, placed the first of a designed set of six 215-megawatt units into operation in November 1975, and is expected to play an important role as a source of electric power for the construction and operation of the Baykal-Amur Mainline. It will be followed by the 2,000-megawatt Talakan hydro project on the Bureya River, where site preparations began in 1976. Aside from power generation, these Far Eastern stations in the Amur River basin will perform an additional function of flood control. The Far East has lagged behind other parts of the Soviet Union in electric power development, accounting for only 2 percent of national electricity production in the mid-1970's. More than 90 percent of the region's electric power was derived from coal-burning stations, of which the largest are the 600-megawatt Luchegorsk station in Maritime Kray (opened in 1974), the Sakhalin central electric station at Vostok near Vakhrushev (450 megawatts; completed in 1972), the Raychikhinsk station (268 megawatts); others in the older coal-mining centers of Artem and Partizansk (the former Suchan) in the Vladivostok area, and heat and power stations at Khabarovsk and Komsomol'sk. Most of the large mainland stations, from the Zeya hydro stations to the Vladivostok area have been linked by a transmission grid since 1971.

Other hydroelectric developments are designed to meet power needs in isolated mining districts. The 750-megawatt Kolyma station, under construction since 1971 and scheduled for completion around 1980, is expected to bolster the power supply of the Magadan grid, which now relies on coal-fired stations (such as the Arkagala plant at Myaundzha) and oil-fired stations (such as the Magadan heat and power plant). A more distant project in the northeast portion of Siberia is the Amguyema hydro station, projected as an additional power source for mining districts of the Chukchi National Okrug, including the Iul'tin tin-tungsten center and the gold producing centers of Leningradskiy and Polyarnyy, on the Arctic coast west of Mys Shmidt (Cape Shmidt). Another gold-mining area, centered on Bilibino is being supplied by a small, 48-megawatt nuclear power station that went into operation at Bilibino in 1974.

In Yakutia, the Vilyuy River hydro power complex, inaugurated in 1967, provides electric power for the diamond-mining district around Mirnyy, which has developed since the mid-1950's. Diamond production began at Mirnyy in 1957, and moved nearly 300 miles north to the Aykhal-Udachnyy area in the 1960's. The first stage of the Vilyuy hydro station, which is situated at Chernyshevskiy, northwest of Mirnyy, reached its designed capacity of 308 megawatts in late 1968, and in addition to Mirnyy began to supply power to the northern diamond fields in 1969. The second stage, of 340 megawatts, went into operation with the first generating unit in 1975. In addition to providing power for the diamond fields, the Vilyuy station is also a source of electricity for the Vilyuy River valley downstream. A power transmission line being built toward Yakutsk, the capital of the Yakut ASSR, reached Suntar in 1972, and Nyurba (300 miles from the station) in 1974.

The Noril'sk complex

Among the significant outlying hydroelectric developments in Siberia are the Khantayka and Kureyka stations of the Noril'sk nickel-platinum complex. The energy needs of Noril'sk have been steadily increasing with expansion of mining, concentrating and smelter operations that began with the discovery of the rich Talnakh ore bodies, 15 miles northeast of the older Noril'sk mines. In an intensive development program that began in the early 1960's, a series of increasingly deep and large underground mines have been built to tap the rich sulfide ores, yielding nickel, copper, cobalt, platinum-group metals and a dozen coproducts. The Mayak mine yielded its first ore in April 1965; the Komsomol mine opened in March 1971, and the Oktyabr' (October) mine started production in early 1974. The Taymyr mine, the fourth in the Talnakh area, has been under construction since 1973 and is expected to reach a depth of 5,000 feet. Since 1960, both metal output and,

33

especially, profits have soared in the Noril'sk operation as a result of the development of the Talnakh ores. The value of output in 1975 was 470 percent of the 1960 level, and a further increase of about 60 percent was envisaged in the five-year plan 1976–80. Profits rose from about 20 million rubles in 1960 to 570 million in 1975. The development of the Talnakh mines produced a surplus of concentrates that could not be handled by the existing smelter capacity, and large amounts of concentrate began to be shipped to smelters in the Kola Peninsula in the 1960's. Increasing icebreaker capacity, including the nuclear icebreakers Lenin and Arktika, was enlisted to extend the normally short shipping season along the Northern Sea Route between Dudinka, the port of Noril'sk, and Murmansk. In some years, the route was kept open from June until December or even early January. The volume of cargo handled by Dudinka rose to nearly 5 million tons a year in the mid-1970's, most of it outgoing concentrates.

The greatly expanded operations at Noril'sk led to the construction of a new nickel and copper smelter on the Nadezhda plateau (site of the old Noril'sk airport), 10 miles west of the city. The smelter, near completion in 1977 with Finnish help, is being supplied with concentrate from Talnakh via a 20-mile slurry pipeline.

Until the expansion starting in the 1960's, Noril'sk relied for its energy needs on local coal mines that yielded about 3 million tons a year in the mid-1960's. The high-cost mining operation yielded a low-calory, high-ash coal that also caused considerable air pollution. The discovery of natural gas in the Messoyakha area, 170 miles west of Noril'sk, provided a cheaper and cleaner fuel. The first of two 28-inch pipelines to Noril'sk was completed in late 1969, and the second in 1973. The original Messoyakha field was supplemented by the nearby Solenaya field in 1972. A natural gasoline plant, processing gas condensate from the Solenaya field, was under construction at Dudinka in 1976. The use of natural gas as a fuel in Noril'sk power stations and smelters reduced the consumption of coal, releasing a large number of the 6,000 workers employed in the coal industry before 1970 for other duties. The labor force engaged in meeting the energy needs of Noril'sk was said to have been reduced by 5,000 by the mid-1970's.

The conversion of fossil-fuel use from coal to natural gas was supplemented by the development of hydroelectric power. In anticipation of the increased electricity needs following the discovery of the Talnakh ore deposits, work began in 1963 on the Khantayka hydro station, about 90 miles south of Noril'sk. The town of Snezhnogorsk was founded in 1964, the first of seven 63-megawatt units went on stream in November 1970, and the station achieved its designed capacity of 441 megawatts in October 1972. It supplies electricity to Noril'sk over a 220-kilovolt transmission line.

In the mid-1970's work began on the construction of a second hydro station, on the Kureyka River, another 90 miles south of the Khantayka River plant. The first supplies moved by truck convoys southward over a temporary winter road from Snezhnogorsk during the winter of 1975–76, and a settlement tentatively named Svetlogorsk was founded on the construction site, which is about 65 miles southeast of Igarka. The start of power production at the station, with a designed capacity of 500 megawatts, is scheduled for 1981.

The expectation is that over the next few decades the Noril'sk mining complex, despite its adverse location in the Arctic environment of northern Siberia, will become one of the world's principal sources of nickel together with platinum-group metals and other co-products like copper, cobalt, selenium, tellurium, gold and silver. Its transport position is likely to be enhanced as the increased use of nuclear icebreakers extends the shipping season along the Northern Sea Route and, especially, after a railroad reaches Noril'sk from the south, possibly in the late 1980's.

Oil and gas development

Beginning in the mid-1960's, West Siberia moved to the fore again as the development of that region's newly discovered oil and gas resources began. The new focus of investment was evident in the allocation of capital resources as the share of East Siberia declined in the second half of the 1960's while that of West Siberia rose slightly (Table 1). But the investment shift became particularly pronounced in the 1970's as the magnitude of oil and gas development increased. Tyumen' Oblast, the major civil division in which the oil and gas fields are concentrated, received more investment resources in the mid-1970's than any other Soviet administrative division except Moscow city and Moscow Oblast. Total investment in Tyumen' Oblast in 1974 was 2.7 billion rubles, which was twice the 1970 level and represented 2.6 percent of all Soviet investment in the economy. The focus on Tyumen' Oblast was also evident in industrial growth figures, as the value of industrial output more than doubled during the five-year plan 1971—75 compared with a national growth rate of 43 percent. Moreover while many parts of Siberia showed a virtual standstill in population growth, the population of the oil and gas region, once virtually unpopulated, displayed rapid growth rates. Khanty-Mansi National Okrug, the ethnic area of Tyumen' Oblast where the oil fields are concentrated, rose in population from 271,000 in the 1970 census to 425,000 in an early 1976 estimate, or by 57 percent. Yamal-Nenets National Okrug, the more northerly ethnic area with the West Siberian gas fields, grew in population from 80,000 in 1970 to 126,000 in 1976, or by 58 percent.

The development of newly discovered oil resources proceeded more rapidly than the development of the more northerly natural gas fields for a number of reasons. The exploration for oil began several years before the search for gas and was motivated by greater urgency because of the leveling off of production in the Volga-Urals oil-producing province, which became the Soviet Union's principal petroleum supplier during the 1950's. The large oil fields, moreover, were situated along the middle course of the Ob' River, in a more accessible, southerly location than the Far Northern gas fields. Although the northern gas fields were the largest in the Soviet Union, their early development did not pose the same urgency as the production of Middle Ob' oil because of the simultaneous discovery of large gas fields in the deserts of Central Asia, notably Turkmenia. A system of gas pipelines had already been laid between Central Asia and Central Russia, beginning in the late 1960's, and the desert environment, though also extreme, posed less of a development obstacle than the remote tundra in the north.

In the West Siberian oil-producing region, early development in the mid-1960's focused on Shaim field in the Konda River valley, where oil had been discovered in 1960 and the oil town of Uray was founded in 1965. In the same year, a 250-mile, 30-inch pipeline was completed from the Shaim fields to Tyumen'. However, oil development in this area did not meet expectations. The population of the town of Uray, which had been planned at 30,000, leveled off at 17,000 in the early 1970's, and oil production did not rise much beyond 5 million tons a year.

The focus of development thus shifted at an early stage to the oil fields in the middle Ob' valley. The first discoveries there were made in 1961 at Megion, west of Nizhnevartovsk, and in the Ust'-Balyk field, southwest of Surgut, where the oil town of Nefteyugansk was founded (it reached a population of 20,000 in 1970 and 28,000 in 1974). The first oil in these Middle Ob' fields—as well as in the Shaim field—was produced in the summer of 1964, when about 200,000 tons moved by tanker barges down the Ob' and up the Irtysh River to the refinery at Omsk. This refinery, the first of any significance in Siberia, was opened originally in 1955 to process crude oil transported by pipeline from the Volga-Urals fields. The pipeline was lated extended halfway across Siberia, and in 1964 reached Angarsk (near Irkutsk), where a second major oil refinery had begun operations in 1961.

Being dependent on barge shipments during the brief summer shipping season, the development of the Middle Ob' fields proceeded slowly at first, reaching 5.8 million tons in 1967. But the rate of production was stepped up when the completion of a 650-mile, 40-inch pipeline from the producing fields to the Omsk refinery in late 1967 provided a year-round outlet. Two years later, the flow through the pipeline was further increased by the completion of a 250-mile, 30-inch feeder line from newly discovered oil fields around Strezhevoy in adjoining Tomsk Oblast. However, the contribution of Tomsk Oblast to West Siberian oil production has remained below expectations. The Strezhevoy field, which began producing in 1966, had been expected to reach an output level of 15 to 20 million tons of crude oil a year by the mid-1970's. However, it leveled off at an average yearly production of 5 to 6 million tons in the five-year plan period 1971—75. Significantly, the oil town of Strezhevoy, founded in 1967 as a workers' settlement, has not been raised to the higher urban status of "city" even though it is reported to have reached a population of 20,000 in 1975. Failure to confer city status may be interpreted as an indication of urban underdevelopment and even a degree of impermanence.

By 1970, West Siberian oil production had risen to 31.4 million tons, of which 28.5 million originated in fields of Tyumen' Oblast and 2.9 million in Tomsk Oblast. The flow of oil roughly met the combined throughput capacity of the refineries at Omsk and Angarsk. In that year, the pipeline system that had brought crude oil from the Volga-Urals fields since the mid-1950's was converted to handle a reverse flow of crude oil from Omsk westward, and the first surplus Siberian oil began to move to refineries in European Russia.

During the five-year period 1971—75, the development of the West Siberian fields was dominated by the upsurge of production in the giant Samotlor field. This field, named for a small lake north of Nizhnevartovsk, was discovered in 1965 and was officially reported in 1970 to have recoverable reserves of 2 billion tons. This disclosure in itself was unusual, for Soviet oil reserves are generally kept secret. Confronted with such a concentration of oil in a single field, the Soviet planners focused development efforts in the early 1970's on Samotlor. Production began in 1969, with 1.3 million tons recovered in that year, and in 1974 the field began to account for more than one-half of all West Siberian oil production. Total regional output rose from 31.4 million tons in 1970 to 180 million in 1976, and production in the single Samotlor field jumped from 4 million in 1970 to 110 million in 1976. Expectations were for Samotlor to level off at about 120 million tons a year in the late 1970's, and its share in total West Siberian output was planned to decline to about one-third as new fields were brought into production (Table 12).

TABLE 12

Crude Oil Production of Siberia
(million metric tons)

	1960	1965	1970	1975	1976	1980 Plan
West Siberia	–	1.0	31.4	147.7	180	310
Tyumen' Oblast	–	1.0	28.5	143	174	
Samotlor	–	–	4	87	110	120
Tomsk Oblast	–	–	2.9	5	6	
Sakhalin	1.6	2.4	2.5	2.5	2+	
Total Siberia	1.6	3.4	33.9	150	182	310
% of USSR	1.1	1.4	9.6	30.5	35	48

The development of the Samotlor field resulted in the rapid growth of the old Siberian village of Nizhnevartovsk, which had been raised to the urban status of workers' settlement in 1964 in connection with the start of production in the nearby Megion oil field. In 1970, Nizhnevartovsk was reported to have a population of 16,000, and two years later it was raised to the urban status of city. By 1976 its population expanded to 63,000. Together with the city of Surgut to the west, Nizhnevartovsk thus became one of the two major management centers of the West Siberian oil industry.

The rapid growth of oil production during the five-year plan 1971–75, when West Siberia's share in total Soviet output rose from 10 percent in 1970 to 30 percent in 1975, required the laying of additional pipelines to refining centers. Following the first pipeline, completed in 1967 to Omsk, the expanding Samotlor field gained a second outlet in 1972 with the opening of a 550-mile, 48-inch line running southeast along the Ob' River to join the Trans-Siberian pipeline system at Anzhero-Sudzhensk. This pipeline was later extended eastward toward Krasnoyarsk and will feed the Achinsk refinery, which was under construction in the mid-1970's. A third outlet from Samotlor was completed in 1973 when a 48-inch pipeline went into operation from the Middle Ob' district westward over a distance of 1,300 miles to join the European Russian pipeline system at the Tatar oil center of Almet'yevsk. A second 48-inch line, running from Samotlor westward to Kuybyshev on the Volga River, was completed in the summer of 1976. Thus far pipelines had been laid either eastward to Siberian refineries or westward toward the major refining centers of European Russia. In the late 1970's, construction was also under way on a pipeline that was to supply West Siberian oil to oil refineries under construction at Pavlodar and Chimkent in Kazakhstan, at Neftezavodsk in Turkmenia, as well as to the existing refineries in the Fergana Valley of Uzbekistan. The first segment, running 275 miles from Omsk southeast to Pavlodar, was scheduled to go into operation in 1977 together with the first stage of the Pavlodar refinery.

Until the mid-1970's, the development of the West Siberian oil fields had proceeded without a year-round transport link with the outside world. Supplies had to be brought in either by water during the six-month summer shipping season (April-October) on the middle Ob' River or by truck convoys over seasonal winter roads. When plans for the exploitation of the oil fields were first laid in the early

1960's, they provided for a rail connection with the city of Tyumen' on the Trans-Siberian, which was to become the gateway to the oil region. The new rail line from Tyumen' reached Tobol'sk in 1967, but progress north of Tobol'sk was slowed by construction problems in the swampy forest, and the railroad reached the south side of the Ob' valley opposite Surgut only in late 1973. It took two more years for the 1.3-mile bridge to be built across the Ob' River floodplain, and the first train from Tyumen' city entered Surgut in August 1975, a decade after the start of West Siberia's oil development.

By this time, Surgut had grown from a quiet Siberian fishing and timbering town of 6,000 people to the principal management center of the oil region, with a population of 67,000, extending over a distance of 10 miles along the right (northern) bank of the Ob'. Together with the oil town of Nefteyugansk, to the southwest, and its tributary pipeline service settlement of Poykovskiy, an urban cluster of about 100,000 had thus developed in the Surgut area. In addition to serving nearby oil fields, Surgut was also the electric power generating center for the entire Middle Ob' region. An electric station burning natural gas associated with oil production started up in late 1972 with the first 200-megawatt unit, and reached a capacity of 1,200 megawatts in late 1975. A second stage of equal capacity was to be added in the five-year plan 1976–80. In addition to serving the growing electric power needs of the oil fields, the Surgut station will transmit surplus electricity into the Urals power grid over a 500-kilovolt line completed between Tyumen' city and Surgut in 1969.

The rail link to the outside world, having reached Surgut in 1975 was then extended 135 miles eastward toward Nizhnevartovsk in 1976 in order to provide year-round overland communication with the region's second major management center. Almost more significant than the rail extension along the north bank of the Ob' River toward Nizhnevartovsk was the start of construction in 1976 of a 400-mile railroad northward toward the great Urengoy gas field. Construction on this line began in April 1976 at the station of Ul't-Yagun, 35 miles east of Surgut along the railroad to Nizhnevartovsk. The decision to proceed with such a major rail project from south to north across the difficult swampy forest terrain of the West Siberian plain was motivated not only by the desire for a rail link with the northern gas fields, but also by the need for pressing northward from Surgut with the development of additional oil resources. During the five-year period of 1971–75, a large portion of the production increase was obtained from the single huge oil concentration in the Samotlor field, and by the beginning of 1976 only 18 fields were being worked in the entire West Siberian oil region out of a total of 78 oil fields discovered. With the Samotlor field approaching peak production, Soviet planners had to take steps to develop a larger number of fields to maintain the rate of growth of the oil industry. Out of an average annual increment of 30 million tons envisaged during the five-year period 1976–80, Samotlor was expected to account for only an 8 million ton increase a year, or about one fourth, with the rest of the growth coming from other fields. Many of these were far from transportation, and the construction of the new railroad was designed in part to speed the development of the more distant fields.

The Surgut-Urengoy railroad was expected to reach the Kogolym field, about 70 miles north-northeast of Surgut in 1977, and the Kholmogory field, 125 miles north-northeast of Surgut in 1978. The target date for reaching the Urengoy gas field was 1980. The development of the Kholmogory oil field, the most promising north of Surgut, did not await the arrival of the railroad. Production started in July 1976 with the completion of a 160-mile pipeline from Surgut.

As is common in Soviet oil fields, the development of gas-processing capacity lagged behind the use of crude oil in the West Siberian fields, and the associated gas was flared off for a decade. Only in the Surgut area was some associated gas collected for fueling the Surgut power station, starting in 1972. The first of a planned series of gas-processing plants did not go into operation until early 1975 at Nizhnevartovsk, with a throughput capacity of more than 2 billion cubic meters a year; its capacity was doubled with the addition of a second stage in early 1976, and another gas plant was nearing completion in the Pravdinsk oil field, southwest of Surgut. The total gas-processing capacity to be completed according to the five-year plan 1976—80 was 14 billion cubic meters, which represented a 50 percent increase over the total capacity installed in the Soviet Union (27 billion in 1974). The dry gas was at first being used in the Surgut power station and the natural-gas liquids were being shipped to petrochemical plants. However, with the projected increase in gas-processing capacity a surplus of both dry gas and natural gas liquids was expected to develop in the late 1970's.

To make use of the surplus dry gas, a long-planned gas pipeline was being rushed to completion from Nizhnevartovsk to the Kuznetsk Basin. The 800-mile, 40-inch line was originally intended to carry natural gas from the Myl'dzhino field, discovered in 1964 in the Vasyugan'ye swamps of Tomsk Oblast. However, the use of the Myl'dzhino gas field was delayed as the vastly greater potential of gas associated with the Samotlor oil field became evident. Construction of the gas pipeline finally began in 1975 and was scheduled to be completed in 1977, with an ultimate carrying capacity of 10 billion cubic meters of gas a year. The natural gas is expected to be used in the Kuznetsk Basin as a fuel in cement kilns, as a source of hydrogen for ammonia synthesis (now based on coke-oven gases) and as a fuel in blast furnaces and steel furnaces, thus reducing the consumption of coke in the iron and steel industry.

Two of the Soviet Union's largest petrochemical complexes were under construction in the late 1970's at Tobol'sk and at Tomsk to make use of the natural gas liquids being generated in growing amounts by the West Siberian oil industry. The Tobol'sk complex, scheduled to go into operation in 1979 with its first gas-fractionating unit, is expected to specialize at first in synthetic rubber monomers (butadiene and isoprene) as well as methanol, and later in synthetic rubber and plastic resins. The petrochemical plant is expected to result in a rebirth of the old Siberian town of Tobol'sk, which dates from 1587. It was the administrative center of West Siberia for 250 years until a southward shift of transport routes and economic activities led to its decline in the early 19th century. The development of the West Siberian oil fields began to stimulate its growth, with the city's population rising from 36,000 in 1959 to 51,000 in 1976. A further increase to more than 100,000 by the early 1980's is expected as a result of the petrochemical project and its supporting activities, with an ultimate population of 200,000 envisaged.

In contrast to the synthetic-rubber orientation of the Tobol'sk complex, the petrochemical project at Tomsk will specialize in plastics, particularly polyethylene and polypropylene. The first stage of the Tomsk plant, scheduled to go into operation in 1980, is expected to produce 350,000 tons of polyethylene, or the

TABLE 13

Natural Gas Production of Siberia
(in billion cubic meters)

	1960	1965	1970	1975	1976	1980 Plan
West Siberia	–	–	9.6	38	46	155
Medvezh'ye field	–	–	–	31	41	70–80
Urengoy field	–	–	–	–	–	30
Komsomol field	–	–	–	–	–	14
Punga-Igrim fields	–	–	9.6	5	3	–
Middle Ob' oil fields	–	–	–	2	2	15
Noril'sk complex	–	–	0.2	1		
Yakutia	–	–	0.2	0.5		
Sakhalin	0.3	0.6	1.0	1		
All Siberia	0.3	0.6	11.0	40	49	158
% of USSR	0.7	0.5	5.0	14	16	36

equivalent of total Soviet production as of 1975, as well as 100,000 tons of polypropylene, which would be 15 times greater than the current Soviet output as a whole. Total investment in the first stage of the Tomsk petrochemical project is expected to exceed one billion rubles ($1.4 billion).

While further exploration for oil was being pressed in the West Siberian province, which is likely to play a key role in the Soviet oil industry over the next few decades, geological prospecting was also under way to the east, in the Tunguska basin of the Siberian platform. The presence of oil was suggested in 1973 with the No. 1 well completed at Kuyumba (Lat. 61°N Long. 97°E) on the Podkamennaya (Stony) Tunguska River. The discovery stimulated a program of geological drilling along both the Podkamennaya Tunguska (Poligus, Ust'-Kamo and Vanavara) and the Nizhnyaya (Lower) Tunguska (near Tura) in an effort to gain a clearer picture of the geology of the region.

Another potential oil-bearing area is believed to be the Ust'-Kut–Kirenga dome in Irkutsk Oblast, where a productive well completed in 1962 at Markovo on the Lena River created a brief flurry of excitement. However, the deposit proved small, and in view of the more significant oil development in West Siberia, exploration was not pressed.

Outside of West Siberia, the only consistent oil production has been taking place in Sakhalin, where the first significant field was discovered in 1923 at Okha, near the northeast coast. Production began in 1926 under a Japanese concession, which was canceled by the Soviet Government in 1928. Under Soviet administration, additional small fields were put into production at Ekhabi, just south of Okha, and at Katangli, 135 miles south of Okha, and by 1940, total production in Sakhalin was 501,000 tons, or 1.6 percent of the Soviet Union's output. Sakhalin oil, even at that low level of production, played a key role in World War II, when a pipeline was completed from Okha across the Tatar Strait to the mainland for use in the refinery at Komsomol'sk.

In the postwar period, additional discoveries such as the Kolendo field, 20 miles north of Okha, raised production to the 1-million-ton mark in 1959 and the 2-million-ton mark in the early 1960's. Since about 1965, Sakhalin has maintained a steady output level of 2.5 million tons a year, or only about 0.5 percent of 1976 Soviet production, covering only about one-third of regional needs of the Soviet Far East. A second oil pipeline from Okha to Komsomol'sk was nearing completion in the mid-1970's. At the same time, offshore exploration began with Japanese survey ships and other foreign assistance both along the east coast shelf and off the south coast in an effort to establish the offshore potential of the Sakhalin shelf. Although both natural gas fields and associated gas represent a potential annual production of about 3 billion cubic meters, gas production has been limited to less than one billion cubic meters because of the limited island market and the lack of a gas pipeline to the mainland. The principal producing gas field is Tungor, 12 miles south of Okha, which has been in operation since 1965 and yields a few hundred thousand cubic meters a year for local consumption. A substantial portion of the gas associated with oil production is injected into wells to stimulate oil flow in so-called gas-lift operations. In 1970, nearly one million tons of crude oil, or 38 percent of the Sakhalin total, was obtained by gas lift.

In West Siberia, the history of natural gas development dates from 1953, when a small gas deposit was discovered at Berezovo. However there was no significant commercial production until the discovery of the Igrim (1959) and Punga (1961) fields, 60 to 70 miles south of Berezovo. Earlier plans for a pipeline from Berezovo to the industrial city of Serov in the northern Urals were abandoned, and instead construction began on a 40-inch pipeline from the Urals to the Punga-Igrim fields. It was completed in 1966, allowing the first West Siberian gas to flow to the Urals industrial cities of Ivdel', Serov and Nizhniy Tagil. These early West Siberian fields, situated a few hundred miles from North Urals industrial centers, had limited reserves and reached a peak production of over 9 billion cubic meters a year in the early 1970's, followed by gradual depletion through the decade.

As these small fields were being developed in the mid-1960's, natural gas resources of incomparably greater magnitude were being identified about 400 miles farther to the northeast, near West Siberia's Arctic coast. The first strike of a relatively small northern field at Tazovskiy in 1962 (initially viewed as a potential source of natural gas for Noril'sk) was followed by a series of field discoveries with reserves in the trillions of cubic meters: in 1965, Zapolyarnoye (60 miles southeast of Tazovskiy) and Gubkin (30 miles southwest of Tarko-Sale); in 1966, Urengoy (35 miles northwest of the old Urengoy settlement) and Komsomol (25 miles west of the Gubkin field); in 1967, Medvezh'ye (50 miles northeast of the old Nadym settlement); in 1968, Vyngapur (on the upper Vyngapur River, 125 miles SSW of Tarko-Sale); in 1969, Yamburg (on the Taz Peninsula, southwest of Yamburg settlement) and Yubileynoye (between the Medvezh'ye and Urengoy fields); and in 1974, Kharasavey (on the west coast of the Yamal Peninsula). While the northern gas fields were generally being developed from the landward side, Kharasavey was the site of an unusual experiment in 1976 when a freighter led by the nuclear icebreaker Lenin delivered a geological exploration party to the field.

The discoveries beginning in the mid-1960's dwarfed the earlier fields of the Berezovo-Punga district, which had total industrial reserves $(B + C_1)$ of 200 billion cubic meters. By 1975, West Siberian reserves in these categories had jumped to 15 trillion cubic meters, or two-thirds of Soviet reserves. Instead of being distributed in many small fields, as in the Berezovo-Punga district, the northern gas resources were concentrated in a few giant fields, of which the largest was Urengoy, with about 5 trillion cubic meters, followed by Yamburg (3.5 trillion), Zapolyarnoye (2 trillion) and Medvezh'ye (1.5 trillion). Despite the harsh Arctic environment under which these fields were to be developed, the large magnitude of the reserves was said to allow economies of scale through the use of extra large diameter drilling pipe and transmission mains. The unusual accumulation of natural gas reserves provided a long-term source of fuel not only for the economically developed regions of the Urals and European USSR, but also for export, both by overland pipelines to Western Europe and by liquefied-gas tankers overseas.

The development of the northern fields began with Medvezh'ye, which was situated closest to the Urals and required the laying of only 300 miles of additional pipeline beyond the Punga field terminal. Construction of the first pipeline, with a diameter of 48 inches and a carrying capacity of 16 billion cubic meters of gas a year, began in 1969, crossing the wide Ob' River floodplain at Peregrebnoye and proceeding generally northeast across the Kazym River toward Nadym. This new town, founded southwest of the old Arctic trading post of Nadym, achieved urban status in 1972. Its population rose from 6,100 in 1970 to about 30,000 in 1976. Nadym was designed not only as the supply base and management center for the Medvezh'ye field, 60 miles to the northeast, but as the principal collecting and transmitting point for natural gas from other northern fields.

On the way from Punga to Nadym, gas pipeline workers laid a 40-mile, 28-inch feeder branch to tap the small Pokhroma field on the Ob' River, opposite Berezovo. The Pokhroma field, discovered in 1960, had reserves of about 20 billion cubic meters, ranking second after the Punga field among the small fields in the Berezovo district.

The development of Nadym and the Medvezh'ye field posed logistical problems because of the lack of transportation in the northern tundra. The only access was in winter by cross-country truck convoys over temporary roads and in summer during the brief shipping season (June to October) down the Ob' River into the Ob' Gulf and upstream along the Nadym River. Bars at the Nadym River mouth and in the stream channel required the transshipment of goods to shallow barges until adequate depths could be assured by dredging. The new town of Nadym was situated on a derelict old rail line that was being built by forcing labor in the late 1940's and early 1950's from the Ob' River town of Salekhard across the tundra eastward toward Igarka on the Yenisey River. By the time the project was abandoned in 1953, following Stalin's death, the line had been completed over a distance of 250 miles from Salekhard to Nadym. When the huge natural-gas potential of the northern region became evident in the late 1960's, there were proposals for rehabilitating the railroad, which would have required replacing rails and crossties and building more permanent concrete bridges instead of the old primitive wooden bridges. However, the reconstruction of the railroad was ultimately rejected as uneconomical, partly because through rail transportation from European Russia would also have required the construction of a major bridge across the lower Ob' River between Labytnangi and Salekhard. Locally, the gas developers in Nadym, in an effort to provide a more efficient transport link between the town and the Medvezh'ye gas field, rehabilitated a segment of the old railroad as far as Khetta, and then built a spur to Pangody, a settlement in the actual gas field. The entire 75-mile line, begun in 1971, went into operation in 1976.

The first gas began to flow from the Medvezh'ye field in April 1972 when the first 48-inch transmission main reached Nadym from the Punga field. A second 48-inch string from Nadym to the Urals was completed in 1974, and a third, with a 56-inch diameter and a carrying capacity of 30 billion cubic meters, opened in 1975. The first Siberian natural gas reached Moscow in October 1974 over a 48-inch pipeline running from the Urals through Perm', Kazan' and Gor'kiy to Moscow. By 1976, the Medvezh'ye field was producing at the annual rate of about 40 billion cubic meters, with a possible goal of 70 billion cubic meters or more by 1980.

The original pipeline plans for the Medvezh'ye field were to run the basic transmission system of several parallel strings through Salekhard across the northernmost Urals and then southwest through Komi ASSR to Ukhta and Torzhok, the great gas-distribution center of central Russia. However, in the early 1970's, priority for this northern alignment was abandoned on economic grounds because of the lack of major gas consumers along the way. Instead the early bundle of pipeline strings ran southwest from Nadym through Punga to the Urals and central Russia, with their developed industrial areas and markets. It was only after a flow of gas to the more southerly developed regions had been provided that the first pipeline was completed in May 1976 across the northern Urals. But instead of crossing the Urals in the extreme north along the rail spur from the Pechora Railroad to Labytnangi on the Ob' (at Lat. 67°N), the pipeline alignment was shifted southward to Lat. 63°N, running between the Punga gas field on the east side of the Urals and the Vuktyl' field in Komi ASSR on the west side. This first pipeline across the northern Urals was part of a 56-inch line, with a carrying capacity of 28 billion cubic meters a year, that will carry West Siberian gas in the general southwesterly direction through Ukhta, Torzhok and Minsk to the western Ukraine for export through Czechoslovakia to Western Europe. Three depleted Carpathian gas fields—Ugersko, 7 miles north of Stryy (with original reserves of 40 billion cubic meters); Dashava, 5 miles northeast of Stryy (15 billion) and Opary, 8 miles northeast of Drogobych (12 billion)—were converted into underground storage reservoirs in 1974—76 to insure a steady year-round flow for export. Gas exports through the West Ukrainian pipeline system totaled 17.5 billion cubic meters in 1975, of which 3.1 billion moved to West Germany, 2.3 billion to Italy and 1.9 billion to Austria. The export flow was expected to rise to about 60 billion cubic meters by 1980, with West Siberia contributing an increasing share.

A major contribution to gas exports was expected to come from the giant Urengoy field, which was next to be developed after Medvezh'ye. The first gas development team reached the Urengoy field in the winter of 1973—74 by cross-country truck convoy from Nadym, and drilling of production wells began in 1975, when construction of a 130-mile pipeline extension from Nadym to the Urengoy also began. The first commercial production in the Urengoy field was scheduled for 1978 from an initial stage with a capacity of 30 billion cubic meters. Ultimate gas output from the field is expected to reach 100 billion cubic meters a year, sometime in the 1980's. A new gas town, tentatively called Yagel'nyy (yagel' is the Russian word for reindeer moss) was under construction on the development site, 35 miles northwest of the old trading post of Urengoy. The initial gas flow was expected to move through Nadym and Punga across the northern Urals into the southwesterly system for export to Western Europe. However, ultimately most of the output from Urengoy was scheduled to be transmitted southward through a new pipeline system running through Surgut, Tobol'sk, Tyumen' to Chelyabinsk and onward into central Russia. This new orientation of the growing gas flow from the

West Siberian fields was decided upon in 1975, when Soviet planners determined the future sequence of development of the region's oil and gas resources. Priority is to be given in the late 1970's and early 1980's to the fields between Urengoy and Surgut, including the Kholmogory oil field in the south and the Vyngapur, Komsomol and Gubkin gas fields farther north. This sequence of development determined both the construction of the Surgut-Urengoy railroad and the parallel gas transmission system. The first 56-inch pipeline from the Komsomol and Vyngapur fields to Chelyabinsk was scheduled to go into operation in 1979, carrying 4 billion cubic meters in that year and 14 billion in 1980.

In addition to providing natural gas for domestic consumption and for overland pipeline transmission to Eastern Europe and Western Europe, the Urengoy field has also been envisaged as a source of gas for overseas shipments in LNG (liquefied natural gas) tankers. The so-called North Star project, first proposed in 1972 by a group of American companies (Tenneco, Texas Eastern, and Brown & Root), called for the construction of a gas pipeline from Urengoy to a liquefaction plant in the Murmansk area and for tanker shipments to the East Coast of the United States. The plan was dormant after Congress put limits on government financing of development projects in the Soviet Union, but was revived in 1976 when financial backing was being sought in West Germany, France and Britain in exchange for a portion of the LNG deliveries to Western Europe.

The significance of the West Siberian developments has overshadowed the use of natural gas elsewhere in Siberia. The development of gas fields for local use in the Noril'sk metals complex of northern Siberia, beginning in 1970, has already been mentioned, as was the limited gas potential of Sakhalin.

However, there are major expectations for significant natural gas development in the Vilyuy River basin of Yakutia. Gas was first discovered in 1956 in a small field (Tas-Tumus) at the Vilyuy-Lena river confluence, and exploratory drilling that continued until 1961 established small reserves adequate for a pipeline to Yakutsk, for use in a small thermal power station, and to a proposed cement plant in the Pokrovsk-Bestyakh area, south of Yakutsk. The 20-inch, 180-mile pipeline from the gas settlement of Promyshlennyy to Yakutsk was completed in January 1968, and a 60-mile extension to the Pokrovsk area was added later that year. The natural gas replaced high-cost coal from the nearby Kangalassy mine as a fuel in the old Yakutsk power station of about 7 megawatts, and was used in a new and larger electric plant equipped with 25-megawatt gas-turbine units; the first unit went into operation in late 1969, and the fourth in late 1971, for a combined generating capacity of 100 megawatts. The other major gas consumer, the cement plant, with a capacity of 200,000 tons, did not go into operation until 1971 in the settlement of Mokhsogollokh, between Pokrovsk and Bestyakh. Although the gas flow from the Tas-Tumus field never exceeded 200 million cubic meters a year (it peaked at 184 million in 1970), the deposit quickly approached depletion in the early 1970's. In an effort to maintain a gas supply, a 120-mile extension was laid westward in 1973 from the depleted field to the larger Mastakh field, on the Vilyuy River at Kysyl-Syr, 30 miles east of the town of Vilyuysk. As a result of the Mastakh connection, the gas flow rose to 435 million cubic meters a year in 1974.

Despite the modest local gas use, potential reserves in the Vilyuy basin have been estimated as 13 trillion cubic meters, rivaling the vast gas resources of West Siberia. However, in contrast to West Siberia, where the presence of such resources has been demonstrated, the Yakutian potential has only been inferred and remains to be established by further drilling. By the mid-1970's, only about one trillion cubic meters (of the inferred 13 trillion) had been indicated, with several hundred billion cubic meters proved for commercial exploitation. The outlook seemed promising enough to induce another group of American companies (El Paso Company and Occidental Petroleum Corp.) to propose an LNG project for the West Coast of the United States, in cooperation with Japan, provided adequate reserves could be proved. An early $400 million plan for geological exploration was put forward in 1972, but failed to obtain financing. However, after the proposed expenditures were scaled down to $100 million, an exploration agreement was signed in 1976 by the Soviet Union, Japanese and American interests. The ultimate plan, with costs running into billions of dollars, would require the construction of a gas pipeline from Yakutia to a liquefaction plant on the Pacific coast, and LNG tanker transport to both Japan and the United States.

Coal and steel developments

Although oil and gas development was going forward at an intensive pace in the mid-1970's, Soviet planners also focused attention increasingly on the use of coal and lignite as a future power-station fuel. Until the upsurge of oil and gas extraction, beginning in the early 1950's, coal had accounted for up to 66 percent of Soviet fuel consumption. Over the next two decades, the share of coal in the fuel balance dropped to a little more than 30 percent while the share of oil rose to 44 percent and natural gas to 21 percent. Minor contributions were made by peat, oil shale and firewood (of the order of one percent each). The realization in the mid-1970's that hydrocarbon resources are more limited than coal resources led to a modification of the energy policy in the Soviet Union. Under that policy, the full impact of which is not likely to be felt until the 1980's, greater reliance was to be placed on the use of coal for power generation while hydrocarbons were to be used more for the production of petrochemicals and for export rather than as a power-station fuel. The new Soviet policy, favoring greater consumption of coal by electric power plants to save the more valuable oil and gas, has its counterpart in the United States, where greater use of coal by electric utilities is being encouraged by the Government to reduce oil imports and move toward energy independence.

The renewed interest in coal in the middle 1970's focused attention on Siberia's vast coal resources, particularly on the high-grade coking and steam coals of the Kuznetsk Basin, which has undergone steady development, and the lower-ranking lignite of the Kansk-Achinsk Basin, which was still awaiting full-fledged development. Kuzbas coal, because of its high heating values and low extraction costs, can support transport costs over long distances and has the largest marketing area of any of the Soviet coal producing areas, covering almost one-half of the USSR—from East Siberia to northwest European Russia. More than one-half of Kuzbas coal is being shipped out of West Siberia, mainly westward. Kansk-Achinsk lignite, on the other hand, though cheap to extract through huge strip-mining operations, has a low heating value and high moisture content and cannot support long hauls, both on economic grounds and for technical reasons (it oxidizes easily and has a tendency to ignite itself in open-air storage and transportation). Although there have been proposals to upgrade Kansk-Achinsk lignite to a drier product or charlike briquets to expand its marketing area, the immediate prospect is for expanded use in onsite power plants and the transmission of the generated electricity westward to the Urals and European Russia over extra high voltage lines.

TABLE 14

Coal Production in Kuznetsk Basin
(in million metric tons)

	1940	1945	1950	1955	1960	1965	1970	1975	1980 Plan
Total production	22.5	30.0	38.5	58.5	84.0	96.9	113	137	161
% of USSR	13.6	20.0	14.8	15.0	16.5	16.8	18.1	19.5	20
Coking coal	5.9	12.9	14.9	21.4	28.5	37.5	46.9	56	
% of USSR	16.7	43.9	28.9	27.5	25.9	27.0	28.5	31	
Strip-mined	—	—	0.9	5.7	16.5	22.4	28	36.7	40
% of USSR	—	—	3.2	8.8	16.2	15.9	16.8	16.7	15

The Kuznetsk Basin has steadily expanded its coal production since World War II, both for its high-rank, low-ash steam coals and especially for its coking coals. The emphasis on coking coals is evident from the data in Table 14, which shows that the percentage share of the Kuzbas in total Soviet coking-coal production has ranged between 26 and 29 percent during the 1950's and 1960's, reaching 31 percent in 1975. By contrast, the share of the Kuzbas in total Soviet coal output has been growing from 15 to 20 percent during the same period. By the mid-1970's, the Kuznetsk Basin had thus firmly established itself as the Soviet Union's second largest coal producer, contributing 31 percent of the nation's coking coal and 29 percent of the bituminous steam coals. (In 1975, the Soviet Union produced about 280 million tons of bituminous steam coals, 180 million tons of coking coals, 77 million tons of anthracite and 164 million tons of lignite.)

In the course of its expansion, the Kuzbas underwent changes both in the geography of its coal industry and in its mining technology. Expansion was associated with a southward movement within the basin, from older northern mining areas near the Trans-Siberian Railroad to newer southern districts. The oldest mining areas were situated around Anzhero-Sudzhensk and Kemerovo, and during the early five-year plans of the 1930's, the center of coal-mining operations had shifted southward to Leninsk-Kuznetskiy, Kiselevsk and Prokop'yevsk. By 1940, these new mining districts accounted for two-thirds of the basin's total output. After the war, expansion proceeded particularly in the southern portion of the basin, with new districts starting production around Belovo and in the Tom'-Usa area, where the new mining city of Mezhdurechensk arose. While the population of most Kuzbas mining cities leveled off or even declined during the 1960's and 1970's (see Table 6), Mezhdurechensk grew from 55,000 in 1959 to 89,000 in 1976.

A large portion of the increase in mining capacity in the postwar period was in strip mines. The first two strip mines of the Kuzbas opened in 1948–49 at Bachatskiy and Krasnobrodskiy, south of Belovo, and within a decade 12 strip mines were in operation. The 17th, Siberginskiy in the Tom'-Usa district, began production in 1971. Of the nearly 100 million tons of coal production added since 1950, roughly one-third represented strip mines and two-thirds deep mines. Virtually all the coking coal is extracted in deep mines, with strip mines contributing only about 2 to 3 million tons; the rest of the strip-mined coal is of the low-ash steam-coal variety. Kuzbas strip mines generally tend to be relatively small, with thin seams and thick overburden compared with the large capacity and thick seams of the basin's deep mines. The largest strip mine, Tom'-Usa No. 7–8, which began production in 1965 near Mezhdurechensk, has a designed capacity of 4 million tons a year. The largest deep mine, Raspadskaya, which went into operation in 1973, also near Mezhdurechensk, has a designed capacity of 7.5 million tons.

Kuzbas coking coal, in addition to being shipped westward to the Urals and into European Russia, has also stimulated the expansion of iron and steel production within the Kuznetsk Basin as a new West Siberian Iron and Steel Plant supplemented the older Kuznetsk plant in the Novokuznetsk area. The new plant started construction in 1957 on a site 10 miles northeast of Novokuznetsk, on the right bank of the Tom' River. The first unit of the plant, the No. 1 blast furnace with a working volume of 2,000 cubic meters and an annual output of one million tons of pig iron, was not completed until 1964, with the No. 2 blast furnace, with identical characteristics, following in 1967. Steel production began only in 1968, with the start of an oxygen converter shop of three 100-ton converters. The plant was not fully integrated until 1970, when blooming and billet mills were in operation. After a third blast furnace, of 3,000 cubic meters and an annual capacity of 2 million tons, was completed in 1971, the West Siberian plant had a pig-iron capacity of 4 million tons. However a pig-iron shortage developed at the plant after a new steel-making section of two large oxygen converters of 300 to 350 ton capacity (equivalent to 3 million tons a year) opened in May 1974, raising the plant's steel-making capacity to 6 million tons compared with 4 million tons of pig iron. To make use of the excess steel capacity, a pig-iron shuttle was set up between the Kuznetsk and West Siberian plants, carrying about 2,000 tons of molten Kuznetsk pig iron a day in specially designed transporters to West Siberian steel furnaces. In an effort to rectify the imbalance, the No. 1 blast furnace at the West Siberian plant was being rebuilt in the mid-1970's to expand its working volume from 2,000 to 3,000 cubic meters.

The construction of a new iron and steel plant required the development of additional Siberian ore sources. The Kuznetsk plant had relied largely on iron-ore mines in the Shor uplands of the southern part of the Kuznetsk Basin (Tashtagol, Sheregesh, Kaz) with a combined capacity of about 7 million tons of crude ore (or 5 million tons of usable ore), which met about 80 percent of the Kuznetsk plant's ore needs. The rest had to be shipped in from the Urals and, starting in the late 1950's, from the newly developed iron-mining complex at Rudnyy in Kazakhstan. The addition of a fifth blast furnace (with an annual capacity of one million tons of pig iron) at the Kuznetsk plant in 1960 and the prospective needs of the new West Siberian plant spurred the development of additional Siberian iron-ore sources.

In neighboring Khakass Autonomous Oblast, the Abaza mine with an ultimate capacity of 2 million tons of usable ore began operations in 1957. The ore first had to move by a roundabout rail route through Abakan and Achinsk to the Kuznetsk plant, until a direct rail link was completed in 1959. On that direct rail link, a second mine, Teya, began operations in 1966, also with a capacity of about 2 million tons of usable ore. In the 1970's two other small iron mines were developed farther east in southern Krasnoyarsk Kray at Krasnokamensk and Irba, near Artemovsk on the Abakan-Tayshet railroad. Krasnokamensk shipped its first ore to the Kuznetsk mill in 1969 and Irba in 1974. Each is to have an ultimate capacity of 3 million tons of crude ore, or about 2 million tons of usable concentrate.

But the biggest iron-ore development was about 1,000 rail miles from the Kuznetsk iron and steel complex at Zheleznogorsk in Irkutsk Oblast, where a concentrator is converting low-grade crude ore of 28–30 percent iron to 62 percent concentrate for shipment to the West Siberian plant. The Zheleznogorsk mining and concentrating complex began operation in early 1965 and, at full capacity in the mid-1970's, was producing 6 million tons of concentrate a year (derived from 16 million tons of crude ore). The Zheleznogorsk iron mine was originally envisaged as an ore source for an iron and steel plant projected for Tayshet, 330 miles away on the Trans-Siberian Railroad. But the Tayshet steel project, though included in the seven-year plan 1959–65, has not materialized, partly because the Zheleznogorsk ore source was committed to the West Siberian. There has been talk of developing the Rudnogorsk iron deposit, northwest of Zheleznogorsk on the rail spur to Ust'-Ilimsk, with slightly higher iron content, but only half the reserves of Zheleznogorsk. A workers' settlement was established at Rudnogorsk in August 1974 suggesting plans for development.

In general, however, a shortage of economical iron-ore resources appears to preclude intensive development of the iron and steel industry in Siberia, where ore development has consistently lagged behind pig-iron output. In the mid-1970's, Siberia still accounted for only about 6.5 percent of the Soviet Union's production of usable iron ore compared with 9 percent of the nation's pig-iron output (Table 2). The balance was made up by shipments from the Rudnyy mines in northwest Kazakhstan.

While the commitment of the Kuznetsk Basin's coking-coal resources to the European iron and steel industry and the general paucity of economical iron-ore resources in Siberia make major expansion of the iron and steel industry unlikely, there appear to be significant prospects for the use of the vast lignite resources of the Kansk-Achinsk Basin as a fuel for minehead power stations and the long-distance transmission of the generated electricity westward over extra-high-voltage lines.

The development of the lignite resources of the Kansk-Achinsk Basin had its beginnings in the late 1930's on the Irsha-Borodino deposit near Zaozernyy, in the eastern portion of the basin. Early development was limited to a few deep mines of limited capacity that yielded 400,000 tons in the war period and reached a peak of 970,000 tons in 1950. After the opening of the first strip mine in that year, the old shaft mines became uneconomical, and underground mining ceased in 1958. The start of strip-mining operations at Irsha-Borodino marked the second phase in the development of the basin. The Irsha-Borodino strip mine yielded 9.5 million tons in 1970 and about 15 million in 1975. Its capacity is to be raised ultimately to 25 million tons. A second strip mine began producing lignite in 1951 at Nazarovo, in the western portion of the basin. This operation yielded 8.6 million tons of lignite in 1970 and 13 million in 1975, with ultimate expansion to about 25 million tons. A substantial portion of the lignite has been burned since 1961 in a minehead power station at Nazarovo that reached an installed generating capacity of 1,400 megawatts in 1968. About 90 percent of the present output of the Kansk-Achinsk Basin is being used as a power station fuel within the southern portion of Krasnoyarsk Kray, with most of the rest moving a short distance to electric generating plants in adjoining Kemerovo Oblast.

Current production, amounting to 28 million tons in 1975, has been restricted by the limited local market and is still far below the potential of the Kansk-Achinsk Basin, which accounts for about three-fourths of the Soviet Union's coal reserves suitable for strip mining. Long-term Soviet forecasts extending to the year 2000 and beyond envisage the basin as the nation's principal coal-mining district with a potential for about 30 giant strip mines with an annual capacity of up to 50 million tons each, or an overall output of the order of one billion tons a year. Favorable mining conditions include the existence of a principal seam of 200 to 300 feet thick that extends almost horizontally over large areas under a relatively thin overburden (250 to 300 feet). The economies of scale made possible by the projected giant strip mines combined with high labor productivity are said to make coal production in the Kansk-Achinsk Basin among the cheapest in the Soviet Union, with the smaller Ekibastuz Basin of northeast Kazakhstan as the only rival.

Large-scale use of Kansk-Achinsk coal, though long urged by some Soviet planners, has been held up by technological problems, including the development of extra-high-voltage power transmission lines that would make it economical to transfer the huge blocks of electricity generated at minehead power stations thousands of miles westward to the Urals and European Russia. Various techniques designed to upgrade the lignite to char or other higher-rank materials that could be transported over greater distances have not been carried beyond the experimental stage to industrial pilot projects.

However, the apparent urgency of conserving valuable hydrocarbons for uses other than power generation and the relatively limited reserves of high-ranking steam coals in the Soviet Union have focused increasing attention on the almost limitless potential of Kansk-Achinsk lignite. After years of hesitation, the construction of a third strip mine finally got under way in 1974 on the Berezovskoye deposit in the western portion of the basin, 50 miles southwest of Nazarovo, on the border of Kemerovo Oblast. A pilot project, with a capacity of 200,000 tons a year, was designed to yield enough lignite for checking its burning characteristics at a test boiler of the Krasnoyarsk Heat and Power Station, a municipal power plant with a capacity of 434 megawatts. The first lignite moved to the Krasnoyarsk thermal station in October 1975. Full-scale development of the Berezovskoye strip mine envisages an annual capacity of 55 million tons by 1990. While the characteristics of the lignite were being tested, ground-clearing work began in 1975 on the site of the first of a series of giant power plants that would burn the lignite for long-distance transmission of electricity westward. The first Berezovskoye station, designed for an ultimate capacity of 6,400 megawatts (eight 800-megawatt units), is to be located near the old Siberian village of Sharypovo, 10 miles south of the strip mine. A city with an ultimate population of 200,000 is envisaged in the Sharypovo area.

The Berezovskoye deposit is the largest in the Kansk-Achinsk Basin, with about 25 billion tons of explored reserves, or one-fourth of the total. By contrast, the Nazarovo deposit has explored reserves of only 0.7 billion tons, and the Irsha-Borodino deposit 3.5 billion tons. Future development of the basin also envisages the excavation of 50-million-ton strip mines in the southern (Barandat) portion of the Itatskiy deposit, across the border in Kemerovo Oblast, 20 miles west of the Berezovskoye pit. In the eastern portion of the basin, large potential lignite development is associated with the Aban deposit, 20 miles north of Kansk. Most of the lignite development is envisaged for the 1980's, with only the first preparatory steps being taken during the 10th five-year plan (1976—80). The plan provides for a production growth of 50 percent, which will come almost entirely from expansion of Nazarovo and Irsha-Borodino, with production rising from 28 million tons in 1975 to about 40 million in 1980. The long-term forecast for Kansk-Achinsk development envisages a tenfold increase during the 1980's, implying a production level of the order of 400 million tons by 1990. Such a lignite output is associated by Soviet long-term forecasts with the construction of about 10 minehead power stations similar to the Berezovskoye electric plant, or a combined generating capacity of the order of 60,000 megawatts, which would be about 10 to 15 percent of the expected Soviet electrical capacity in 1990.

Plans for the disposition of the vast amounts of electric power to be generated in the Kansk-Achinsk Basin have gone through several stages. Early designs envisaged a direct transmission system from the Kansk-Achinsk power-generating complex over a distance of 2,000 miles westward to the Urals and the European electricity grid of the Soviet Union, which would have been in addition to a similar transmission system from the proposed power complex of the Ekibastuz Basin in northeast

Kazakhstan. However it emerged in the early 1970's that priority would be given to an extra-high-voltage link between Ekibastuz and Central Russia and that, in the initial phase at least, Kansk-Achinsk would feed electricity through an interconnection into the Ekibastuz transmission system. Proposed voltages on these long-distance transmission lines have also risen over the years as the technology advanced. By the mid-1970's, both 1,500-kilovolt DC and 1,150-kilovolt AC lines were being tested, with the latter type being given priority in development. The 10th five-year plan (1976—80) calls for the construction of a 1,150-kilovolt AC intertie between the Kansk-Achinsk Basin and Ekibastuz through the Kuznetsk Basin, capable of carrying up to 6,000 megawatts, or about 40 billion kilowatt-hours of electricity a year. However, pending the completion of this line, as well as the transmission system at extra high voltage between Ekibastuz and Central Russia, which is not expected until the 1980's, the Kansk-Achinsk Basin (and the central Siberian power grid generally) is to be linked with Ekibastuz by a 500-kilovolt line through Barnaul and Rubtsovsk. At the same time a 500-kilovolt link was opened in 1976 from Ekibastuz through Tselinograd and Rudnyy to the Urals, thus interconnecting for the first time the power systems of central Siberia, northern Kazakhstan and the Urals at 500 kilovolts, which has become a standard voltage for interconnection between Soviet regional power systems.

The lignite-based power generation that is to be carried out on a giant scale in the Kansk-Achinsk Basin during the 1980's is already being implemented in smaller strip-mining operations extending through southern Siberia along the Trans-Siberian Railroad. In Irkutsk Oblast, the Azey lignite field at the town of Tulun went into operation in 1956 and was producing 10 million tons a year in the mid-1970's, or 40 percent of the total coal output of Irkutsk Oblast. Most of the Azey lignite is being burned in nearby electric power stations. East of Lake Baykal, two small lignite basins are being developed with associated minehead power stations. The Gusinoozersk deposit in Buryat ASSR began strip-mining operations in 1965, after earlier deep mining on the site, and the first 200-megawatt generating unit of a 1,200-megawatt minehead power station went into operation in 1976. The strip mine is being expanded to an annual capacity of 3 million tons to supply the electric plant. The Kharanor lignite field in southeast Chita Oblast started strip-mine production in 1957, reaching an annual output of 5.5 million tons in the mid-1970's. A minehead thermal power station, with a designed capacity of 1,200 megawatts is under construction. Both the Gusinoozersk and Kharanor power plants, which will be the largest thermal stations east of Lake Baykal, are intended to meet the increased power needs of the region in connection with the construction of the Baykal-Amur Mainline and associated activities.

In the Soviet Far East, the principal strip-mining operations are under way at Raychikhinsk in Amur Oblast and in the Bikin deposit at Luchegorsk. The Raychikhinsk coal district, in operation since the 1930's, yielded 13—14 million tons of lignite a year in the mid-1970's from four strip mines. The coal is used both in a minehead heat and power station (268 megawatts) and on the nonelectrified eastern segments of the Trans-Siberian Railroad. Also in Amur Oblast, work began in 1976 on the development of a new lignite deposit, the Nylga field, 30 miles northwest of Svobodnyy. The lignite in this area is of low heating value and must be used in an on-site power station. The reserves in the Svobodnyy-Nylga field, though of lower rank, are the largest of any lignite surface deposit in the Soviet Far East, about four times larger than those of Raychikhinsk. In Maritime Kray, the Bikin lignite deposit at Luchegorsk went into operation with a first-stage capacity of

51

3.3 million tons a year, to be expanded ultimately to 8 million tons. The minehead thermal station started up its first generating unit of 200 megawatts in 1974, and reached an installed capacity of 800 megawatts in 1976.

Siberia's Contribution to the Soviet Economy

The foregoing review of Siberian resource developments suggests uneven contributions to the Soviet economy, with a strong role in the provision of energy resources, some nonferrous metals and nonmetals, but not in the iron and steel industry and in such key ferroalloy ores as manganese and chrome. In general, Siberian resource development west of Lake Baykal is oriented westward toward the European part of the USSR while the exploitation of resources east of Lake Baykal, a great overland distance away from the industrial and population centers of the European zone, is likely to be oriented increasingly eastward toward the Pacific basin, particularly as a result of the construction of the Baykal-Amur mainline.

All three major fossil fuels—coal, oil and gas—are expected to make increasingly significant contributions to the Soviet economy. In the case of coal, the Kuznetsk Basin is assuming growing importance as a producer of both high-quality steam coals and coking coals, with over one-half of the total output moving out of Siberia, mainly westward to the Urals and the northern half of European Russia, but also southwest into eastern Kazakhstan and even to Central Asia. Other Siberian coal basins produce for local consumption, and overall Siberian coal output in the mid-1970's was about one-third of Soviet production. This proportion is expected to rise in the future, particularly as the Kansk-Achinsk lignite basin goes into large-scale production during the 1980's. Siberia will thus continue to contribute a wide range of coals to the Soviet economy, ranging from the high-grade steam coals and coking coals of the Kuznetsk Basin to the lignite for on-site power generation in the Kansk-Achinsk Basin and smaller production areas. During the 1980's, the South Yakutian Basin, after being reached by a branch of the BAM, will supplement the output of the Kuzbas with coking coals and high-grade steam coals, but mainly for export through Pacific Coast ports.

Siberia has become an increasingly important Soviet producer of petroleum since the start of the West Siberian fields in the mid-1960's. By 1970, when West Siberian output reached about 30 million tons a year, about 10 percent of total Soviet production, it was already adequate for Siberian needs, meeting the throughput capacities of Siberia's two major refineries at Omsk and Angarsk. Since then West Siberian oil has been moving in growing amounts to the European part of the USSR, at first through a reversal of flow in the old pipeline system that carried crude oil from the Volga-Urals field to Siberian refineries. This was supplemented by a 48-inch pipeline in 1973, and another in August 1976. Additional pipeline construction from the West Siberian fields to the European USSR is projected as production grows. In 1975, the West Siberian fields contributed 30 percent of total Soviet oil production, and the Siberian share is planned to reach nearly one-half of national output by 1980. Surplus crude, estimated at about 100 million tons in 1975, will also begin moving to new refineries in Kazakhstan (Pavlodar and Chimkent) and in Central Asia as well as in Siberia itself (Achinsk) in the late 1970's and early 1980's. If present plans hold, West Siberian crude oil will also be moving eastward through Siberia by a combination of pipelines and BAM tank-car unit trains starting in the mid-1980's, both to the refineries in the Far East and for export through Pacific tanker terminals.

The development of West Siberian natural gas resources has been lagging behind the development of the oil, partly because Central Asian gas fields also provide a substantial source of gas for the Soviet economy (30 percent in 1975), but also because of the more remote location of the gas fields near the Arctic Circle. Following the start of production in 1972 in West Siberia's first giant gas field—Medvezh'ye—the region's output rose to 13 percent of Soviet gas production in 1975, and is planned to reach about 35 percent of the national total in 1980. The initial gas-transmission system from the Medvezh'ye field ran southwest to the middle Urals and on into Central Russia, with one pipeline (completed in 1976) running along a more northerly alignment directly to the western Ukraine for export to Eastern and Western Europe. With the development of the second giant gas field, at Urengoy, the basic transmission alignment will shift to a new string of pipelines running south from Urengoy through Surgut, Tobol'sk and Tyumen', and then west through Chelyabinsk into European Russia. The only gas pipeline serving Siberia is one carrying associated gas from the West Siberian oil fields to the Kuznetsk Basin; it was scheduled to be completed in 1977. In addition to the overland transmission of natural gas to the European part of the USSR and to other European countries, Siberia's resources also held out the prospect of overseas tanker shipments of liquefied natural gas. One project, under discussion in the mid-1970's, would involve the use of West Siberian gas for transmission to a coastal liquefaction plant on the Barents Sea for onward tanker transportation to Western Europe and the East Coast of the United States. Another project, still dependent on detailed exploration of reserves, would involve the use of Yakutian gas for pipeline transmission to a liquefaction plant on the Pacific coast, and tanker shipments to Japan and the West Coast of the United States.

The start of hydroelectric development of Siberia's Angara-Yenisey river basin in the 1950's has placed the region in the forefront of electric power production, especially low-cost waterpower, attracting power-intensive industries. By the mid-1970's, Siberia was generating nearly 19 percent of the Soviet Union's electric power, including close to 40 percent of the nation's hydroelectricity. In the absence of extra-high-voltage transmission lines to the European part of the USSR, not expected before the 1980's, Siberia's electric power was being consumed entirely within the region, particularly in aluminum plants and in other power-intensive industries like chlorine and caustic soda production, calcium carbide, ferroalloys and electric steels. In the 1980's, with the large-scale development of lignite-based power stations in the Kansk-Achinsk Basin and the construction of long-distance transmission lines to the European part of the USSR, Siberia will feed electricity into the nation's European power grid. The transfer may reach the order of 200 billion kilowatt-hours a year after the installation of four or five extra-high-voltage transmission lines by the 1990's, representing about 10 percent of the power consumption in the European regions of the Soviet Union at that time.

In contrast to energy resources, Siberia has been playing a relatively minor role in the Soviet iron and steel industry, mainly because of the absence of adequate iron-ore resources. The discrepancy between the region's share in Soviet iron-ore production and pig-iron output is evident from Table 15. In the early period of the Urals-Kuznetsk Combine, until the late 1950's, the imbalance was made up by ore shipments from the Urals, particularly Magnitogorsk. With the increasing depletion of Urals ore resources and the rise of the Rudnyy iron-ore complex in northwest Kazakhstan, iron ore has been moving to the Kuznetsk Basin from Kazakhstan. In the mid-1970's, this movement amounted to 1 or 2 million tons a year. The general

TABLE 15

Siberia's Contribution to the Soviet Economy
(in percent of national output)

	1940	1950	1960	1970	1973	1975
Energy resources						
Coal	23	27	28	32	33	34
Coking coal	17	29	26	29	30	31
Oil	1.6	1.6	1.1	9.6	21	31
Natural gas	–	1.5	0.7	5.0	8.5	14
Electric power						
capacity	7.2	12	15	20	19	
output	6.6	11	15	18	18	
hydro output	4.4	3.6	10	36		
Iron and steel						
Iron ore	1.6	5.5	5.7	6.5	6.9	6.4
Pig iron	10	10	7.1	8.5	9.5	9
Crude steel	10	13	8.4	8.1	8.3	9
Rolled steel	9.1	15	10	8.9	10	
Chemicals						
Sulfuric acid	1.1	1.7	3.8	5.9	5.2	
Soda ash	2.5	8.2	3.1	1.2	7.2	
Caustic soda	–	8.9	9.1	10	12	
Fertilizer	6.8	6.7	4.4	5.0	4.0	
Man-made fibers	–	–	16	13	11	
Machinery						
Machine tools	1.4	5.2	4.3	2.3	2.6	
Metallurgical equipment	–	7.2	4.8	5.2		
Tractors	–	9.5	8.8	7.3	7.4	
Tractor-drawn plows	19	22	43	37	38	
Tractor-drawn drills	–	31	18	26	14	
Grain harvesters	–	5.0	15	18	27	
Wood products						
Roundwood	23	23	26	33	34	
Sawnwood	23	19	23	26	27	
Pulp	–	4.3	9.3	20	22	
Paper	0.1	5.2	7.3	8.9	7.0	
Paperboard	0.5	4.3	8.0	16	18	
Building materials						
Cement	8.8	13	13	12	12	
Textile and leather products						
Cotton fabrics	0.8	2.0	2.9	3.6	3.2	
Wool fabrics	0.5	1.1	1.1	0.8	3.3	
Man-made fiber fabrics	–	–	2.8	3.7	4.1	
Linen fabrics	1.7	1.1	0.8	0.6	0.7	
Leather shoes	3.1	5.1	5.2	5.2	4.7	
Consumer durables						
Radios	–	13	19	24	20	
Refrigerators	–	–	–	18	15	
Washing machines	–	–	13	13	15	
Food products						
Meat	13	12	11	9.1	10.1	
Butter	23	17	13	12	12	
Population	8.9		10.8	10.5	10.5	

Note: Official statistical tables listing the Siberian share of selected commodities appeared regularly in Soviet statistical yearbooks until 1973; these regional breakdown tables have since been omitted.

trend for pig iron and crude steel, as a share of national production, was downward from 1940's to the mid-1960's, when the West Siberian Iron and Steel Plant went into operation. Since then the Siberian share has risen by a few percentage points, with a more rapid rise in the case of crude steel because of large scrap inputs. Although rolled steel production, at about one-tenth of the Soviet level, appeared adequate for Siberian needs, the type of rolled products turned out by the Siberian plants was not always geared to the region's needs. The Kuznetsk plant specialized originally in rails and beams to support the Siberian railroad and construction program. As machine-building developed in Siberia and the rail-building program declined, Siberia exported rails to other parts of the Soviet Union and imported various shapes needed for its metal-fabricating industry. The imbalance was rectified by the construction of the West Siberian plant, which acquired a small-shapes mill in the mid-1960's and one of the world's largest medium-shapes mills in 1976. However, Siberia's needs for sheet and, since the oil and gas program began, particularly for pipe are still being met to a large extent by shipments from the Urals and the Ukraine.

Although Siberia does not mine either manganese or chrome, the two most common ferroalloy ores, the electric smelting of ferroalloys such as ferrochromium, ferromanganese and ferrosilicon is a power-intensive activity that would tend to be attracted by the low-cost power sources of southern Siberia. Although ferroalloy manufacture in Siberia has thus far been limited to the ferroalloys plant established in World War II in the Kuznetsk Basin, it is likely that further such production may be attracted to the Siberian power-generating complex, particularly the new Sayan district. Among the metals used as ferroalloys, Siberia provides substantial shares of tungsten, which is recovered both from tungsten-molybdenum ores (Transbaykalia) and tungsten-tin ores (Far East); columbium and tantalum (Transbaykalia) and molybdenum (the Sorsk district of southern Krasnoyarsk Kray, in addition to Transbaykalia).

The Noril'sk district is an important source of export metals, including platinum-group metals and growing amounts of nickel, as well as copper and cobalt and a host of coproducts such as gold, silver, tellurium, selenium. Cobalt is also recovered from a mine in operation at Khovu-Aksy in Tuva ASSR since 1970.

Among nonferrous metals, Siberia occupies a key position in aluminum reduction plants (more than one-half of all Soviet aluminum production in the mid-1970's) even though the raw-material base is limited to a nepheline-based alumina plant at Achinsk. Most of the alumina used in the Siberian aluminum industry is brought in from the Urals or from abroad. Except for copper from Noril'sk, zinc from Belovo, and lead from the Dal'negorsk (formerly Tetyukhe) operation in Maritime Kray, Siberia is now making no significant contribution to the Soviet base-metals industries, which are strong in Kazakhstan, Central Asia, the Urals and the Caucasus. However, the large Udokan copper deposit, to be developed in the 1980's with the arrival of the BAM, offers an important future prospect both for domestic consumption and for export through Pacific ports. Siberia has a virtual monopoly position in Soviet tin, which originates mainly in Solnechnyy (near Komsomol'sk), Khingansk (near Obluch'ye), Kavalerovo (near Dal'negorsk), northern outposts like Iul'tin (Chukchi Peninsula) and Deputatskiy (Yakutia), with concentrates converging at a tin-smelting plant in Novosibirsk. For a long time, Siberia also had a virtual monopoly in gold mining, with the focus of activity shifting increasingly northeastward from the Baley and Darasun mines of

Transbaykalia to the Aldan district in the 1920's, the Kolyma district in the 1930's and the Chukchi Peninsula in the 1960's, with centers at Bilibino and the Polyarnyy-Leningradskiy district near Cape Shmidt. Other Siberian gold mines are in Yakutia, in the Allakh-Yun' district in the southwest and at Kular in the Far North. However, since the 1960's, major gold-mining operations have also been started outside Siberia, notably the lode mines of Zarafshan in the Kyzyl Kum (put in operation in 1969), Altynkan in the Fergana Valley (opened in 1970) and the Armenian lode mine at Zod, with a mill at Ararat, put on stream in 1976.

Siberia also makes significant contributions in some nonmetallic minerals, again with a virtual monopoly position in diamonds (from the Yakutian mines of Mirnyy, Aykhal and Udachnyy), boron (from Dal'negorsk in the Maritime Kray) and lithium (from Chita Oblast). Significant shares of national output are also provided by Siberia in the case of fluorspar (from Chita Oblast and the Yaroslavskiy mine of Maritime Kray), as well as mica, with the muscovite variety (potassium mica) coming from the Mama River district of Irkutsk Oblast and phlogopite (magnesium mica) from the Aldan district of southern Yakutia. Asbestos is contributed by the Tuva ASSR, where the Ak-Dovurak mine went into operation in 1964 and reached a capacity of 250,000 tons of spinning grade asbestos fibers in 1976, or about 10 to 15 percent of Soviet output. Siberia also furnishes a substantial share of the Soviet Union's natural graphite from the Noginsk mine on the Lower Tunguska River, where the mining of Iceland spar also began in 1976.

Except for some agricultural machinery, notably tractors and tractor-drawn implements at Rubtsovsk and grain harvesters at Krasnoyarsk, Siberia does not account for an unusually large share of Soviet machinery. There has been some emphasis on heavy machinery, such as metallurgical equipment, but Siberia's production of a universal machinery category like machine tools has been unusually low (2 to 3 percent of Soviet output in the mid-1970's). Exceptions may be found in a few specific machinery items; for example, the Soviet Far East accounts for about one-third of all casting equipment produced in the Soviet Union, 17 percent of gantry cranes and substantial portions of the nation's diesel engines. However, half of the machinery output of the Soviet Far East is now being shipped westward across Siberia, with exports going as far as Eastern Europe, greatly adding to transport costs. A greater share of Far Eastern equipment may be exported directly to the Pacific basin in the future, provided that the quality of production conforms to world standards.

In the chemical industry, Siberia's contribution has been limited largely in the past to the coke-based chemical industry of the Kuznetsk Basin and some power-intensive chemicals like chlorine and caustic soda in the East Siberian power-generating complex. The chemical center of Usol'ye, in Irkutsk Oblast, contributed about 12 percent of the Soviet Union's caustic soda in the mid-1970's, with construction under way on a similar complex at Sayansk, near Zima. Soda-ash production was limited in the past to natural sodium carbonate recovered from soda lakes in Altay Kray, whose share in Soviet production was down to little more than one percent in the late 1960's. However, the use of nepheline as a raw material for alumina production starting in 1970 yielded large amounts of soda ash as a byproduct, thus enhancing Siberia's contribution of this chemical. Fertilizers are limited largely to nitrogenous fertilizers, based either on coke gases of the Kuznetsk Basin or on oil refinery gases of Angarsk. Sulfuric acid output is limited by the absence of a significant phosphatic fertilizer industry, although this situation may change with the start of development of Siberia's apatite resources, either in Buryatia or in the Aldan district. Chemical fibers include viscose at Krasnoyarsk and viscose and polyamide fibers at Barnaul, with cellulose from Siberia's growing woodpulp industry providing the material for viscose fibers, and coke-based caprolactam from the Kuznetsk Basin supplying the basis for polyamide fibers. Both in Krasnoyarsk and in Barnaul, the man-made fibers provide cord fabric for local tire plants using synthetic rubber from the petrochemical complex at Omsk and from an old wood alcohol-based plant at Krasnoyarsk. Future chemical developments in Siberia will focus increasingly on petrochemicals based on the oil and gas potential of West Siberia, with complexes under development at Tomsk and Tobol'sk, and on power-intensive chemicals like chlorine-caustic production and its derivatives at Sayansk, near Zima.

Siberia's forest products industry has been distinguished by a low level of processing activities and the costly shipments of unprocessed roundwood out of the region. In the mid-1970's, Siberia accounted for 34 percent of the Soviet Union's roundwood, but only 27 percent of the nation's sawnwood. Since the 1960's, the situation has improved somewhat with a rapidly growing share of woodpulp as well as paperboard. However, paper production, which tends to be more highly market-oriented, has not received much attention (Table 15).

Consumer goods production has generally been below Siberia's population share, implying that a substantial portion of daily necessities is being shipped into Siberia from other parts of the Soviet Union, adding transport costs and raising prices. Basic fabrics range between 3 and 4 percent of national output for a population that represents about one-tenth of the Soviet Union. Significant cotton-textile production is limited to small mills at Barnaul and Kansk, and man-made fiber fabrics to a mill at Krasnoyarsk, using local viscose. Siberia's share in some consumer durables (Table 15) is higher than the region's population share.

West Siberia was once an outstanding producer of butter, but its share in national output has been declining as other regions of the Soviet Union, notably Central Russia and the Volga valley, have gained greater significance. Siberia's share of meat production has declined for the same reason. As for grain production, Siberian harvests tend to fluctuate sharply together with Soviet harvests in general; in good years, Siberia contributes 15 percent or more to the national grain crop, in bad years 10 percent or less.

Bibliography

Alekseyev, Veniamin V. *Elektrifikatsiya Sibiri. Istoricheskoye issledovaniye* [The Electrification of Siberia, a Historical Study]. Part I: 1885–1950. Novosibirsk: Nauka, 1973, 308 pp.

Barr, Brenton M. *The Soviet Wood-Processing Industry*. University of Toronto Press, 1970, 135 pp.

"Basic directions of the development of the economy of the USSR for 1976–80," *Ekonomicheskaya Gazeta*, 1976, No. 11.

Bogorad, David R. *Voprosy spetsializatsii i kompleksnogo razvitiya narodnogo khozyaystva Sibiri* [Problems of Specialization and Complex Development of the Siberian Economy]. Moscow: Nauka, 1966, 193 pp.

Borisovich, Grigoriy F.; Mikhail G. Vasil'yev; Aleksey G. Dedov. *Devyataya pyatiletka khimicheskoy promyshlennosti. Ekonomicheskiye problemy*

[The Ninth Five-Year Plan of the Chemical Industry; Economic Problems]. Moscow: Khimiya, 1973, 215 pp.

Boyarskiy, Vladimir A. *Razvitiye otkrytoy dobychi rud, 1950–70* [Development of Open-Pit Ore Mining, 1950–70]. Moscow: Nauka, 1975, 297 pp.

Braun, Grigoriy A. *Zhelezorudnaya baza chernoy metallurgii SSSR* [The Iron-Ore Base of the Iron and Steel Industry of the USSR]. Moscow: Nedra, 1970, 310 pp.

Brenner, Mark M. *Ekonomika neftyanoy i gazovoy promyshlennosti SSSR* [Economics of the Oil and Gas Industry of the USSR]. Moscow: Nedra, 1968, 382 pp.

Bruyev, Gennadiy G.; Valentin. S. Kudryavtsev; Mikhail N. Larionov; Moisey G. Turbiner. *Kansko-Achinskiy basseyn–toplivnaya baza strany* [The Kansk-Achinsk Basin–the Nation's Fuel Base]. Krasnoyarsk, 1972, 84 pp.

Bushuyev, Viktor M. *Khimicheskaya industriya v svete resheniy XXIV s"yezda KPSS* [The Chemical Industry in Light of the Resolutions of the 24th Party Congress]. Moscow: Khimiya, 1974, 310 pp.

———— and Georgiy V. Uvarov. *Sovetskaya khimicheskaya promyshlennost' v tekushchem semiletii* [The Soviet Chemical Industry in the Current Seven-Year Plan]. Moscow: Ekonomizdat, 1962, 197 pp.

Central Intelligence Agency. *Soviet Long-Range Energy Forecasts.* A(ER) 75–71. September 1975. 27 pp.

Conolly, Violet. *Beyond the Urals.* London: Oxford University Press, 1967, 420 pp.

————. *Siberia Today and Tomorrow.* London: Collins, 1975, 248 pp.

Dal'niy Vostok [The Far East]. Edited by Fyodor V. D'yakonov; Vadim V. Pokshishevskiy and Aleksandr S. Khomentovskiy. Moscow: Mysl', 1966, 493 pp.

Dal'niy Vostok. Edited by Adol'f B. Margolin. Moscow: Mysl', 1971, 396 pp.

Dienes, Leslie. "Energy self-sufficiency in the Soviet Union," *Current History*, August 1975, pp. 10–14, 47–51.

————. "Soviet energy resources and prospects," *Current History*, September 1976.

"Draft basic directions of the development of the economy of the USSR for 1976–80," *Pravda*, December 14, 1975.

Dunayev, Vladimir P. *Samyy severnyy (geograficheskiy ocherk o zapolyarnom gorode Noril'sk)* [The Northermost (a Geographical Essay About the Arctic City of Noril'sk)]. Moscow: Geografizdat, 1960, 71 pp.

Ekonomicheskaya zhizn' SSSR. Khronika sobytiy i faktov, 1917–1965 [Economic Life of the USSR; a Chronicle of Events and Facts, 1917–1965]. Moscow: Soviet Encyclopedia Publishers, 1967, 2 vols., 931 pp.

Ekonomicheskiye problemy razvitiya i razmeshcheniya khimicheskoy promyshlennosti [Economic Problems in the Development and Location of the Chemical Industry]. Edited by Nikolay P. Fedorenko. Moscow: Nauka, 1968, 398 pp.

Ekonomicheskiye problemy razvitiya Sibiri [Economic Problems in Siberian Development]. Edited by Boris P. Orlov. Novosibirsk, Nauka, 1974, 262 pp.

Ekonomika chernoy metallurgii [Economics of the Iron and Steel Industry]. Edited by Nikolay P. Bannyy. Moscow: Metallurgiya, 1975, 469 pp.

Elektrifikatsiya SSSR, 1917–67 [Electrification of the USSR, 1917–67]. Edited by Pyotr S. Neporozhnyy. Moscow: Energiya, 1967, 541 pp.

Elektrifikatsiya SSSR. Edited by Pyotr S. Neporozhnyy. Moscow: Energiya, 1970, 543 pp.

Elektroenergeticheskaya baza ekonomicheskikh rayonov SSSR [The Electric Power Base of the Economic Regions of the USSR]. Edited by V. K. Savel'yev. Moscow: Nauka, 1974, 226 pp.

Energeticheskiye resursy SSSR [Energy Resources of the USSR]. Vol. 1.–*Gidro-energeticheskiye resursy* [Hydroelectric Resources]. Edited by Andrey N. Voznesenskiy. Moscow: Nauka, 1967, 598 pp.

Energetika SSSR v 1971–75 godakh [The Electric Power Industry of the USSR in 1971–75]. Edited by A. S. Pavlenko and A. M. Nekrasov. Moscow: Energiya, 1972, 261 pp.

Exploitation of Siberia's Natural Resources. Main Findings of a Round Table Held Jan. 30–Feb. 1, 1974, in Brussels. Edited by Yves Laulan. NATO, Directorate of Economic Affairs, 1974, 199 pp.

Gerasimova, Nina K.; Aleksandr A. Myterev; Lyudmila M. Savel'yeva. *Ekonomiche-skaya geografiya Kuzbassa.* Kemerovo, 1966, 84 pp.

Gladyshev, Anatoliy N.; Aleksandr V. Kulikov; Boris F. Shapalin. *Problemy razvitiya i razmeshcheniya proizvoditel'nykh sil Dal'nego Vostoka* [Problems in the Development and Location of Productive Forces of the Far East]. Moscow: Mysl', 1974, 214 pp.

Gosudarstvennyy pyatiletnyy plan razvitiya narodnogo khozyaystva SSSR na 1971–1975 gody [The State Five-Year Plan of Development of the Soviet Economy for 1971–75]. Moscow: Politizdat, 1972, 454 pp.

Gramoteyeva, Liliya I. *Tekhniko-ekonomicheskiye problemy razmeshcheniya vazhneyshikh otrasley khimicheskoy promyshlennosti* [Technical-Economic Problems in the Location of the Principal Sectors of the Chemical Industry]. Moscow: Nauka, 1970, 223 pp.

Grigor'yev, Klavdiy N. *Kansko-Achinskiy ugol'nyy basseyn* [The Kansk-Achinsk Coal Basin]. Moscow: Nedra, 1968, 183 pp.

Holzman, Franklyn D. "Soviet Urals-Kuznetsk Combine; a study in investment criteria and industrialization policies," *Quarterly Journal of Economics*, August 1957, pp. 368–405.

Kazanets, Ivan P. *Chernaya metallurgiya v devyatoy pyatiletke* [The Iron and Steel Industry in the Ninth Five-Year Plan]. Moscow: Metallurgiya, 1972, 110 pp.

Kistanov, Viktor V. *Budushcheye Sibiri: razvitiye khozyaystva v semiletke* [The Future of Siberia: Development of the Economy in the Seven-Year Plan]. Moscow: Gosplanizdat, 1960, 108 pp.

Kortunov, Aleksey K. *Gazovaya promyshlennost' SSSR* [The Gas Industry of the USSR]. Moscow: Nedra, 1967, 322 pp.

Kuznetsov, Konstantin K. et al. *Ugol'nyye mestorozhdeniya dlya razrabotki otkrytym sposobom* [Coal Deposits For Strip-Mining Operations]. Moscow: Nedra, 1971, 308 pp.

Lebedinskiy, Vladimir N., and Pyotr I. Mel'nikov. *Zvezda Zapolyar'ya* [Stars of the Arctic] (about Noril'sk). Moscow: Profizdat, 1971, 108 pp.

Lelyukhina, Nina D. *Ekonomicheskaya effektivnost' razmeshcheniya chernoy metallurgii* [The Cost-Effectiveness of Location of the Iron and Steel Industry]. Moscow: Nauka, 1973, 295 pp.

Livshits, Raisa S. *Razmeshcheniye chernoy metallurgii SSSR* [Location of the Iron and Steel Industry of the USSR]. Moscow: Academy of Sciences USSR, 1958, 374 pp.

L'vov, Mikhail S. *Resursy prirodnogo gaza SSSR* [Natural Gas Resources of the USSR]. Moscow: Nedra, 1969, 221 pp.

Margolin, Adol'f B. *Problemy narodnogo khozyaystva Dal'nega Vostoka* [Problems in the Economy of the Far East]. Moscow: Academy of Sciences USSR, 1963, 253 pp.

Mazòver, Yakov A. *Toplivno-energeticheskiye bazy Vostoka SSSR* [Fuel and Energy Bases of the East of the USSR]. Moscow: Nauka, 1966, 205 pp.

Misevich, Korney N., and Valentina I. Chudnova. *Naseleniye rayonov sovremennogo promyshlennogo osvoyeniya Severa Zapadnoy Sibiri* [Population of the Regions of Contemporary Industrial Development in the North of Western Siberia]. Novosibirsk: Nauka, 1973, 208 pp.

Morozova, Ta'tyana G. *Ekonomicheskaya geografiya Sibiri.* Moscow: Vysshaya shkola, 1975, 261 pp.

———— and Dina M. Zakharina. *Novaya geografiya Sibiri* [The New Geography of Siberia]. Moscow: Prosveshcheniye, 1972, 221 pp.

Moskovskiy, Aleksey S. *Promyshlennoye osvoyeniye Sibiri v period stroitel'stva sotsializma (1917–1937)* [Industrial Development of Siberia in the Period of Construction of Socialism (1917–1937)]. Novosibirsk: Nauka, 1975, 262 pp.

Narodnoye khozyaystvo RSFSR [The Economy of the RSFSR], statistical yearbook, various years.

Narodnoye khozyaystvo SSSR [The Economy of the USSR], statistical yearbook, various years.

Nekotoryye voprosy predplanovogo obosnovaniya osvoyeniya neftegazovykh resursov Zapadnoy Sibiri [Some Problems in the Preplanning Study of the Development of Oil and Gas Resources in West Siberia]. Novosibirsk, 1973, 162 pp.

Nekrasov, Nikolay N. *Problemy Sibirskogo kompleksa* [Problems of the Siberian Complex]. Novosibirsk, 1973, 221 pp.

Nesterov, Ivan I.; Farman K. Salmanov; Kal'man A. Shpil'man. *Neftyanyye i gazovyye mestorozhdeniya Zapadnoy Sibiri* [Oil and Gas Deposits of West Siberia]. Moscow: Nedra, 1971, 462 pp.

Nikonov, Semyon P.; Georgiy N. Tarasenkov; Ivan V. Cherezov. *Geografiya Tyumenskoy oblasti* [Geography of Tyumen' Oblast]. Sverdlovsk, 1966, 142 pp.

Orlov, Boris P. *Sibir' segodnya: problemy i resheniya* [Siberia Today: Problems and Solutions]. Moscow: Mysl', 1974, 207 pp.

Osintsev, Arkadiy S. *Ekonomika chernoy metallurgii SSSR* [Economics of the Iron and Steel Industry of the USSR]. Moscow: Metallurgiya, 1969, 342 pp.

Osmolovskiy, Valentin V. *Ekonomika zhelezorudnoy promyshlennosti* [Economics of the Iron-Ore Industry]. Moscow: Nedra, 1967, 311 pp.

Osvoyeniye neftyanykh mestorozhdeniy Zapadnoy Sibiri [Development of the Oil Deposits of West Siberia]. Moscow: Nedra, 1972, 181 pp.

Pervushin, Sergey A., et al. *Ekonomika tsvetnoy metallurgii SSSR* [Economics of Nonferrous Metallurgy of the USSR]. Moscow: Metallurgiya, 1970, 447 pp.

Pomus, Moisey I. *Zapadnaya Sibir'* [West Siberia]. Moscow: Geografgiz, 1956, 640 pp.

Popov, Vitaliy E. *Problemy ekonomiki Sibiri* [Problems in the Siberian Economy]. Moscow: Ekonomika, 1968, 215 pp.

Prirodnyye usloviya i osobennosti khozyaystvennogo osvoyeniya severnykh rayonov Zapadnoy Sibiri [Natural Conditions and Peculiarities of Economic Development of the Northern Regions of West Siberia]. Edited by Leonid F. Kunitsyn. Moscow: Nauka, 1969, 242 pp.

Rabkina, A. L.; O. B. Braginskiy; Ye. P. Shchukin. *Ekonomicheskiye problemy perspektivnogo razvitiya neftekhimicheskoy promyshlennosti* [Economic Problems in the Long-Term Development of the Petrochemical Industry]. Moscow: Khimiya, 1973, 180 pp.

Razvitiye toplivnoy bazy rayonov SSSR [Development of the Fuel Base of the Regions of the USSR]. Edited by Abram Ye. Probst. Moscow: Nedra, 1968, 322 pp.

Rodnoy kray: ocherki prirody, istorii, khozyaystva i kul'tury Tomskoy oblasti [Our Region; Essays on the Natural Environment, History, Economy and Culture of Tomsk Oblast]. Tomsk University, 1974, 400 pp.

Ryl'skiy, Vyacheslav A. *Ekonomika mezhrayonnykh elektroenergeticheskikh svyazey v SSSR* [The Economics of Interregional Electric Power Linkages in the USSR]. Moscow: Nauka, 1972, 128 pp.

Savin, Stanislav I. *Formirovaniye territorial'no-proizvoditel'nykh kompleksov Vostochnoy Sibiri* [Formation of Territorial-Production Complexes in East Siberia]. Moscow: Nauka, 1972, 125 pp.

Shabad, Theodore. *Basic Industrial Resources of the USSR.* Columbia University Press, 1969, 393 pp.

————. "News Notes," *Soviet Geography: Review and Translation*, various issues.

————. "Raw material problems of the Soviet aluminum industry," *Resources Policy*, December, 1976.

Shelest, Vasiliy A. *Ekonomika razmeshcheniya elektroenergetiki* [Economics of Location of the Electric Power Industry]. Moscow: Nauka, 1965, 266 pp.

Smith, Alan B. "Soviet dependence on Siberian resource development," paper delivered at annual meeting of the American Association for the Advancement of Slavic Studies, Atlanta, October 1975, 38 pp.

Sokolikova, Valeriya V. *Sayanskiy narodnokhozyaystvennyy kompleks* [The Sayan Economic Complex]. Moscow: Mysl', 1974, 205 pp.

Sosvinskoye Priob'ye [The Sos'va Portion of the Ob' Basin]. Edited by Yuriy P. Mikhaylov. Irkutsk, 1975, 511 pp.

Statisticheskiy yezhegodnik stran-chlenov SEV [Statistical Yearbook of Member Countries of Comecon], various years.

Tarasov, Georgiy L. *Territorial'no-ekonomicheskiye problemy razvitiya i razmeshcheniya proizvoditel'nykh sil Vostochnoy Sibiri* [Territorial-Economic Problems of Development and Location of Productive Forces in East Siberia]. Moscow: Mysl', 1970, 230 pp.

Urvantsev, Nikolay N. *Noril'sk–istoriya otkrytiya i osvoyeniya medno-nikelevykh rud Sibirskogo Severa* [Noril'sk; History of the Discovery and Development of the Copper-Nickel Ores of the Siberian North]. Moscow: Nedra, 1969, 87 pp.

Vostochnaya Sibir' [East Siberia]. Moscow: Geografizdat, 1963, 885 pp.

Vostochnaya Sibir'. Edited by Vadim V. Pokshishevskiy and Vladimir V. Vorob'yev. Moscow: Mysl', 1969, 492 pp.

Yegorov, Valentin I. *Ekonomika neftegazodobyvayushchey promyshlennosti* [Economics of the Oil and Gas Industry]. Moscow: Nedra, 1970, 236 pp.

Zapadnaya Sibir' [West Siberia]. Edited by Moisey I. Pomus. Moscow: Mysl', 1971, 428 pp.

Zapadno-Sibirskiy ekonomicheskiy rayon [The West Siberian Economic Region]. Edited by Adol'f B. Margolin. Moscow: Nauka, 1967, 249 pp.

Zayonchkovskaya, Zhanna A., and Viktor I. Perevedentsev. *Sovremennaya migratsiya naseleniya Krasnoyarskogo kraya* [Contemporary Migration in Krasnoyarsk Kray]. Novosibirsk: Siberian Division of the Academy of Sciences USSR, 1964, 104 pp.

Zubkov, Anatoliy I., and Boris B. Gorizontov. *Promyshlennyye uzly Krasnoyarskogo kraya* [Industrial Nodes of Krasnoyarsk Kray]. Moscow: Academy of Sciences USSR, 1963, 108 pp.

Chapter 2

THE BAYKAL-AMUR MAINLINE: CATALYST FOR THE DEVELOPMENT OF PACIFIC SIBERIA

Victor L. Mote

The concept of complementarity was introduced into the field of economic geography well over a quarter century ago. The notion presupposes that before spatial interaction can occur, there must be a need to exchange a product or products between one place and another. The key to this relationship is some means of transportation.

A glaring example of complementarity is one that exists between the temperate, developed industrial nations and the resource-rich but agriculturally poor Soviet Far East and Eastern Siberia, labeled "Pacific Siberia" by Dibb[51] (Fig. 1). Long before the 20th century, enterprising Western businessmen pondered the commercial possibilities inherent in this areal association. The Trans-Siberian Railroad, for instance, was constructed not without the urgings of European and American capitalists. Immediately prior to the Russian Revolution of 1917, it was chiefly the railway and Western capital on which the economy of Western Siberia hinged. All the subsequent, considerable development of what today is called the West Siberian Major Economic Region (*krupnyy ekonomicheskiy rayon*) has been either directly or indirectly dependent on the Trans-Siberian and its feeders.

In contrast, Pacific Siberia, comprising nearly one-half the territory of the USSR, remains largely untapped and unexplored. Despite well-organized geological expeditions in the area since 1896, only 10 to 20 percent of the important Sayan-Stanovoy mountain complex has been surveyed thoroughly.[254] Adequate exploration simply cannot be conducted without better access. Moreover, once discoveries have been made (and they have been numerous), the resources lie unaltered without transportation. In further contrast to Western Siberia, a great lowland across which the Trans-Siberian passes more centrally, Pacific Siberia is mountainous and is traversed by the railroad along its southern rim. The impact of the rail network has thus been less effective in the regions east of the Yenisey River than in those to the west.

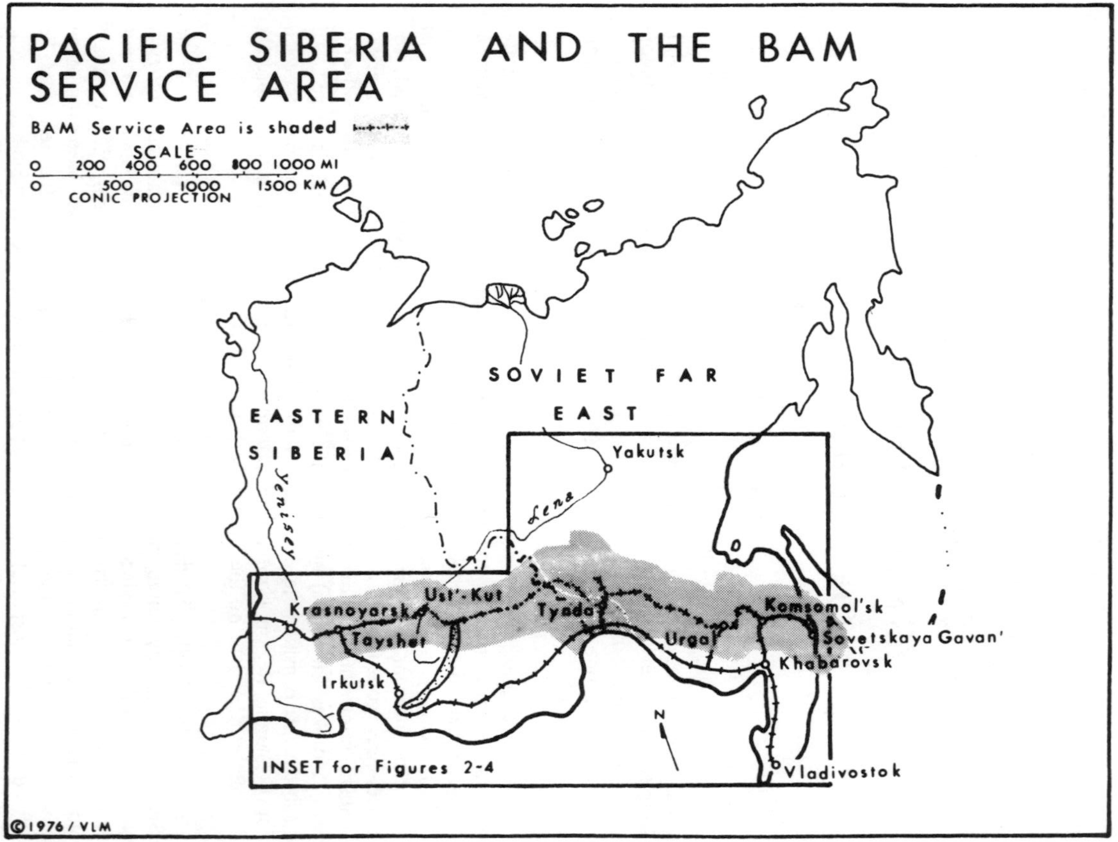

PACIFIC SIBERIA AND THE BAM
SERVICE AREA

BAM Service Area is shaded

SCALE
0   200 400 600 800 1000 MI
0   500   1000   1500 KM
CONIC PROJECTION

EASTERN
SIBERIA

Yenisey

Krasnoyarsk
Tayshet
Irkutsk
Ust'-Kut
Tynda

INSET for Figures 2-4

SOVIET FAR

EAST

Yakutsk

Lena

Ural

Komsomol'sk
Sovetskaya Gavan'
Khabarovsk
Vladivostok

N

© 1976 / VLM

Fig. 1.

64

To say that there has been no progress in Pacific Siberia, however, would be an error. The fishing and timber industries, though heavily subsidized, pay for themselves and for many of the region's imports, the most critical of which is food.

Pacific Siberian farmers produce only 40 percent of the food needs of the population of the region. This should not be surprising since only one percent of the territory is considered arable.[51]

In contrast to the food deficit, the resources of Pacific Siberia are varied and abundant. Even accounting for geological ignorance, the resource base appears great enough to prompt some observers to call it an "Eastern El Dorado." Because of it, the Soviet Union should have a surplus of nearly every strategic mineral well into the next century. This development will occur while the industrialized West becomes increasingly resource-poor and dependent on raw material imports.

As the population of their country expands, however, Soviet leaders will have to reckon further with their seemingly hopeless agricultural problems. An even greater food deficit may be expected in Pacific Siberia, if economic development proceeds as anticipated. Simultaneously, food surpluses are likely in North America for years to come.

This analysis has been intentionally simplistic, ignoring potential technological innovations, because the complementary relationship between Soviet mineral resources and Western food may remain a reality through the year 2000. It is fundamental to the Soviet policy of détente and should be understood in that context. There will be an increasing number of "grain deals" and perhaps offers of raw materials in return for advanced technology and expertise, the model for which is being created even now between the USSR and Japan.

The burden of these interchanges rests on transportation. The Trans-Siberian is still the only artery of any consequence that reaches the Soviet Pacific. The limits of its freight-carrying capacity have been exceeded in many instances. Since 1945 freight volumes on the Trans-Siberian have increased on the average by 7 to 10 times.[2] Yet, with the exception of double-tracking and extensive electrification, the general appearance and orientation of the old rail line are not much different from what they were in 1904 when it reached the Pacific.

Obviously, transportation alternatives are required. Air transport, with the possible exception of dirigibles under intermittent discussion in the Soviet Union, is restricted to high-value, low-bulk freight, is inhibited by vagaries of the weather, and is too expensive a solution. Truck transport is economically feasible only over short distances because of high costs of fuel and maintenance; in Pacific Siberia, where the few adequate highways are the rivers in winter, "roadlessness," moreover, is a formidable obstacle. Though there is no shortage of navigable rivers in Pacific Siberia, this mode of transport is slow and is restricted by ice for six months or more.[51] Indeed, according to their own economic analyses, the Soviet planners have concluded that another railroad and a set of rail and motor-road spurs are the best choices for Pacific Siberian conditions. Rail transport is relatively swift, hauls a wide variety and great quantities of freight, performs well in almost any weather, spans vast distances while requiring comparatively less fuel and maintenance than its chief rival, motor transport, and is competitive in comfort with the airplane.

65

Thus, albeit anachronistic in the space age, a huge, new railroad is under construction in Pacific Siberia. It is known as the Baykal-Amur Mainline or, simply, the BAM.

As if the implicit, aforementioned complementarity and obsolescence of the old Trans-Siberian were not enough, there are other reasons that underlie the construction of the BAM. Shabad is no doubt correct in rating the BAM's primary purpose as the opening up of much needed mineral resources in the Soviet Pacific.[175] An equally compelling reason, and perhaps a more important one in the short run, is the strategic vulnerability of the Trans-Siberian. In part because of their border disputes with China, Soviet military authorities have stationed an estimated 92 divisions, or some 62 percent, of their armed forces in Asia. Of these, 40 percent face China directly.[96] Within Pacific Siberia, the Trans-Siberian is less than 80 miles from the China border for over half its length. The BAM will be positioned at least 110 miles north of the Trans-Siberian and, even though such distances mean little in the face of modern missiles, the new railroad will be in less immediate danger from ground attack.

A third underlying purpose for the building of the BAM is an apparent renewal of the much disputed notion of planned proportional development, at least as far as Soviet eastern regions are concerned.[181] Prior to 1945 there was a pronounced eastward movement of Soviet industry. In the wake of World War II, the industry of the European regions had to be rebuilt at the expense of Siberian economic growth. In the meantime, a controversy had arisen over the advantages of scale economics in already developed areas (western emphasis) versus the idealistic Marxist-Leninist precept of developing proportionally (eastern emphasis). For the time being, although the costs perhaps far outweigh the benefits, the latter proponents in the dispute appear to have won out. Since 1965, investment in eastern regions has risen dramatically to 40 percent of the total, and more of the same trend is promised in the 10th Five-Year Plan.[101] Thus, the BAM will play an important part in opening up new areas of Pacific Siberia for settlement, agriculture, and forestry.

Finally, Soviet officials long thought that it would be more economical to build a large diameter pipeline and an "ordinary railroad" in the BAM zone to ease the load on the Trans-Siberian. At first glance there seems to be no doubt about the correctness of this position. A pipeline was built parallel to the old railroad as far as Irkutsk. Maps in some Soviet textbooks and atlases still reflect a projected pipeline along the Trans-Siberian from Irkutsk to Khabarovsk and Nakhodka.[130] But the planned Irkutsk-Khabarovsk pipeline segment was evidently abandoned recently as a result of a report by a study group of Gosplan, the Soviet Government's planning agency. That group found that it would be more economical to build a railroad specially equipped to haul fluids than it would be to construct an ordinary railroad and a pipeline. "Under the decision taken by Soviet planning authorities, crude oil will be moved by pipeline from the West Siberian fields to Tayshet, where it will be transshipped to [8-axle] tank-car trains taking the oil to Urgal. There it will be transferred again to pipelines [via Khabarovsk] for transmission to refineries and port terminals."[23]

Regardless of the motives behind the construction of the BAM, there is no more ambitious or costly endeavor being attempted in the world today. The BAM between Ust'-Kut and Komsomol'sk together with its two previously finished terminal segments (Tayshet–Ust'-Kut and Komsomol'sk-Sovetskaya Gavan') will be 2,670 miles long, slightly more than half the Trans-Siberian. Some of the world's most difficult terrain, including major mountain ridges, permafrost zones, thousands of water courses, and innumerable bogs, will be negotiated. The climate is cold enough in winter to shatter ordinary steel, and warm and humid enough in summer to make life uncomfortable.

In terms of time and investment, both human and fiscal, the BAM has no modern global counterpart. Upwards of 500,000 workers and dependents are supposed to be linked directly to the route by 1977.[115] Early estimates revealed that 6 billion rubles ($8 billion) would be spent on the railroad proper before the last mile of track is laid in 1983.[54] More recent analyses have indicated that the BAM as well as associated construction in its service area (feeder roads, stations, towns, etc.) will cost around $5.7 million (1971 dollars) per mile, or more than $15 billion for the entire project.[71] For comparison, the Trans-Alaska pipeline, one-third as long, will cost $5 billion, suggesting that the latest Soviet statistics are reasonable.

If the Gross National Product of the USSR approximates $655 billion, computed according to a 3.5 percent adjusted annual growth rate since 1970, an immediate expenditure of the BAM monies would represent almost two-thirds of the income added to the economy in 1975, or nearly the equivalent of the officially publicized defense budget.[247] More meaningfully, averaging the BAM outlay over the next decade and dividing the annual cost by an estimated net fixed investment for the country of $150 billion (23 percent of GNP), the BAM funds would equal 1 percent of the total yearly investment—no small sum for a single project.

Though it is expected that the BAM will pay for itself eventually in foreign exchange income, outlays in the meantime will be derived, as they traditionally have been for heavy industry, from low priority sectors of the economy. Preliminary reports on the 10th Five-Year Plan indicate that some of the investment will come from the long-lagging consumer sector, whose growth during the period is projected at 5 to 7 percent less than that suggested for the previous five-year period.[156]

Whatever the cost, the BAM is the latest of grandiose Siberia projects. Like the Urals-Kuznetsk Combine, Bratsk and Samotlor before it, news about the railroad fills the Soviet press. So rich is the written record, Soviet authorities are compiling a bibliography devoted entirely to the BAM. Almost comically, a BAM Yearbook has been announced and will be published annually throughout the years of construction. In Moscow, exhibition space in the Museum of the Revolution has been dedicated to BAM models, photographs, and assorted paraphernalia. A "Scientific Siberia" exhibit has toured the United States, ostensibly to teach Americans about their nearest Soviet neighbor. A common topic of conversation between visitors to the Soviet Union and their guides is the BAM.[148]

Because of Americans' woeful ignorance of Siberia and its potential role in their future, few may have seen the real significance of the "Scientific Siberia" exhibit. Visitors probably viewed it merely as a friendly gesture in times of détente. Some recognized its true meaning: a recognition of geographic complementarity, the linchpin for which may well be the Baykal-Amur Mainline.

What follows is a partly general, partly detailed description and analysis of the BAM and its service area. Included are sections devoted to the physical geography of the region, a history of the BAM, the route, proximal natural resources, the BAM's likely impact on Pacific Siberia and international trade, human and environmental problems associated with the project, and the importance of comprehensive planning to the BAM and its region.

Physical Geography of the BAM Zone

Encompassing almost one-half the total area of the Soviet Union but including less than 6 percent of the population, Pacific Siberia composes one of the largest and least densely populated regions in the world. The BAM will affect the southern quarter of the territory, traversing, at least in part, five political and administrative subdivisions of the Russian Republic (RSFSR): Irkutsk Oblast (a segment of 180 miles); Buryat ASSR (320 miles); Chita Oblast (250 miles); Amur Oblast (840 miles); and Khabarovsk Kray (375 miles). In addition, the "Little BAM," running perpendicular to the mainline from Bam to Tynda and Berkakit (250 miles), enters the Yakut ASSR. The mainline will parallel the Trans-Siberian at a distance of 110 to 310 miles to the north. Its tributary area will comprise a zone 95 to 125 miles north and south of the track, some 600,000 square miles, or more than three times the size of France.[205]

The physical geography of a region as large as the BAM zone may not be summarized adequately in a study of this nature. Probably the most complete work on the area was done in the 1940s by Suslov.[219] More recently, in line with their impact analyses of the BAM on its service area, Sochava and associates at the Institute of Geography of Siberia and the Far East have produced the best material.[205]

According to these surveys, the BAM zone is part of three large natural provinces: Middle Siberia; Baykal-Dzhugdzhur; and Amur-Sakhalin. Soviet research in the 1960s further delineated 26 subprovinces in the region.

The Middle Siberian natural province already has been spanned by a railroad between Tayshet and Ust'-Kut, the western leg of the BAM. The area is composed of a horizontal, elevated plateau which has been deeply incised by tributaries of the Angara and Lena. This is the ancient Siberian Platform (commonly known to geographers as the southern extension of the Anabar Shield), consisting of some of the oldest rocks in existence. The climate of the province is continental with wide annual ranges of temperature [Bratsk, $-24°C$ $(-10°F)$ in January, $18°C$ $(64°F)$ in July] and scanty precipitation [300 mm (12 inches)], with a pronounced summer maximum (80 percent of annual total).[142] The vegetation is characteristically southern tayga, including spruce, fir, Siberian stone pine, and larch. In cleared areas, a second growth of coniferous pine and larch or deciduous birch and aspen appears. The rare expanses of true soil are decidedly podzolic. Most of the landscape is covered with intrazonal or azonal gleized bogs, regosols or lithosols, underlain by permafrost. The poor soils and short growing season (105 days or less) limit agriculture to isolated thermal and pedogenic anomalies, such as in valleys just north of Tayshet, Bratsk, and Ust'-Kut. There it is possible to raise spring wheat, barley, oats, flax, hemp, peas, beans, apples, tubers and berries along with stall-fed cattle and sheep. Despite some potential for expanded agricultural production in the province, Middle Siberian farms are providing only 13 percent of their own potatoes, 18 percent of their vegetables, 17 percent of their egg needs, and a dismal 6 percent of their requirements for milk.[207]

The longest and most difficult segment of the BAM lies in the Baykal-Dzhugdzhur natural province. In comparison with the railroad's Middle Siberian service area, which includes only three fairly homogeneous subprovinces, the BAM's Baykal-Dzhugdzhur province comprises 14 subregions, 6 of which intersect the railway itself. Overall, the province is a typical mountain realm running from Ust'-Kut to the headwaters of the Nyukzha and generally northeastward to the Dzhugdzhur Mountains. It consists of a highly complex geomorphology with dissected plateaus and uplands in the west and high faulted mountain ranges from Lake Baykal east to the Olekma River. Between the principal ranges (Baykal, Muya, Kodar, and Stanovoy) is a chain of narrow, block-faulted depressions, through which the railroad will pass. This is the Baykal Rift, heart of the Sayan-Stanovoy orogenic zone, a regional exposure of the Archeozoic and Proterozoic basement rocks of the Anabar Shield, 900 million to 3 billion years old.[131] The climate of the Baykal-Dzhugdzhur province, like its neighboring western province, remains continental, but is slightly influenced by the Pacific monsoon. Temperatures at Bodaybo range from −33°C (−28°F) in January to 18°C (64°F) in July. Reflecting the effect of the monsoon, precipitation totals rise to 425 mm (17 inches), with 80 percent falling in the high sun period. The vegetation is dominated by larch tayga except in the Kirenga River basin where there are promising commercial stone-pine stands. Higher elevations are either bald, tundra-clad or shielded by a sparse larch growth. As in Middle Siberia, true soils are uncommon with most of the depressions veneered with boggy *mari*. Though agricultural potential may be found in a few of the rift valleys, as in the Muya-Kuanda depression where melons are said to grow, this activity is limited by an extremely short growing season of 95 days or less. This period is sufficient for cultivating potatoes, barley, early oats, and flax, but little else. The most promising agricultural activity in the region is the raising of livestock. At present, however, farmers cannot raise enough food to satisfy even the most austere needs of the very small population.[207]

The third and most hospitable natural province in the BAM zone is Amur-Sakhalin, flanking the railroad between Tynda and Sovetskaya Gavan'. Here the relief is characterized by low mountains and broad waterlogged depressions (*mari*). The entire region is formed of folded Mesozoic rocks. Though strongly influenced by the Pacific monsoon, the climate remains severe, with January temperatures below −20°C (−4°F) and those for July above 20°C (68°F) except on the coast. Precipitation is nearly everywhere over 450 mm (18 inches), with a peaked July maximum. Larch tayga predominates in the folded interior, with the vegetation becoming more luxurious, diverse, and commercially valuable near the coast. Soils, once again, are commonly waterlogged, but reflect more nearly zonal features (brown forest, true podzol, etc.). Many of them, when drained, should prove fertile. This is especially true of the pseudo-chernozems of the Zeya-Bureya plain.[112] Despite its coastal position, the Amur-Sakhalin province still reflects a short growing season, varying from 95 days near Bomnak to 120 days at Komsomol'sk. Nevertheless, potential agricultural productivity and variety are much greater here than in the two provinces to the west. Soviet experts predict that settlements in the BAM service area will depend heavily on the agricultural, especially vegetable, output of the Amur-Sakhalin region.[167] However, it is doubtful that the agricultural base of this area will ever satisfy the food needs of its own future population, much less the demands of the population of the rest of the BAM zone.

Although functionally and geographically encompassed by the BAM service area, the "Little BAM" spur railroad from Bam to Tynda and Berkakit should be described here in some detail as well. Proceeding almost due north from the Trans-Siberian, the "Little BAM" links the Amur-Sakhalin and Baykal-Dzhugdzhur natural provinces. Thus, its route may be divided into two parts: a southern (Amur) segment and a northern (Aldan) segment.

By the end of 1976, the southern segment of the "Little BAM" was completed as far north as the Yakutian border and for some distance beyond.[135] It crosses the western flank of the Amur-Zeya plateau, formed of Tertiary sand and clay on a bedrock of conglomerate, granites, gneisses, and Jurassic sandstone. The vegetation on this part of the route is larch-pine tayga. This forest persists to the foothills of the Yankan-Tukuringra Ridge, which is composed chiefly of schists and a variety of sedimentary formations, all of Paleozoic or Mesozoic age. Here the vegetation is a potentially exploitable mountain tayga. Beyond this ridge, the spur joins the BAM at Tynda, situated on a high plateau clad with larch and pine and drained by the Gilyuy River and its tributaries. Despite relatively temperate conditions along the southern end of the "Little BAM," agriculture is limited by unfavorable soil and relief factors.

Having crossed the Stanovoy Range at the end of 1976, the "Little BAM" descends onto the Aldan upland, an important subprovince of Baykal-Dzhugdzhuria. Composed basically of highly fractured pre-Cambrian schists and gneisses penetrated by intrusions and, in part, extrusions, the Aldan upland is a highly dissected plateau containing dome-shaped, bald mountains, often covered with talus. Where forests are found, they are dense stands of larch, pine, and fir of some commercial value. Agriculture is limited and of secondary importance to the mining industry.[167]

An Old Idea: A New Railway

The Russians first considered building a railway that would skirt the northern extremity of Lake Baykal in the 1880s.[3] Years earlier, there were similar proposals for mainlines by which Europe and the Far East could be connected via the Soviet heartland, but none was taken seriously. In 1888, though, a respected commission of the Russian Technological Society published a document recommending a northern route for the proposed Trans-Siberian that would be shorter by 300 miles. However, the more severe climate and relief of the northern alternative simply were too much of an obstacle for the railroad construction technology of the time.

After the Alaska purchase, entrepreneurs of the Western Union telegraph company had aspirations of linking North America and Europe by cable across the Bering Strait and Siberia.[200] However, before a proper survey could be conducted, the Trans-Atlantic cable was laid by the Great Eastern Company, and the Siberian plans were abandoned.

Nevertheless, the plans may have provided inspiration for the ideas of a syndicate of American railroad magnates. In 1904 the syndicate, through a French spokesman, suggested the construction of a Siberian-Alaskan railroad from Cape Prince Wales in Alaska through a tunnel under the Bering Strait and across northeastern Siberia to Irkutsk via Cape Dezhnev, Verkhnekolymsk, and Yakutsk.[3] The proposal might have been more appealing to the conservative Czarist government had it not been for the preconditions. As compensation for the expenses incurred, the syndicate adjured not only a 90-year lease of the right-of-way and associated buildings and communication lines, but also claimed exclusive mineral rights within 8 miles on each side of the right-of-way. It would seem that such a bold proposal would have been refused outright, but it was debated by Czarist officials until March 20, 1907, when a negative decision was given.

Between 1911 and 1914 the Czarist Railroad Ministry worked out a preliminary plan for the construction of the Angara-Lena railroad, the western segment of the future BAM. Two alternative routes were included in the report, one of which was the Tayshet-Bratsk-Ust'-Kut alignment, destined to be completed some 40 years later. Final selection of the route was forsaken by the Russians because of World War I.

With the Soviets in power in the early 1920s, a plan for the construction of a super-mainline railroad, apparently running parallel to, and north of, the Trans-Siberian was included as part of the GOELRO project, a program for electrification and associated industrial development. The idea did not specify a route, and merely envisioned it as passing through "regions extraordinarily rich in natural resources and whose economic accessibility by means of an electrified mainline would create totally new conditions for the future structure of the economy, not only in Russia but in world trade."[18]

While ascribed to Lenin, the notion of a second Siberian railway was not considered seriously again until 1932. With Komsomol'sk then under construction, a decision was made to extend a railroad to the new city from Urusha Station on the Trans-Siberian in Transbaykalia. The geology of the route was studied and good maps of the regions to be crossed were produced. But, in view of terrain difficulties and technological inadequacies, this particular proposal was tabled. One of the accomplishments of these surveys of the early 1930s was the establishment of basic reference points for the BAM. A spur line from the vicinity of Skovorodino, a siding on the Trans-Siberian, to Tynda, 110 miles to the north, was to be the first leg, to be followed by an easterly alignment, through Urgal and Komsomol'sk to Sovetskaya Gavan'. The course that the western half of the BAM would take was cause for debate. Several alternatives were suggested, but the one ultimately decided on would begin at Tayshet, pass through Ust'-Kut, circle the north end of Lake Baykal through Nizhneangarsk, and reach Tynda at the 1,650-kilometer marker (1,015 miles).

The railroad work in Pacific Siberia during the 1930s was apparently responsible for much of the misinformation that later surrounded the BAM. In a confusing transfer of names, the label BAM was applied in 1933–35 to a project of double-tracking the Trans-Siberian east of Lake Baykal. The construction was carried out largely with the use of forced labor.[211]

Prewar detailed surveys were conducted between Tayshet and Sovetskaya Gavan' by a special agency, *Bamproyekt* (later known as *Zheldorproyekt*). Between 1938 and 1942, the agency carefully determined the alignment of the Tayshet—Ust'-Kut and Tynda-Sovetskaya Gavan' segments. Agreement on the alignment of the difficult Ust'-Kut—Tynda section was not reached until 1944.

Meanwhile construction was begun on a projected 600-mile spur northward from the Trans-Siberian at Bam Station (so designated as the jumping-off point for the BAM mainline itself), just west of Skovorodino, through Tynda to Yakutsk. This line, now called the "Little BAM," was conceived as a bridgehead from which work would proceed both west to the Lena and east to the Pacific. As World War II began, track had been laid between Bam and Tynda, but in 1942, during the battle of Stalingrad, incredibly the rails were pulled up and hauled to the Volga, where they were urgently needed for a supply line built from Saratov to the besieged city.[178] Even anti-tank weapons were forged from the rails.[2]

Also, in the early days of the war (1940), a spur line of the Trans-Siberian was completed between Khabarovsk and the new city of Komsomol'sk. Simultaneously, construction was begun (but not finished until 1945), on the easternmost segment of the BAM from Sovetskaya Gavan' and its adjacent Pacific port of Vanino to Pivan', on the right bank of the broad Amur River opposite Komsomol'sk.

In the 1940s, as well, work was begun on the Tayshet—Ust'-Kut segment of the BAM, a spur line northward from the Trans-Siberian station of Izvestkovaya to the coal mines of Urgal and Chegdomyn, and an extension of the eastern BAM on the left bank of the Amur from Komsomol'sk to Berezovka. The last-mentioned line, used for hauling timber from the Amgun' valley, has not appeared on Soviet maps, apparently because it has not been a common carrier under the Railroad Ministry.

Many of the facts surrounding the early construction of the BAM were complicated by the events of the war and the clandestine world of Stalinist Russia. The BAM was to be the most important building project of the third Five-Year Plan (1938—1942). Thus, while the war raged, conflicting reports regarding its status reached the West. Maps, including a National Geographic map of the Soviet Union, were published showing the railroad as completed.[173] Supposedly knowledgeable Soviet *émigrés*, indeed, no less than the son of the first president of the Soviet Academy of Sciences and organizer of the first geologic surveys along the Trans-Siberian, insisted that the railroad had been finished.[212,85] Evidently, with news of construction on the western Tayshet—Ust'-Kut segment (completed in 1954, but not formally opened to permanent use until December 1958) and of the completion of the eastern link between Pivan' (the right bank suburb of Komsomol'sk) and Sovetskaya Gavan' combined with the earlier false BAM reports emanating from the Soviet Union, it was deemed logical by some that the segment between Ust'-Kut and Komsomol'sk had also been traversed. As late as 1961, a widely used Western textbook for courses in geography of the USSR asserted: "In Siberia, the BAM branches off at Tayshet and after serving the Bureya Valley reaches Komsomol'sk."[83]

Although the final plans for the BAM were ready when the war ended in 1945, they had to be revised completely. Updating, in fact, took more than 25 years and the labor of 3,000 surveyors and designers. The line had been laid out for steam locomotives instead of diesel and electric traction, and planned for light loads. It could not take the weight of 8-axle tank cars for hauling Western Siberia's new-found oil. The designers had underestimated the seismic dangers and failed to provide for reinforced construction. The dismantled spur from the Trans-Siberian to Tynda in the middle of the route was overgrown, and its reinforced concrete supports had cracked. At the western end, the spur from the Trans-Siberian to Ust'-Kut had to be double-tracked to carry supplies to the railhead.[71] (Most of BAM will be single-track, but the roadbed is to be built for eventual double-tracking.)

Despite this activity, no official recognition of it was given by the Soviet press, and when the BAM was not included in the fourth five-year plan (1946–50) and subsequent five-year plans, the railroad was all but forgotten in the West. In 1961 the Bratsk segment of the Tayshet–Ust'-Kut line was shifted northward in connection with the Bratsk hydro project. Then, rather quietly, in 1967, design work on the central BAM began anew. This nearly coincided with the announcement of the planned construction of a Tyumen'-Komsomol'sk (North Siberian) rail route. "The trace of the BAM seemed to form the eastern section of this railway."[44] Between 1967 and 1974, surveys and inspections were made of the BAM, "Little BAM," and their tributary areas.

Actual construction of the Bam-Berkakit railroad began in 1971, apparently spurred by Japanese interest in the coking coal of southern Yakutia.[180] There are now only very distant plans to extend this railway ultimately to Yakutsk, as was envisioned in the blueprints of the 1930s.

Heading up the survey and design work was *Mosgiprotrans* (The Moscow Transport Design Agency), including institutes in the Ministry of Transport Construction, the Ministry of Railroads, and others. A subdivision of the overall agency, *Giprotranstei*, calculated prospective freight flows for the BAM and may have been largely responsible for arousing new interest in the project among the highest government leaders.[18]

These leaders registered their approval of the BAM when Leonid I. Brezhnev in March 1974 proclaimed that the railway would be one of two major projects of the 10th five-year plan (1976–80).[27] (The other was to be rural development of the backward non-chernozem zone of European Russia.) A few weeks later, appearing at the 17th congress of Young Communist League (Komsomol), he issued a challenge to the youth of the country to join in the building of the BAM, "the construction project of the century."[28] Finally, as thousands of young persons were induced to respond to the summons, on July 8, 1974 a formal resolution concerning the construction of the railway was adopted by the Central Committee and Council of Ministers.[88] Thus, following nearly a half-century of sporadic deliberation, the construction of the BAM was sanctioned officially by the Soviet regime.

Since the issuance of those decrees, perhaps as many as 50,000 young people—there were 156,000 applicants at the end of 1974[71]—have been attracted to the BAM and its service area. In 1975 and in 1976, the plan was fulfilled. Both the Amur and Lena bridges were built. Some 85 miles of track between Ust'-Kut's Lena station and the rail siding of Nebel', in the western section of the mainline. On the transverse line to the South Yakutian coal field, rail-laying crews crossed the border into Yakutia and reached the settlement of Nagornyy. Near Urgal and Chegdomyn, teams had cleared 75 miles of forest and had laid 30 miles of track. The first 215-megawatt generator went on line at the Zeya hydroelectric station from which the eastern half of the BAM service area eventually will be supplied with electric power via high-voltage lines. Altogether, 28 new settlements and forward bases were inaugurated; 70 new bridges, ranging from several feet to nearly a mile long, were finished; and 110 miles of track were laid.[135]

Despite these achievements, the BAM workers must nearly triple their track-laying capacity between now and 1983, if they are to meet their deadline. After all, the central BAM from Ust'-Kut to Komsomol'sk is 1,965 miles long and well over 50 miles remain on the "Little BAM." Projected work schedules are: Ust'-Kut–Komsomol'sk (BAM), 1974–1983; Bam-Tynda-Berkakit (Little BAM), 1974–1977; Tayshet–Bratsk–Ust'-Kut (second track, 1974–1983); Komsomol'sk-Sovetskaya Gavan' (improved freight handling), 1974–1983.[94]

The BAM Route

The BAM begins at Lena station, which serves the Lena River port of Osetrovo at Ust'-Kut. Perhaps 15 miles east, at Yakurim, the rails cross the 1,375-foot concrete span bridge completed over the Lena in 1975 (Fig. 2). Another 25 miles or so east, at Kilometer 64 (Mile 40), the railroad reaches the new urban settlement of Zvezdnyy (Tayura Station), near the fork of the Tayura and Niya rivers. At the end of 1975, this was as far as the track had been laid.

From Zvezdnyy, the BAM follows the Niya River to its headwaters, passing through the forward base of Niya and reaching Nebel' at Kilometer 135 (Mile 85). Nebel' was reached at the end of 1976. From that point, construction crews were descending into the Kirenga River basin in 1977, crossing the stream near the new urban settlement of Magistral'nyy (founded in 1975), south of the older village of Kazachinskoye. The goal of the 1977 construction program was the urban settlement of Ul'kan (founded in 1976) at kilometer marker 208 (Mile 130). Continuing in a south-southeasterly direction, the BAM arrives in Kunerma, on the Kunerma River, which drains the western face of the Baykal Range. This point is to be reached from the west by 1979.

The Baykal Range is the first obstacle of any consequence on the route east of the Lena River. The trains will be conducted up the Kunerma River valley and then, by means of a 4-mile tunnel, through the range, from Irkutsk Oblast into Buryat ASSR. Construction workers of the Leningrad Subway Design Agency (*Lenmetroproyekt*) are responsible for this and all the route's tunnels, which cumulatively stretch for 15 miles.[204]

Emerging from the tunnel, the BAM proceeds due east along the Goudzhekit River to the Tyya, where it turns south along the left bank of the stream and descends to its mouth on Lake Baykal. Here on Cape Kurly the new town of Severobaykal'sk was founded in September 1975. Some 2,000 BAM workers were already in residence there at that time.[33]

From Severobaykal'sk, the railroad skirts the shore of the lake in a northeasterly direction to the depot of Nizhneangarsk. The BAM will be electrified from Ust'-Kut to this point on the basis of power supplied by a high-tension line from the dam at Ust'-Ilimsk.[94] From Nizhneangarsk, the BAM negotiates the broad Upper Angara valley for about 130 miles to the east, passing through the villages of Chencha and Uoyan before encountering the North Muya Range, the most formidable obstruction along the entire route.

Planners examined a dozen possible traverses of the North Muya and ultimately decided on a 9-mile tunnel based on the stability of its subgrade. When finished in 1983, the conduit will rank as the fourth or fifth longest railway tunnel in the world. Workers are blazing an approach road to the tunnel site from Sakhuli in the Barguzin lowland via Taza. The BAM will be electrified in the long tunnel, otherwise, exhorbitant expenditures of power would be required for ventilation systems. Ultimately, the entire western segment of 405 miles between Lena station at Ust'-Kut and Muyakan station, at the eastern end of the North Muya tunnel, will be electrified, both because of the two tunnels and because of steep 16-percent grades. For the time being, steam traction will be used everywhere east of Muyakan.

Emerging on the eastern face of the North Muya range, the BAM descends into the Muya-Kuanda basin following the Muyakan and Muya rivers, tributaries of the Vitim, crossing the latter at Vitim station, south of Ust'-Muya, via a 1,620-foot bridge into Chita Oblast. East of the Vitim, the alignment ascends the Syul'ban River valley to a spur of the Kodar Ridge, to be traversed by yet another tunnel, of 5,400 feet. Thence, the railroad proceeds into the isolated Chara River basin. In the center of the lowland is the town of Chara, which, together with Ust'-Kut, Sevorobaykal'sk, Tynda, and Urgal, will be one of the five largest towns on the mainline.[17] From the north end of the Chara basin, the BAM continues eastward over the Udokan Ridge, a spur of the Stanovoy Mountains, down the Khani River valley to the Olekma in Amur Oblast. Pending the arrival of the railroad, a temporary winter road from the Trans-Siberian town of Mogocha now supplies the Udokan copper mine development, 20 miles southeast of Chara.[4]

After following the Olekma for 60 miles, the BAM crosses the river and proceeds along one of its right tributaries, the Nyukzha River. The route parallels this stream until it reaches the Lena-Amur divide, where a huge cut was under excavation in 1976–77 to accommodate the railroad as it pursues a southeasterly course to Tynda. Several forward bases have been established along the line between the Olekma River and Tynda, including Lopcha, Larba, Khorogochi and Kuvykta. Kuvykta has been designated as a future station and was linked in 1975 to Tynda by a 25-mile secondary road.[152]

From Tynda and its junction with the "Little BAM," the mainline runs together with the Yakutian branch railroad as far as Sivachkan on the upper course of the Gilyuy to the northeast, then generally east past Marevaya (reached in late 1976), Dipkun and Tutaul to the Zeya River at Zeysk station, just west of old Bomnak. The original BAM alignment of the 1940s between Tynda and Urgal was along the Zeya River, but because of the reservoir created by the Zeya Dam, it has been relocated to the north.[102] From Zeysk, the railway ascends the gentle slopes of the Tukuringra-Dzhagdy Ridge in a southerly direction along the Izhak River, intersecting the ridge in a low-elevation gap. Then it follows a meandering course along the Dep and Tungala rivers to the Nora-Dugda confluence. From this point, it passes southeastward across several rivers to the Selemdzha River at Fevral'sk, west of Selemdzhinsk.

Fevral'sk was linked to the Trans-Siberian at Svobodnyy by an access highway in 1975. This means that now the BAM construction teams in Amur Oblast can be supplied by three feeder routes, including the new highway, the Bam-Tynda rail route, and the Zeya River water route.[229]

The mainline continues its southeasterly course from Fevral'sk along the Isa River and across the Turan Ridge, which divides Amur Oblast from Khabarovsk Kray. Descending the ridge via the valley of the upper Tuyun River, the railway reaches the Bureya River at Alonka, halfway between Ust'-Niman and Ust'-Urgal. From Alonka, the BAM turns south to Ust'-Urgal (Urgal II station), then east to Urgal (Urgal I) and, finally, upstream along the Soloni River through the Bureya

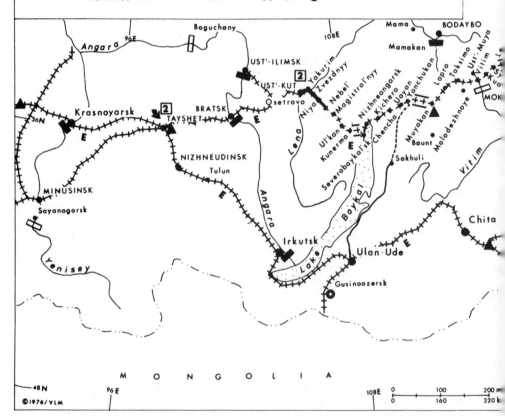

THE BAYKAL-AMUR MAINLINE
as of January 1, 1977

++++ RAILROADS: ▲++++▲ ELECTRIFIED OR SOON TO BE ELECTRIFIED.

▼++++++++▼ THE BAM: ■■■■ FINISHED; ++++ UNFINISHED;

oooooo ORIGINAL TRACE; ±± TUNNELS;

▲+++▲ TO BE ELECTRIFIED FIRST;
  E

1++++1 TO BE IMPROVED;

2++++2 TO BE DOUBLE-TRACKED.

MAJOR MOTOR TRANSPORT ROUTES: —— FINISHED; ------ UNFINISHED
OR USED ONLY IN WINTER.

POWER PLANTS:

HYDROELECTRIC: ■FINISHED;▢UNDER CONSTRUCTION OR PLANNED;

PLANNED THERMAL — MAJOR BAM SUPPORT: ◉.

Boguchany

Angara 96E

108E

Mama   BODAYBO

Mamakan

UST'-ILIMSK

UST'-KUT

Osetrovo

Yakurim

Zvezdnyy

Niya

Nebel'

Magistral'nyy

Nizhneangarsk

Kichera

Uoyan

Yanchukan

Taksimo

Ust'-Muya

MOK

Krasnoyarsk

TAYSHET

BRATSK

Lena

Ul'kan

Kunerma

Severobaykal'sk

Chencha

Muyakan

Baunt

Molodezhnoye

Lapro

56N

E

NIZHNEUDINSK

Tulun

Sakhuli

Vitim

MINUSINSK

Sayanogorsk

Angara

Lake Baykal

Chita

Irkutsk

Ulan-Ude

E

Yenisey

Gusinoozersk

M   O   N   G   O   L   I   A

48N

96E

©1976/VLM

108E   0   100   200 m
       0   160   320 k

Fig. 2.

76

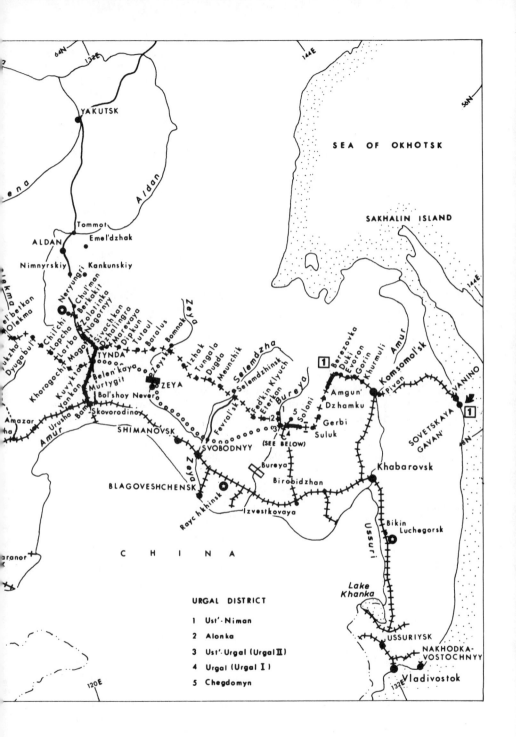

SEA OF OKHOTSK

SAKHALIN ISLAND

YAKUTSK

Tommot
Emel'dzhak
ALDAN
Nimnyrskiy Kankunskiy

Neryungri
Chul'man
Berkakit
Zolotinka
Nagornyy
Sivachkan
Dzhalinara
Dipkun
Tutaul
Baralus
Bomnak

TYNDA

Zeyo

Aizhak
Tungala
Dugda
Meunchik

Selemdzha

Selemdzhinsk

Fedkin Klyuch

Eterkan

Soloni

Khorogoch
Mogot
Kuvykta
Yankan
Murtygit
Bol'shoy Never
Bam
Urusha
Skovorodino

Belen'kaya
ZEYA

Fevral'sk

Bureya

Amgun'
Dzhamku

Barezovka
Duki
Evoron
Gorin
Khurmuli

Komsomol'sk

Pivan

Gerbi
Suluk

VANINO

SOVETSKAYA
GAVAN'

SHIMANOVSK

SVOBODNYY

(SEE BELOW)

Zeya

Bureya

Birobidzhan

Khabarovsk

BLAGOVESHCHENSK

Raychikhinsk

Izvestkovaya

Ussuri

Bikin
Luchegorsk

C H I N A

Lake
Khanka

URGAL DISTRICT

1   Ust'-Niman

2   Alonka

3   Ust'-Urgal (Urgal II)

4   Urgal (Urgal I)

5   Chegdomyn

USSURIYSK

NAKHODKA-
VOSTOCHNYY

Vladivostok

Amazar

Amur

Olekma

Dyugabul'

Chilchi
Lopcha
Larba

77

divide by means of the 1.3-mile Dusse-Alin' tunnel, which was being approached by rail-laying crews from Urgal by the end of 1976. The tunnel, the fourth major tunnel along the mainline, was originally excavated in the early 1950s by forced labor working on the original BAM project. It is now being refurbished. One report, in the summer of 1976, said 32,000 cubic meters of ice, accumulated in the unattended tunnel over the last two decades, had already been removed.

Emerging from the tunnel, the mainline proceeds downstream along the Amgun' River northeast to Berezovka, the terminus of the old logging railroad from Komsomol'sk, which is to be modernized to fit the BAM specifications. Rail crews from Berezovka have been advancing southwest along the Amgun' toward the Dusse-Alin' tunnel. They reached Amgun' station by the end of 1976, leaving a 125-mile gap. The entire Urgal-Komsomol'sk segment is scheduled to be completed by 1979.

Formerly, flatbeds bearing timber from the Amgun' valley and bound for Sovetskaya Gavan' or Vanino were carried from the Komsomol'sk (left-bank) side of the Amur via ferries in summer, or over the ice on temporary rails in winter, to the right-bank railhead of Pivan'. During spring and fall, communications were severed by floating ice. With the completion of the Amur River bridge on Sept. 26, 1975, all this changed.[155] The latter structure is a 4,550-foot Eiffel bridge supported by reinforced-concrete spans. Begun in 1972, it was completed 3 months ahead of schedule.

Some 1,100 miles by rail to the west of Komsomol'sk, the "Little BAM" begins its nearly 250-mile journey to the north at Bam Station, west of Skovorodino, on the Trans-Siberian. Though eventually to be electrified, the "Little BAM" now runs on steam traction and is capable of negotiating slopes of 9 percent.[37] From the junction at Bam, the spur road ascends the Yankan Ridge on its way to a bridge over the Tynda at the way station of Belen'kaya, a growing logging center. It is then a short 30 miles farther to Tynda, the so-called "capital of the BAM."

Railroad construction crews reached Tynda from the south in early May 1975, in time for the 30th anniversary of the end of World War II. The first freight train arrived from the Trans-Siberian on May 8.[37] Construction work has proceeded along three axes from Tynda ever since: north, east, and west.

The Tynda-Sivachkan segment, which combines the alignments of the BAM mainline and the Yakutian rail branch, was completed in early 1976, and the construction crews proceeded northward through Mogot, crossed the Yakutian border and by the end of 1976 reached the urban settlement of Nagornyy, an old highway post at the intersection of the Yakutian road and the Timpton River. The original construction schedule called for completion of the line to Berkakit by 1979. But an accelerated program called for the completion of a 1.25 mile tunnel through the Stanovoy divide between Nagornyy and Zolotinka so that rail crews would reach the coal terminus of Berkakit by the end of 1977. The actual coal center, extracting high-grade coking coal from a huge strip-mining operation, is the new city of Neryungri, on the Chul'man River, a few miles northwest of Berkakit. The spur may also be extended ultimately 25 miles farther north to the small town of Chul'man, which was the regional center, with a small thermal power station, before the rise of Neryungri.

All along its trace, the "Little BAM" is flanked by the Amur-Yakutian (Aldan) motor road, running from Bol'shoy Never to Yakutsk. The region has been served by the highway since the development of gold mining in the 1930's.[207] Though ostensibly a surfaced highway, it requires frequent repairs and is flooded or iced over many times during the year.

Design and Construction

By the time the BAM is completed—by 1983 if it is on time—it will have linked 200 stations and sidings, 64 of which will become central places or urban settlements. Seven ridges will have been crossed, including: the Baykal; North Muya; Kodar spur; Udokan; Tukuringra-Dzhagdy; Turan; and Dusse-Alin'. About one billion cubic-feet of earthwork will have been done; 3,700 bridges and culverts will have been built; 15 miles of tunnels will have been dug; 70 million square feet of work space and residences will have been constructed; and 2,500 miles of railroad superstructure will have been laid. In addition, 250 bridges and artificial structures, including the Stanovoy tunnel, will have been built along the trace of the "Little BAM." These statistics in every case are easily more than triple the engineering requirements of the controversial Trans-Alaska oil pipeline.[43] Such enormous obligations obviously require considerable organization.

The Olekma River has been considered by Soviet authorities as a convenient physical dividing line for allocating responsibilities for the design of the railroad. *Tomgiprotrans* (Tomsk Transport Design Agency) and *Sibgiprotrans* (Siberian Transport Design Agency) are accountable for planning the mainline on the plateaus of Central Siberia from Lena station to the Upper Angara. *Sibgiprotrans* is wholly obligated to design the segment from the Upper Angara to Chara. From Chara to Tynda, the duties are conferred on *Lengiprotrans* (Leningrad Transport Design Agency). Responsibility for the longest stretch (620 miles), between Tynda and Urgal, and for the "Little BAM" has been given to *Mosgiprotrans* (Moscow Transport Design Agency), whereas the final leg from Urgal to Komsomol'sk will be supervised by *Dal'giprotrans* (Far East Transport Design Agency). All bridges of more than 300 feet, of which there are 142 over the entire route, will be designed by *Giprotransmost* (State Bridge Transport Design Agency) and *Lengiprotransmost* (Leningrad Bridge Transport Design Agency).[17]

In charge of overall construction is *GlavBAMstroy* (Main BAM Construction Administration) of the Ministry of Transport Construction, with headquarters at Tynda.[262] The move from Moscow in 1975 was predicated, at least in part, on a lack of communications between the ministry in Moscow and the various construction agencies in the BAM zone.[59] *BAMstroyput'* (BAM Railroad Construction Agency) has been directly responsible for all work in the field, including the labor on both the BAM and "Little BAM."[136] This agency is also situated at Tynda, but its subcontractors are scattered throughout the BAM service area.

Much of the subcontracting has been allocated along ethnic lines. For instance, the BAM has been publicized as a "national project (*stroyka vsenarodnaya*)" and has attracted young people from at least 20 nationalities.[14] Perhaps for reasons of intracommunication or socialist competition, the ethnic teams more or less have been segregated. For example, Azeris are working at Ul'kan; Donbas Ukrainians are

79

at Urgal II; in neighboring Alonka, there are Moldavian crews; Lithuanians are found at Uoyan; and the Russians predominate in the Tynda area.[1]

Though there are problems among the various construction agencies and, certainly, difficulties with equipment, the BAM is intended as an ultramodern, highly automated railroad of the first category. Along with the plans for electrification, the mainline will possess automated block signaling, centralized electric switching, and automatic train stops and controls.

The BAM will be built at the rate of nearly a mile a day, once construction is fully organized. However, on the difficult segment west of the Olekma, half that rate is anticipated because of special structural, grading and track-curvature requirements. Soviet authorities hope that the use of new light-weight, prefabricated structures, corrugated metal pipe, and imported heavy equipment will help to maintain the high rates of construction.[94] The roadbed will consist almost exclusively of road-metal ballast, which will be supplied at the rate of 400,000 tons per year. Other annual building material requirements are 80 million bricks, 11 million cubic feet of rock, and 40,000 tons of lime.

Heavy equipment needs are summarized as follows: 1,200 excavators; 435 bulldozers; 320 graders; 835 cranes; 72 mine-loading machines; 60 rock crushers and sorters; 950 mobile compressors; 7,440 8-ton trucks; 310 tractors; 100 1,200-horsepower switching locomotives; 1,550 dumper cars; and 300 4-axle flatcars. West Germany will supply 600 dump trucks and 1,000 lorries. The United States has promised the delivery of 600 310-horsepower bulldozers. And Japan will provide 166 excavators and 600 mobile cranes, 320-horsepower tower cranes, and 420-horsepower bulldozers.[97]

The Impact of the BAM on Resource Use

The resource base of Pacific Siberia is undeniably awesome, comprising perhaps as much as half of the USSR's potential reserves of coal, major ores and timber. As new regions are made accessible by the BAM, "Little BAM," and their feeder routes during the rest of this century, these potential reserves are expected to become geologically established and even increased. Obviously, of greatest importance to the development of this massive region are its mineral resources (Fig. 3).

The most important readily exploitable resource in the BAM service area is the Udokan copper deposit, which, with an estimated 1.2 billion tons of ore over a 14-square-mile area, is comparable in size and quality to the Soviet Union's largest site at Dzhezkazgan in Kazakhstan. Udokan was discovered in 1948 at Naminga, 20 miles southeast of Chara. A seasonal winter road from Mogocha on the Trans-Siberian went into operation in the winter of 1959—60 during a period of further exploration of the site. Since that time, three additional copper-ore associations have been discovered near Udokan: Syul'ban, Unkur and Krasnoye. As a result of these and future expected findings, Udokan easily may be the country's richest copper area.

Because its copper sandstones lie close to the surface, the site will be worked by open pits. The first pit is anticipated to yield 20 million tons of 2 percent copper ore, or 400,000 tons of refinable copper annually. A pilot concentrator is planned to be in operation by the time the BAM arrives in the early 1980s. In the

80

meantime, Udokan will be supplied by the Mogocha truck convoys for at least four winter months out of each year.[65]

Because of its large size and remoteness from the principal markets in the USSR (as close to Anchorage as it is to Moscow), Udokan has been proposed by Soviet authorities as a joint development project to several Western nations, most notably to Japan. No doubt discussions of this proposal will increase as the BAM approaches completion.[51]

The second most significant resource in the service area of the mainline is the coking coal of southern Yakutia, the estimated reserves of which exceed 40 billion tons. This is already comparable in size to the Karaganda basin, even though southern Yakutia is relatively unexplored. The most promising site is the Neryungri deposit, which lies in seams more than 150-feet thick and may be extracted by strip-mining operations. There are numerous, less investigated deposits in the area, but Neryungri, with 500 million tons of high-caloric coal in reserve, will be developed first. Projected annual output from the site is 12 million tons, giving it a 40-year lifetime at present. As with Udokan, Soviet trade officials have proposed southern Yakutia as a project for joint development.[51]

Approximately 60 miles north of Neryungri, near the Amur-Yakutian motor road, are the Aldan iron ore deposits, whose long-range potential reserves may equal 20 billion tons.[94] Current economically extractable reserves are estimated at 3 billion tons, and only 1.5 billion of these are proven. The latter are associated chiefly with the Tayezhnoye deposit of 42 percent ore and three sources of magnetite: Pionerskoye, Sivagli, and Desovskoye. Questionable iron-ore deposits have been found 220 miles and 250 miles west and northwest of Neryungri. The former, known as Chara-Tokko, and the latter, named Olekma-Amga, are composed of iron quartzites similar to those at Krivoy Rog and are reckoned at 10 billion tons of long-range potential reserves, but these are far from being geologically established. The bulk of the Aldan ore may be extracted by the open-pit method. The proximity of cheap iron ore and coking coal in south Yakutia may provide the basis for the establishment of a new iron and steel plant somewhere in Pacific Siberia in the 1980s.[233]

Expected to assist economic development throughout Pacific Siberia is the relative nearness of natural gas in the Vilyuy basin and perhaps petroleum farther south along the Lena not far from Ust'-Kut. Potential reserves of natural gas in the Vilyuy area have been estimated at nearly 460 trillion cubic feet, but as of January 1973 only 30 trillion had been geologically established.[174] Moreover, only 8 trillion cubic feet have been proven in the field. Soviet officials have induced Japan and the United States to provide credit for exploration and extraction of the fuel. Many Western mineral fuels experts have been skeptical about the prospects because of the gap between estimated and proven reserves. As Soviet exploratory techniques improve, this skepticism may fade.

The BAM also will give access to a major chrysotile asbestos deposit at Molodezhnyy on the Mudirikan River, a right tributary of the Muya on the northern face of the South Muya Range. An open-cut mine and beneficiation plant are planned for the site, which was explored thoroughly between 1960 and 1964. Molodezhnyy asbestos is an unusually high grade of long-spinning textile-quality ore that is no less rich than the Thetford and Black Lake deposits in Canada.[118]

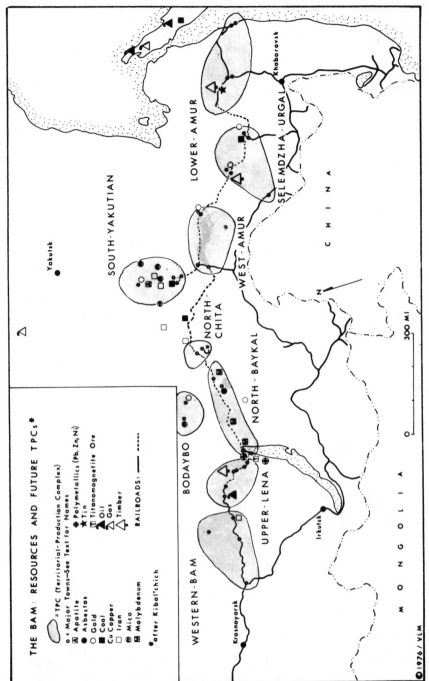

THE BAM: RESOURCES AND FUTURE TPCs*

▱ = TPC (Territorial-Production Complex)
o = Major Towns—See Text for Names
Ⓐ Apatite   ⊛ Polymetallics (Pb, Zn, Ni)
● Asbestos   ★ Tin
○ Gold   ▣ Titanomagnetite Ore
■ Coal   ▲ Oil
Cu Copper   △ Gas
□ Iron   ▽ Timber
Ⓜ Mica
Ⓜ Molybdenum   RAILROADS: ------

*after Kibal'chich

WESTERN-BAM

BODAYBO

UPPER-LENA

NORTH-BAYKAL

NORTH-CHITA

SOUTH-YAKUTIAN

WEST-AMUR

LOWER-AMUR

SELEMDZHA-URGAL

Yakutsk

Khabarovsk

C H I N A

M O N G O L I A

Krasnoyarsk

Irkutsk

N

0   300 MI

©1976/ VLM

Fig. 3.

82

Roughly 120 miles north of Berkakit, again on the Amur-Yakutian motor road, is the Seligdar apatite deposit. Estimated at 3 billion tons, the reserves of Seligdar are comparable in quality to the ores of the Kola Peninsula and Karatau. A processing plant with a yearly capacity of 60 million tons of crude ore may be constructed near the site, which is only 15 miles southwest of the settlement of Aldan. With superphosphates now being shipped to Siberia from the Urals and European Russia, a great savings in rubles, time and energy should result from the production of fertilizer at Seligdar.[21]

Another nonmetallic that will be made more accessible by the BAM is phlogopite (magnesium) mica on the Aldan upland, one of the Soviet Union's few phlogopite sources. The deposits are found mainly at Emel'dzhak, 30 miles southeast of Tommot on the Amur-Yakutian motor road; and at Kankunskiy on a spur of the highway, 90 miles south-southeast of Tommot. The Emel'dzhak and Kankunskiy deposits have been worked in open pits and underground mines since the 1940s. The pits and mines have yielded 40 to 60 percent raw mica, respectively. The ore is shipped out of southern Yakutia for processing.[41]

South Yakutian placer gold deposits are near depletion, but lode-gold output persists around Aldan on the Amur-Yakutian motor road.[92] The BAM may also foster the mining of gold in the vicinity of Selemdzhinsk in Amur Oblast; on the upper reaches of the Bureya and Zeya rivers; in northern Chita Oblast; in the Baunt area of Buryatia; and in the Bodaybo Region in Irkutsk Oblast.[170]

The BAM zone also is well endowed with lesser known ores. One of the most important is found in the Far East near the Berezovka-Komsomol'sk railway. Here in the Myaochan Mountains lie the Badzhal-Komsomol'sk tin deposits. The ore from these sites is mined and concentrated at the towns of Gornyy and Solnechnyy, and construction of a tine smelter, was begun in 1976. Elsewhere, in the Mam-Chuya district along the Vitim River, muscovite (potassium) mica is mined, yielding 75 percent of the country's muscovite output. Large, but dispersed, deposits of the important ferroalloy, molybdenum, are found throughout Transbaykalia, with those at Orekitkan and Katugin to be exploited first. Finally, hydrothermal veins in the Baykal Range are rich in polymetallics, for example, the titanomagnetites in the Tyya River valley and the lead-zinc-nickel associations in the mountains to the north and south.

Other promising minerals in the BAM service area have been enumerated by Odintsov and Bukharov.[131] Because of the great potential for hydroelectricity in Pacific Siberia, reputedly 56 percent of the total for the entire country,[51] the energy-intensive processing of light metals, such as aluminum and magnesium, has an auspicious future, given new discoveries of alumina-bearing bauxite (Kirenga River basin), kaolin (the same location), and nephelite (Synnyrskiy intrusions of the Baykal upland).[131] However, the quantity and quality of these ores remain to be proven. Also located in Pacific Siberia are deposits of manganese carbonate, which are presently of no value because the compound cannot be refined economically with current technology. The BAM zone, furthermore, is endowed with nonmetallic salts, building materials and abrasives.

Extensive stands of tayga will be thrown open to exploitation by the BAM. Estimates of the potential volume of timber located within 100 million acres of forest flanking the railway vary between 1.4 billion cubic meters of mature timber and a total of 15 billion cubic meters.[34] The best stands are found along the Kirenga River, the Selemdzha River, and in the Amgun' basin.

The Impact on the Domestic Economy

Obviously, the BAM will have no small impact on the local economy. It will serve as an artery over which labor and materials may be channeled to exploit the rich Pacific-Siberian resource base.

First priority for the region lies with the creation of what Soviet planners call "territorial-production complexes," or TPCs, integrated geographical units in which the various industries jointly would be responsible for local investment, housing, services, and community facilities, instead of each industry owing its exclusive allegiance to its own ministry in Moscow. According to N. N. Kolosovskiy, the originator of the concept, a production complex is an economic (interrelated) combination of establishments in a particular industrial center or in an entire region that achieves a certain economic effect as a result of an appropriate (planned) selection of establishments based on the region's physical and economic conditions and its economic-geographic and transport situation.[196]

The concept is fundamental to long-range regional development in the USSR. Concomitant with the realization of an adequate transportation network, highest priority in the creation of such complexes is given to the power base. Understanding this priority lends meaning to the otherwise inane statement of Lenin that Soviet power plus electrification equals communism. Next in line is the materialization of energy-intensive industrial complexes based on local raw materials. Finally, these pioneer enterprises stimulate the formation of large-scale complexes with common raw-material and power resources.[224]

As regards the power base of Pacific Siberia, since the 1950s major emphasis has been placed on capturing the hydroelectric capacity of the rivers. Huge blocks of power, much of which has been wasted because of insufficient local demand, have been created at such places as Irkutsk, Bratsk and Krasnoyarsk. Others, such as Ust'-Ilimsk and Zeya have begun generating electricity, and the Sayan-Shushenskoye station at Sayanogorsk is under construction. In addition, site preparation work is under way at the Boguchany station on the Angara River and at the Talakan station on the Bureya River.[151a] Finally, there are long-range blueprints for the construction of the Mok hydro station on the Vitim River, south of Ust'-Muya. The name is a contraction of *Mnogoobeshchayushchaya Kosa*, "Promising Spit (of Land)". All of these sites are or will be at least medium capacity and will be supplemented with power from large coal-fired central electric plants, like the ones planned at Neryungri in southern Yakutia and in operation at Luchegorsk near Bikin in northern Maritime Kray.[106] Altogether, some 4,000 miles of high-voltage transmission lines will be strung across the tributary area of the railroad.

In the western sector of the BAM service area, pioneer energy-intensive enterprises have been or are being established at Bratsk (pop. 195,000) and Ust'-Ilimsk (pop. 30,000). The Bratsk aluminum refinery, for example, is the Soviet Union's largest. Additionally, huge wood-pulp and associated wood-processing establishments are in operation at Bratsk and under construction at Ust'-Ilimsk. Located east of Bratsk at Zheleznogorsk-Ilimskiy is the Korshunovo iron mine and concentration plant with a rated annual capacity of 17 million tons of 32 percent crude magnetite ore. Thanks to the availability of cheap hydro power from Bratsk, the low-grade iron ore of the Korshunovo deposit may be beneficiated into 62 percent concentrate.[172] Additional mines and concentration plants are planned for the area.[224] The output from the Zheleznogorsk vicinity is now shipped to the ore-deficient Kuznetsk Basin for smelting. With the ultimate construction of the on-again, off-again iron and steel plant at Tayshet (pop. 35,000), the anticipated greater ore production from Korshunovo and neighboring deposits will go there for processing. Finally, though a copper concentration plant will be built near the source of the ore at Udokan, a copper smelter may be constructed in the vicinity of Tayshet, Bratsk or Ust'-Ilimsk.[225] There is also the possibility it will be built outside the service area in Lesosibirsk or Minusinsk.[94]

Such pioneer operations have laid the foundation for production complexes in the western part of the BAM zone. Projected regional development programs illustrate similar intentions for the rest of the service area.

Kibal'chich includes the upper Lena and Kirenga river regions in an Upper Lena complex (Fig. 3). Towns in the area include Ust'-Kut (pop. 38,000), embracing the Upper Lena port of Osetrovo; Zvezdnyy (pop. 5,000); Magistral'nyy; Kazachin-skoye; Ul'kan (pop. 2,000) and Kunerma. The future economic base of this part of the BAM will depend on the rich stands of stone pine in the Kirenga River valley and, prospectively, on further discoveries of oil and natural gas along the upper Lena near Ust'-Kut. Power requirements for the timber and potential petrochemical industries will be satisfied initially by Bratsk and Ust'-Ilimsk and, later, by dams on the Lena and Kirenga.[94]

The North Baykal complex comprises the northern part of Buryat ASSR and will include such urban settlements as Severobaykal'sk (pop. 2,000), Nizhneangarsk (3,500), Ust'-Muya and Molodezhnyy. The economy of the region will be based on the mining of asbestos and nonferrous and precious metals. Except for the Muya depression, the region will be electrified eventually via high-voltage lines from Bratsk, Ust'-Ilimsk, and, later, closer hydro-power sources. The Muya valley no doubt will depend on local compressors and small power plants until the completion of the Mok station, with a possible capacity of 1,500 to 2,000 megawatts, some distance to the south.

In the extreme northeast section of Irkutsk Oblast, on what is named the Patom upland, will be the Bodaybo complex. The principal towns of the region are Bodaybo (pop. 18,000 in 1959) and Mama. Bodaybo is in the center of the Lena goldfields and was the focus of numerous pre-revolutionary railroad proposals, some of which complemented the ideas that led to the BAM.[3] Mama is famed for the muscovite-mica mining in its vicinity. These elements will continue to figure prominently in the economic base of the region. Nonferrous metallurgy may play a role also. The Mamakan hydro station, the only notable power plant in the area, presently generates a mere 86 megawatts, but may be expanded to 450 megawatts in the future.[51]

The North Chita complex will specialize in the mining beneficiation of Udokan copper. The most important towns will be Chara (planned population of 60,000) and Udokan (Naminga; planned population of 20,000). Because of its extreme isolation, this complex will be powered by local generators until it can be assimilated into the Central Siberian electric power grid.

The great diversity of raw materials in southern Yakutia provides an ample base for a stable economic community. Highlighting the economy of the South Yakutian complex will be the mining and concentration of coal and iron ore, but the production of nonferrous metals, phlogopite mica, apatite, refractory clays, and precious ores will remain important, too.

The demand for such consumer-oriented by-products of ferrous metallurgy as coke chemicals, mineral fertilizers and metal fabrication militates against the placement of an integrated iron and steel plant in the South Yakutian complex, much to the chagrin of Yakutian Government and party leaders.[41] The latter favor locating the plant at Neryungri, but officials in Moscow prefer a more developed site, like Komsomol'sk or Svobodnyy, on the Trans-Siberian. In either case, the plant, with an eventual annual output of 9 million tons of pig iron, 10 million tons of steel, and 9 million tons of rolled metal, is a distant project.

Electric power production in the South Yakutian complex will be derived from coal-fired power plants. A small 20-megawatt thermal electric station at Chul'man has been supplying electricity to the Aldan gold and mica district. In the future, a planned 600-megawatt station will be based on the expanded coal mining activities at Neryungri (pop. 11,000; future population 50,000–100,000) and will supply other towns in the area, for example, Berkakit (pop. 1,200) and Aldan (pop. 20,000).

The western half of Amur Oblast will contain the West Amur production complex. The principal towns of the complex will be Tynda (pop. 30,000; future population 70,000), Mogot (future population 2,000), Zeya (pop. 18,000) and the town of Zeysk. The economic base of the region will be dominated by sawmilling at Tynda and Zeya, and gold mining on the Upper Zeya plain. Machine building and metal fabrication also are expected to evolve at Tynda and Zeya. Finally, with reclamation, agriculture will be expanded in the south on the Zeya-Bureya plain. The region's chief power source will be the Zeya hydroelectric station with an ultimate capacity of about 1,300 megawatts.

The Selemdzha-Urgal complex will comprise eastern Amur Oblast and western Khabarovsk Kıay. The towns of this region will be Fevral'sk, Svobodnyy (pop. 70,000), Chegdomyn (17,000) and Urgal (which, together with Chegdomyn, is expected to exceed 100,000 by the year 2000). The economy is now based on the mining of coking coal at Sredniy Urgal, a few miles northwest of Chegdomyn. In the future, logging and wood processing, the latter including sawmilling and plywood manufacturing, will become important along with the extraction of nonferrous and precious metals (chiefly gold). Energy for the complex will be derived from the planned Talakan hydroelectric station on the Bureya River, with an ultimate capacity of 2,000 megawatts.

Eastern Khabarovsk Kray will be dominated by the Lower-Amur complex, whose center will be at Komsomol'sk (pop. 246,000). Other towns in the complex are Sovetskaya Gavan' (pop. 31,000), Vanino (pop. 16,000), and Amursk (pop. 25,000). The region's economy will be based on local and imported raw materials. In the Amgun' valley, three mechanized wood-processing centers will be established. These centers will produce not only building materials but viscose fiber and fabric as well. There will be a continued emphasis on tin mining at Gornyy and Solnechnyy and a possible expansion of steel output at Komsomol'sk. Additionally, the processing of woodpulp will persist at Amursk. Transportation equipment and hoisting machinery also will be manufactured in the complex.

In the future, new and expanded manufacturing dependent on Tyumen and Sakhalin petroleum and Vilyuy natural gas is expected to develop. The processing of these hydrocarbons promises to yield fertilizer, urea, lavsan (a dacron-like fiber), formaldehyde, and other (petro) chemicals. A peat-based chemical industry, producing resin, paraffin, and anthracene, has also been suggested.[34]

Finally, Soviet authorities believe an alumina plant based on imported bauxite, with an annual capacity of 1.1 million tons, is feasible somewhere in the Far East. The alumina would be carried via the BAM and the Trans-Siberian to Bratsk and Krasnoyarsk for conversion into aluminum. In time, an aluminum refinery, whose output would be shipped abroad, may be built in Khabarovsk Kray.[54] The notion of an aluminum refinery in the Lower Amur complex, however, may be altogether too optimistic because the region is energy-deficient, restricting the potential spread of energy-intensive industries like aluminum refining. In fact, without promising hydro-power sites on either the Amur or its tributaries in this area, the complex must rely on imports of expensive coal-fired electricity from large steam-electric plants, like the Luchegorsk station near Bikin or draw from small-to-medium size thermal plants within its own boundaries.

The Impact on Foreign Trade

The BAM should have at least as much influence on the development of Pacific Siberia in the last quarter of the 20th century as the Trans-Siberian had on Western Siberia during the first quarter. This includes the realm of foreign trade.

A University of Hawaii historian, John J. Stephan, wrote "If current trends persist, the Soviet Union could replace the United States as the leading presence in the Pacific Basin."[215] Indeed, if Soviet authorities realize their goals in Pacific Siberia, they may obtain hegemony in the Pacific Ocean within the next 25 years. Even now, the Soviet Pacific Fleet exceeds the United States Seventh Fleet in tonnage, and reflects as much mobility. These accomplishments have occurred within the last decade simultaneously with the construction, enlargement and modernization of the ports of Vostochnyy (near Nakhodka), Sovetskaya Gavan', and Vladivostok. At the same time, Soviet diplomats have tried to obtain, with some success, visitation privileges at harbors in the Indian and Pacific oceans.

Publicity over the increasing visibility of the Soviet Navy has overshadowed the USSR's inroads into Pacific commerce. Formerly dependent only on China in this part of the world, Soviet economic relations have been expanded to include trade ties with Japan, the United States and other members of the Pacific community.

For many years Soviet economists have complained that it is neither logical nor economical to transport by rail the low-value bulk resources of Pacific Siberia to European Russia when there are favorable opportunities for shipping the same goods by sea to Pacific-rim countries. In fact, "the impact of transport costs on goods produced in Pacific Siberia and freighted to European Russia is to add 100 percent to 200 percent to the extraction costs of timber, 30 percent to 40 percent to coal and cement, and up to 5 percent to the production costs of machine tools."[51] This involves a doubling of the price of the goods if they are shipped more than 2,000 miles. The average length of haul of Pacific-Siberian products is more than 3,000 miles, or over three times the national average.[96]

Given these relative disadvantages for domestic trade, except for high-value, low-bulk metals like gold and tin, Pacific Siberia is disposed auspiciously for long-range expansion of maritime commerce. Japan is two days' sail away. By great circle from Vladivostok to Vancouver, the distance is 4,800 miles, and to Sydney from the same port it is 5,800 miles, nearly equal to the Moscow-to-Vladivostok rail run.[51] These comparatively long distances are rendered advantageous by the cheapness of sea transport. To top it off, the aforementioned complementarity exists and awaits resolution.

In this respect, Japan is the leading contender for dominance of Soviet-Pacific trade. Poorly endowed with industrial resources of their own, the Japanese are blessed with superior technology, machinery, consumer goods, and capital. Even though Pacific commerce represented less than 10 percent of total Soviet foreign trade in 1975, Japan accounted for nearly half of it.

With successfully negotiated agreements for the exportation of Amur timber (1968) and for the construction of the new port of Vostochnyy, on the Gulf of Nakhodka (1970), Soviet and Japanese trade officials have engaged actively in discussions of joint resource-development programs in Pacific Siberia since the 1960s. An Australian expert on the USSR, Paul Dibb, surmised that prior to 1972, Soviet negotiators were handicapped in meaningfully coming to terms with the Japanese because the resources in concern (for example, Udokan and Neryungri) were so inaccessible.[51] Thus, the BAM has been recognized by Soviet authorities as not only an important conduit for domestic development, but also as a principal artery upon which their complementary relationships with Pacific-rim countries ultimately may be realized.

Dibb illustrated the huge regional imports of foodstuffs into Pacific Siberia from other parts of the Soviet Union. Some of the food deficit is satisfied by foreign imports from Mongolia, North Korea, and Manchuria; but imports from Australia, New Zealand, Canada, and the United States have only just begun. What with the unreliable harvests in the eastern regions of the USSR, the Pacific-Siberian food deficit will have to be filled either from increasingly scarce interregional surpluses or from overseas.[51]

Until the BAM is completed, all imports into Pacific Siberia from foreign sources will be exchanged for roundwood and some processed wood products, fish, and some minerals. The imports in concern doubtlessly should be food, some technology, and capital from the western United States; technology, consumer goods, and capital from Japan; grain from western Canada; wool, grain, and meat from Australia and New Zealand; natural rubber, tin, and rice from Southeast Asia (Malaysia, Thailand, Cambodia, Vietnam, and Indonesia); and coffee from Latin America.[51]

Such crude exchanges should persist until 1983. Thereafter, during the so-called "first stage" of BAM operation, 70 to 75 percent of the freight movements in ton-kilometers will be composed of Western Siberian crude oil, bound for Far Eastern refineries and export. The second most important export commodity on the BAM during the early stage will be timber (10 to 18 percent), comprising primarily coniferous roundwood from the Kirenga, Selemdzha and Amgun' basins. Thirdly, coking coal from Neryungri will play a major role in commerce between the USSR and Japan. Lastly, paper, pulp, wood chemicals and fiberboard processed from larch trees found in permafrost areas of northern Buryatia, northern Chita Oblast, and northwest Amur Oblast will be exported. Later on, the second stage of BAM freight operations may be characterized by exports of pig iron, fertilizers, chlor-organic products, machinery, and paper.[18]

It should be emphasized that these are planned exports. In fact, in light of fuel shortages in the European USSR, it is doubtful that the Soviet Union will be able to afford petroleum exports of the magnitude envisioned for the BAM. It is even more doubtful because of the unusually high per-capita fuel requirements of a country as far north as the USSR. Unable to rely on solar energy because of thermal deficiencies (except in Central Asia), possessing only isolated sources of geothermal power, lacking adequate locations for generating tidal power, etc., Soviet authorities surely must realize that fossil fuels eventually are far more important to them than they are to persons living in more temperate locations.[51a]

Aside from bilateral and, perhaps, multilateral trade relations with Pacific-rim countries, Soviet officials have allowed expanded utilization of the Trans-Siberian and, when it becomes operable, the BAM as transit routes for goods moving between Europe and Japan. In 1975 an estimated 3.5 million tons of freight were shipped by rail in 20-ton and 30-ton containers from Japan to Western Europe. This was a threefold increase over 1974. As an indication of their enthusiasm for containerization, the Russians are now manufacturing flat cars designed for containers at a new railroad car plant at Abakan and they have completed the construction of a plant that will assemble 20-ton containers at Il'yichevsk on the Black Sea. Until now, they have had to buy or lease heavy-duty containers from abroad. Moreover, Nakhodka and its new outer port of Vostochnyy will specialize in the transshipment of containers, and Sovetskaya Gavan' will be equipped to do the same before the BAM is finished.[45]

Regarding joint-development agreements in Pacific Siberia, thus far the Japanese have been the only real takers. Since the 1970 decision to build Vostochnyy, Soviet and Japanese negotiators have discussed at least six different Siberian projects: joint development of the petroleum and natural gas on the continental shelf off Sakhalin Island; the development of South Yakutian coking coal; joint development of Pacific-Siberian timber resources; the construction of a big pulp mill in Eastern Siberia; development of Vilyuy natural gas; development of Tyumen' petroleum and the associated construction of a $3 billion, 4,100-mile pipeline from Tyumen' to Nakhodka.

In 1972, Soviet and Japanese representatives signed a memorandum on geological prospecting for offshore natural gas and oil in the vicinity of Sakhalin Island. In accordance with the document, the two countries would share the responsibilities for equipping, drilling, extracting, and ultimately transporting the fuels to Japan. Potential oil deposits on the Sakhalin shelf were estimated at 3 to 5 billion tons. Deliberations continued until January 28, 1975, when a general agreement was attained.

On April 22, 1974, officials from the two countries devised a preliminary agreement on long-term credit for developing the South Yakutian coal fields, commercial prospecting for natural gas in the Vilyuy Basin, and the development of Siberian timber resources. Under the terms of the protocol, Japan would extend $1.1 billion credit to the USSR for the purchase of Japanese motor-transport equipment, hoisting and excavating machinery, devices for the construction of bridges and drilling rigs, and included $110 million worth of consumer goods. In exchange, a share of the resources extracted by this equipment would go to Japan. This credit agreement was the largest in the history of Soviet foreign trade.

Eight days later, a general agreement on South Yakutian coking coal was reached. As part of the overall extension of credit, $450 million worth of capital would be invested in Neryungri and environs. On the Soviet side, $4 billion worth of coking coal, or 100 million tons at 5 million tons per year for 20 years, would be shipped to Japan. The generous coal allotment would allow the Russians to pay off the loan quickly to obtain the equipment necessary for future development of the Siberian economy. Initially, the funds would go into the construction of the Neryungri coal-agglomerating plant with a planned capacity of 9 million tons.[188] Finally, on June 3, 1974, the agreement to develop the Yakutian coal fields was concluded.

The Japanese had been purchasing coking coal from the Kuznetsk Basin, 1,500 miles west of Neryungri, at the rate of 3 million tons per year. Ostensibly, they will continue to receive Kuzbas coal until 1983, when, via the "Little BAM" and the BAM, they will obtain Neryungri coal.[94]

Upon termination of the 1968 Amur timber agreement in 1973, Soviet-Japanese deliberations on this subject began anew. It was not long before a new five-year contract was drawn up. Under the agreement, which was signed on July 30, 1974, the remainder of the protocol funds ($550 million) would be utilized to purchase Japanese-made logging and sawmilling equipment in exchange for 17.5 million cubic meters of roundwood and 900,000 cubic meters of sawnwood.[94]

As regards the final three objectives of commercial negotiations between Japanese and Soviet representatives, little has been decided conclusively. The Vilyuy gas and Tyumen' oil pipeline ventures in part involved the United States, since the Japanese insisted that they alone could not provide all the required credit, including $400 million initially requested for preliminary natural gas exploration in Yakutia and $3 billion for the oil pipeline from Tyumen'.

The latter, bigger project appears to have been abandoned. In view of the decision to construct the BAM as an obvious alternative to any pipelines through Pacific Siberia, Soviet planners, for the time being, have determined not to press this issue.

The Vilyuy gas proposal remains alive. In 1976, the Russians scaled down their cost estimate for gas exploration to $100 million and credits were granted by the United States and Japan. Under the terms of the Yakutian proposal, if adequate reserves can be identified, some of the gas recovered from the Vilyuy Basin would be transmitted by a pipeline from Yakutsk to a liquefaction plant on the coast, and thence by tanker to Japan, where half the fuel would be retained. The other half of the output would be shipped to the West Coast of the United States. Under the 1976 accord, preliminary exploration will be paid for by $50 million of Soviet investment and $25 million from Japanese banks, with a matching sum from commercial banks in the United States. The $100 million is only a beginning investment. The project would cost billions before the gas begins to flow.

In the meantime, the Japanese have expanded their petroleum imports from China, whose principal oil fields are situated on or near the coast, far more favorably than the Soviet Union's oil fields in remote, interior Western Siberia. China, with a weaker industrial base and, for the time being, a smaller requirement for petroleum products, may acquire a substantial share of the Pacific market before the BAM opens up a potential transport route for West Siberian crude oil to tanker terminals on the Pacific coast in the mid-1980s.

However, as was stated earlier, for many reasons Soviet hopes to export large amounts of petroleum and natural gas to the Pacific basin may not materialize. The export outlook is more promising in connection with surpluses of metallic and nonmetallic minerals in Pacific Siberia. Provided they can influence expanded cartelization of these minerals among the third-world nations, Soviet planners may be able to influence the world price of a number of strategic raw materials by the year 2000. The "energy crisis" of the 1970s, therefore, is merely an omen of what industrialized Western nations will have to face in terms of minerals within the next 25 years. In fact, the BAM is less interesting as a feat of engineering than it is as a manifestation of Soviet aims in the realm of foreign commerce.

The Labor Problem

The building of a new economy east of the Yenisey River is not without its difficulties, perhaps the gravest of which is a reliable source of labor. Traditionally thought of as "over-employed" in many sectors, the Soviet Union as a whole will face a considerable labor shortage in the 1980s "should current plans for growth be continued," for it is then that the reduced number of children born in the 1960s will be reaching the age of employment.[62] In fact, the Soviet demographer Viktor Perevedentsev estimates that the annual increase of able-bodied labor in the USSR between 1985 and 2000 will be one-seventh the rate for 1970 to 1985. "And nothing can be done about it, for those who will be 20 in 1995 have already been born."[138]

In a recent article, Leo Gruliow stated that when BAM construction began, aside from urban concentrations at Ust'-Kut, Tynda and Komsomol'sk, consisting of an estimated 265,000 persons, only 4,000 people resided along the BAM route.[71] By mid-1975, this population had increased by 30,000.[149] In fact, if Soviet planners' estimates are correct, at least 1 million persons must gravitate to the BAM service area within the next decade.[108]

Yet, if traditional trends are indicative of the future, such in-migration will be more than counterbalanced by out-migration. For instance, between 1959 and 1970, net in-migration into Pacific Siberia was only 8,000 out of a total growth of more than 1.9 million.[179] Moreover, because of the expected labor deficit in western regions of the USSR, except for some skilled personnel, young university graduates, and construction specialists, the future employment needs of Pacific Siberia must be met from within the region itself. That is, the requirements must be satisfied by increased labor productivity (mechanization, automation, and best available technology), rational labor distribution, and a high rate of natural increase.

Concerning the latter element, Vorob'yev has shown that at least with respect to Eastern Siberia, aside from no significant in-migration, the natural increase of the population will be adverse as well.[253] Although, typically, the region produces a rate of natural increase that is higher than the average for the Russian Republic, it does reflect similar overall growth trends. Thus, as will be true for the country as a whole, the annual increase of employable persons in Eastern Siberia between 1980 and the year 2000 will be declining relative to the 1970s.

Because of the problem of out-migration, including at times over 75 percent of the workers in the West Siberian oil fields,[133] a situation no less grim in parts of Pacific Siberia, Soviet authorities have raised the incentives for work in the BAM service area. If an individual volunteers for at least three years, he can earn a salary that is up to 2.5 times the national average (350 rubles per month compared with 146 rubles per month). If he opts for less than three years, he obtains only half that, or 1.25 the average. BAM workers are granted privileges analogous to those provided residents of the Far North. They may obtain low interest loans of up to 500 rubles and take up to three years to pay off the debts. Additionally, higher bonuses for extraordinary work on the project are appealing motives.[235] Perhaps as a result of these incentives, during the first year of work on the BAM, returnees to western regions of the Soviet Union amounted to only 15 percent of a total work force of around 20,000.[143]

Another reason why labor turnover in the BAM zone has been low thus far may be an idealistic spirit that pervades the project, attractive to young, educated, and adventurous men and women. Roughly 80 percent of the workers in 1975 were under 30. A similar percentage had high school educations. A sense of community among these workers must be high, for they are given almost daily attention by the news media and, though logistics on the project can be improved, an effort is being made to keep them comfortable.

Unfortunately, even the best plans can go awry. Mail and telegraph service in the tributary area of the BAM is reportedly terrible. Helicopters frequently are grounded. Roads, if they exist, are poor. New machinery sent from European Russia, notably from Voronezh and Chelyabinsk, becomes defective as soon as it is off the railroad platforms. Compounding this problem, spare parts, as everywhere in the USSR, are almost impossible to obtain. Even such basic necessities as toothpaste, shoes, jackets, and headwear cannot be purchased in the stores of supposedly well-supplied Tynda. Because of the burgeoning stock of new BAM recruits, Tynda cafeterias cannot seat more than a third of their customers at a time. The situation is far worse in the backwaters because they rely on places like Tynda and Ust'-Kut for their logistical support.[152]

Such disorganization may have to be tolerated in the early stages of BAM construction, but unless the situation is improved soon, the adventure of working in the wilds of Pacific Siberia will wear off, and high rates of out-migration may be experienced once again. For this reason, articles of the current five-year plan (1976–80) adjure stricter attention to amenities and infrastructures, often sorely lacking, in Pacific Siberia.[168a]

Even these efforts will be insufficient, if labor productivity is not increased. Thus, the mainline is to be so automated that a maximum of 35,000 railroad operators and maintenance crews is envisioned for the BAM once it goes into full operation.[17] If, after this, more workers are required, there is the possibility that labor from Eastern Europe will be imported.[99] This has occurred already at Ust'-Ilimsk, where workers from member nations of the Council for Mutual Economic Assistance (Comecon) are employed.[168a]

Some of the industrial labor force may be attracted from indigenous populations. These include several thousand Evenki in isolated parts of the service area between Ust'-Kut and Komsomol'sk; at least as many Yakuts in the Chara and Chul'man vicinities; perhaps 11,000 Nanay and Nivkhi on the lower Amur between Khabarovsk and Nikolayevsk; and a few thousand Orochi, Negidals, Ul'chi, and Udegey in the Amgun' and Amur river valleys. Most of these people are associated with hunting and fishing collectives. Some are engaged in the raising of livestock and crops. And at least one-quarter of the autochthonous peoples along the Amur are employed in Soviet industry.[190a]

There is no doubt that the BAM will have an impact on the lives of these people. An Izvestiya reporter in early 1976 dealt sensitively with the problem.[190a] A few Soviet geographers have expressed their concern.[206] Their analyses have concluded that the advent of the BAM will improve the living standards of the isolated minorities in the service area of the railroad, but the authors hesitated to speculate on the potential assimilative aspects. A few of the ethnic groups number less than a thousand.

Natural Hazards

The BAM will be confronted with potential hardship over almost every mile of its length. There is imminent danger from earthquakes, tremors, and ground shaking, during which landslides, avalanches, earthflows, talus cones, and soil creep may be created. These, in turn, disrupt the thermal regime of the permafrost and ground ice (*naledi*), spawning complex chain reactions of solifluction, frost heave and thermokarst.

The capacity of permafrost to block the infiltration of meltwater yields the extensive bogs called *mari* during Pacific-Siberian summers. In the same season, the rivers exceed flood stage. These temporary to semi-permanent reservoirs further disrupt the permafrost.

In the spring and autumn, when the ice breaks up on Siberian rivers, ice dams are formed in downstream locations. In winter, shallow reaches in streams and rivers freeze solidly. Moving water, therefore, is forced around or over such blockades in shallow layers. Some types of river icings are created in this way.

Finally, not all natural hazards need be inorganic. Disease-carrying insects and other communicable agents are prevalent throughout the BAM service area, especially in the high sun period.

In all, 745 miles of the BAM route has been designated as endowed with conditions that are unsatisfactory for purposes of engineering. This is nearly the equivalent of the entire length of the Alaska pipeline.[162]

Earthquakes and faults

The western leg of the BAM will traverse the rugged Mongolian-Baykal seismic belt, including major fault zones and grabens in Lake Baykal itself, the Barguzin

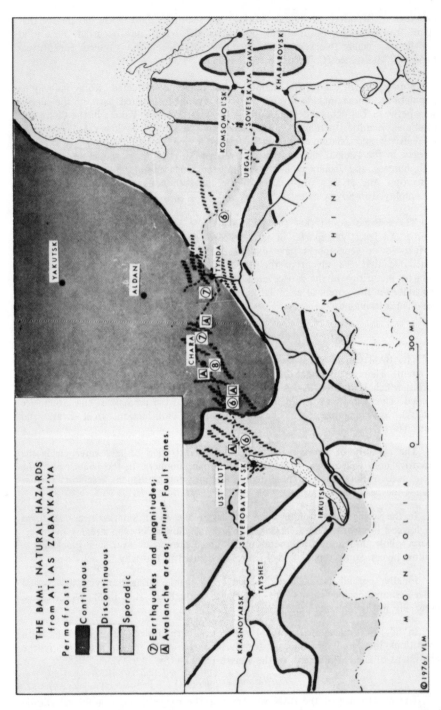

THE BAM: NATURAL HAZARDS
from ATLAS ZABAYKAL'YA

Permafrost:
■ Continuous
□ Discontinuous
▨ Sporadic

⑦ Earthquakes and magnitudes;
Ⓐ Avalanche areas; ⊪⊪⊪⊪ Fault zones.

© 1976/ VLM

Fig. 4.

300 MI

YAKUTSK
ALDAN
KOMSOMOL'SK
SOVETSKAYA GAVAN
KHABAROVSK
URGAL
TYNDA
CHARA
UST'-KUT
SEVEROBAYKAL'SK
IRKUTSK
TAYSHET
KRASNOYARSK

C H I N A

M O N G O L I A

lowland, the Upper Angara depression, and the Muya-Kuanda and Chara river basins. This is easily one of the most seismically active regions on the globe. Since seismographic record-keeping began in this century, at least 30 devastating surface earthquakes of 6 or more on the Richter scale have been witnessed on or near the projected trace of the BAM between Lake Baykal and the Olekma River.[210] (Fig. 4). In the same region, ground shaking, including all forms of seismic activity, is recorded up to 1,500 times annually. The most severe earthquakes, of magnitudes greater than 7 on the Richter scale, are likely to occur in the Muya-Kuanda and Chara basin vicinities. A surface quake of 7.9 seriously disrupted these areas in 1957. Vertical displacements of 30 to 50 feet have been measured in the Lake Baykal region and the potential displacement is even greater in the vicinity of Udokan.[263] Cracks and craters of up to 60 feet wide have been observed after the strongest upheavals.

Much less is known about the eastern leg of the BAM, from the Olekma River to Komsomol'sk. Yet, quakes of up to 5.8 have been recorded in the Tukuringra-Dzhagdy Ridge area. The Zeya Dam is situated tremulously near the epicenters of disruptions of this magnitude. Nevertheless, seismicity definitely decreases east of the Olekma, the earthquakes here being associated with Stanovoy-Dzhugdzhur vulcanism instead of the more dangerous Baykal rifting.[210]

Seismic activity in more temperate zones of the earth does not necessarily pose danger of any particular consequence to railway construction. However, in periglacial environments like the BAM zone, they are of importance not so much because of the isolated consequences in the immediate vicinity of the event itself, but because of subsequent responses that encompass broader territories. For example, an earthquake may occur in the Udokan region, and hundreds of landslides, avalanches, and landslips may be spawned over a wide radius away from the epicenter. The same thing happens in temperate zones, but high latitude locations are complicated by ancillary disruption of the permafrost, which leads to almost perpetual differential subsidence of the land within the area affected by the quake. Needless to say, transportation lines in such regions must be watched constantly for corrugation and buckling and are more expensive to maintain than are similar networks in hospitable environments.

Seismically triggered avalanches, and no doubt landslides as well, are more frequent along the western segment of the BAM than in any other part of Pacific Siberia. Between the North Muya and Udokan ridges, an average of 350 avalanches take place every year.[238a] Worse yet, avalanches and landslides breed other avalanches and landslides.[210] The steep slopes of the BAM's western sector are weakened and weathered intensely, making construction especially hazardous and difficult in youthful stream valleys.[32] Loose talus cones are often a nuisance.

Permafrost

Permafrost will be a factor in decision-making for over two-thirds of the BAM route (1,300 miles). In contrast, the Alaska pipeline will be elevated over similar areas for only 350 miles.[43] Because of the subfreezing temperatures in Pacific Siberia during most of the year, moisture within the soil and bedrock exists in a frozen rather than liquid state. Only the upper few feet thaw with the advent of summer. This so-called "active zone" varies from 3—6 feet in the nearly soilless mountains to 11—13 feet in the boggy *mar'* regions. These thawings on slopes may

95

give rise to substantial earthflows or their moderate form, solifluction. Soil creep may appear on gradual, vegetated slopes. On flat-lying surfaces, where there are sufficient moisture-bearing soils and sediments, "quick ground" (analogous to quicksand) is a factor.

Throughout the central third of the BAM route, permafrost is continuous with maximum depths reaching 1,000 feet in the Chara basin. However, average thicknesses beneath the railway will be less than 250 feet.[4]

Complex processes that begin with the freezing of the active zone and end with the discharge of ground water onto the surface in winter give rise to various forms of ground ice. The differences between the temperature of ground-ice water (32 to 34°F) and that of the air (−40°F) create steam fogs known as "ground-ice boils." As the frozen upper layers press downward, more ground water is conducted to the surface, spreading liberally in continually growing layers across the landscape. Ground ice may affect areas ranging in size from a hundred to a million square yards and up to 15 feet thick. In addition, the thicker the overlying mass of ice, the faster the water flows to the surface, reaching at times 300 gallons per second.[219]

Ground ice is particularly hazardous to engineering and winter supply convoys. During the winter of 1974, two cranes collapsed into a ground-ice patch just south of Belen'kaya on the "Little BAM." "The equipment could not be retrieved for a long time, and only the two metal booms sticking out of the ice indicated the site of the catastrophe."[2]

Owing its origin to the 9 percent volume change when water converts to ice and to the growth of ice crystals when additional water is drawn from the active zone or water table, frost heave is another factor critical to construction in the BAM area. Differential heaving may cause buckling of the track and destruction of buildings. It is also responsible for the periodic ejection of telephone poles, pilings, and fence posts. The process largely depends on ground that is susceptible to various drainage characteristics. For instance, well-drained edaphic deserts are less conducive to frost heave than are poorly drained *mar'* surfaces.[147]

Another response to the differential melting of permafrost is the thermokarst landscape, similar to true karst regions underlain by limestone. Many of the features characteristic of the latter are also associated with thermokarst areas, for example, mounds, caverns, disappearing streams, funnel-shaped pits, elongated troughs, and large flat-floored valleys with steep sides. "The fundamental difference is that karst is formed through chemical processes while thermokarst is formed by physical processes in permafrost."[147]

When the thermal regime of the permafrost has been disrupted, thermokarst is a common development. Familiar causes include earthquake damage, climatic change, changes in vegetation, shifts in stream channels, fire and disruptive human activities. Thermokarst development in the BAM zone is particularly prevalent on the Aldan upland.

Just as there is a definite correlation between earthquakes and permafrost problems, there seems to be a positive correlation between disruption of the permafrost and ground shaking. It, therefore, behooves BAM engineers and construction workers to disrupt overlying surfaces as little as possible.

Rivers and streams

The mainline will span more than 3,700 swamps, gorges, streams and rivers, 142 of which are broader than 300 feet. Of the rivers remaining to be bridged, the Upper Angara, the Vitim, the Olekma, the Selemdzha, and the Zeya are at least a quarter-mile wide. Following the river valleys for most of its trace, the BAM will be subjected to seasonal stream flow fluctuations. During the long winter (September through April), the eastern Siberian rivers are frozen solidly, but with the coming of spring, they become raging torrents carrying away snow and ice accumulated in the low sun period. The most destructive activity of the rivers occurs during the flood season in June and July when their levels rise by 25 to 35 feet, with crests of up to 40 feet. Their velocities exceed 12 feet per second.[32] Therefore, not only do the rivers flood the adjacent plains and scour their beds and banks, but they also unload deep layers of alluvium, some of which become placer deposits. In such areas, the railroad will have to be laid upon high, coarse ballast to avoid the flood waters. Serving as dams, the roadbeds will create temporary reservoirs, which will accelerate thawing of the permafrost and serve as breeding grounds for mosquitoes. To permit drainage of the surface water, there will have to be culverts through the ballast.

Disease and pest problems

Under the supervision of the Gamaleya Institute of Epidemiology and Microbiology, some 28 research institutes are studying the disease-carrying potential of various insects endemic to the tributary area of the railroad. Researchers are particularly concerned with a species of encephalitis-bearing tick. Numerous individual instances of the disease, including at least one epidemic, occurred in the Upper Angara depression prior to the 1967.[115] Although reportedly contained by innoculation, the disease still remains to be eradicated.

In addition to the tick problem, a species of gnat attains worrisome dissemination in summer. Fierce and offensive, the insects have sent visitors into near-suffocating panic by clogging their nostrils, throats and eyes. These blood-sucking animals are also known for their painful bites. Chemical sprays supposedly eliminated them in 1975, but as late as September of that year a team of doctors, chemists, microbiologists and entomologists was working on an effective means of controlling the pest. Ironically, the use of insecticides against mosquitoes apparently is banned in the BAM zone for ecological reasons.[44]

In addition to tick-borne encephalitis and the nuisances brought on by other blood-sucking insects in the BAM service area, there are problems with rabbit fever; tick-borne rickettsiosis; toxoplasmosis; trichinosis; a variety of mite fever; endemic goiter; snow conjunctivitis; and periodic invasions of midges, horseflies, and lice. Medical geographers are involved in delimiting the spatial confines of these problems in the BAM zone.[6]

Forest fires

Fires, of course, may be initiated by both natural and artificial means. In the relatively arid, periglacial environment of the BAM area, human beings most often are the instigators. As their numbers climb in the next decade, fire potential will rise as well.

Whatever the cause of the fire, it may prove to be disastrous in a periglacial environment because of its effect on subterranean ice and permafrost. The trees, mosses, and lichens that serve as insulators for the subsoil may take decades to return after the occurrence of a single fire.

Potential Environmental Disruption

Confronted with prospects of large-scale heavy industrial enterprises developing in Pacific Siberia as a result of the construction of the BAM, Soviet planners have concerned themselves with air and water pollution. In respect to the problem of atmospheric contamination, the physical geography could not be less suitable. The major potential industrial centers—Molodezhnyy, Chara-Udokan, Tynda, Neryungri-Berkakit-Chul'man, and Urgal-Chegdomyn—are situated in poorly ventilated basins into which air drainage occurs nightly. Moreover, during the 7-month winters, long nights averaging 16 to 21 hours, persistent high atmospheric pressure in excess of 30 inches, and a thin, but durable snow cover lasting for 5 months or more, combine to create almost continuous surface and above-surface temperature inversions, which, in the presence of low wind speeds, render atmospheric diffusion nearly impossible.[112] The length of winter and the long nights also will require greater expenditures of energy, producing greater air pollution per capita than in more hospitable climates. Finally, owing to the short growing season and, as a result, the relative lack of photosynthesis, the comparative availability of oxygen per unit area is less, and the atmosphere's capacity for self-cleansing is low.[100]

Regarding water pollution, the situation may be more auspicious. Research in the United States indicates that as a river gets colder, oxygen becomes increasingly soluble in water. For example, at $4°C$ ($40°F$), fully saturated water contains 13 ppm oxygen, while at $27°C$ ($80°F$), it contains 8 ppm.[36] Thus, an oxygen-rich stream can oxidize greater quantities of Biochemical Oxygen Demand (BOD). Even if dissolved oxygen levels momentarily drop, a river's capacity for recovery is much greater in wintertime. This happens because the further away water is from saturation, the faster the oxygen diffuses into the river to redress the imbalance. Therefore, if dissolved oxygen is 4 ppm and saturation is 16 ppm, oxygen will diffuse three times more rapidly into the stream than if the saturation level is 8 ppm, as it is in summer.

Soviet findings reveal that in harsh climates water pollution may remain in rivers everywhere from 8 to 10 times farther from its source than it will in mild-temperature regions. This is because oxygen-consuming microorganisms that degrade pollutants are not as active in water at colder temperatures. The result is that wastes are oxidized more slowly in winter, and, even though a river may not smell or change color (owing to its high oxygen content), the effluents will persist for longer time periods and, therefore, over longer distances than they would in summer. Hence, Soviet scientists justifiably are concerned that industrial wastes and domestic sewage be treated properly before being discharged into the water bodies of Pacific Siberia.

Impact of earthwork

Deposits of limestone, perlite, vermiculite, and building stone may be found at numerous points along the route. More than 30 enterprises of the construction industry, depending on hundreds of quarries, are under construction in the BAM zone and on the Trans-Siberian. At their disposal are multibucket excavators, rock crushers, graders, and bulldozers, capable of moving and processing the millions of tons of earth and rock required to build the BAM and its incipient economy. As is the case in any project of this size and scope, there is a danger of engineers becoming infatuated with their attack on the landscape. Consequently, excavation of upland areas may alter the slope of the terrain, produce thaw areas in the permafrost, and accelerate local erosion. The turbidity created by such erosion will be enhanced by quarrying for sand and gravel, which are most readily obtainable in stream channels.

Though admittedly an anomaly, dune development is a common occurence in the depressions of the Baykal Rift, owing to deflation and transport of sand and dust particles from regions where permafrost has been disrupted. Clearing landscapes in the Barguzin lowland resulted in the formation of semi-desert conditions on the eastern shore of Lake Baykal in the 1960s.[69] Mismanagement of quarrying, dredging, mining, and earth-moving operations in the BAM service area could inadvertently increase the consequences of wind and water erosion.

Mismanagement of timber resources

When the latest construction on the BAM began early in 1974, the headlines of various newspapers and periodicals in the USSR declared: "The Tayga Is Retreating!"; "Submit, Move Along, Tayga!", etc. This prompted Soviet scientists to remind the BAM workers and the media of the manifold purposes and relative exhaustibility of the forests of the region.[64]

For one thing, timber reserves along the route are not distributed evenly, with more than half of them located in the mountainous western section. Here, of course, they protect slopes against severe erosion and streams against being clogged with sediment. The trees of these areas, chiefly larch, are not particularly well suited for processing and they mature slowly. One scientist, upon felling a tree with a circumference of 5 feet, discovered that it was 200 years old.[197] Naturally, clearcutting a forest of this age and character on the slopes of the Udokan or South Muya ranges would be of questionable merit.

Until now, the attention of the forest industry has been directed at the stone-pine stands of the Kirenga River basin. Although implored by the Academy of Sciences to cut only 50 percent of the mature trees on their timber tracts, officials of the Wood and Wood-Processing Ministry have decided to leave only 7 percent. This amounts to clearcutting and paves the way for "thaw halos" in the permafrost, liquefaction, earthflows, and frost heave. Furthermore, the impact on wildlife will be considerable because of habitat disruption.

A model of environmental disruption in the BAM service area

In a periglacial environment like the BAM service area, engineering is infinitely more difficult than it is in more hospitable realms. Figure 5 has been designed to add some perspective to the seemingly discrete factors just covered. Note that in a temperate climate the damage to the environment largely ceases with the "immediate effects," there being no permafrost. But, in periglacial regions, owing to the presence of permafrost and/or ground ice (naledi), complex chain reactions are initiated by the "disruptive forces" and their immediate effects, so that in time a

A MODEL OF PERPETUAL DISRUPTION IN A PERIGLACIAL ENVIRONMENT

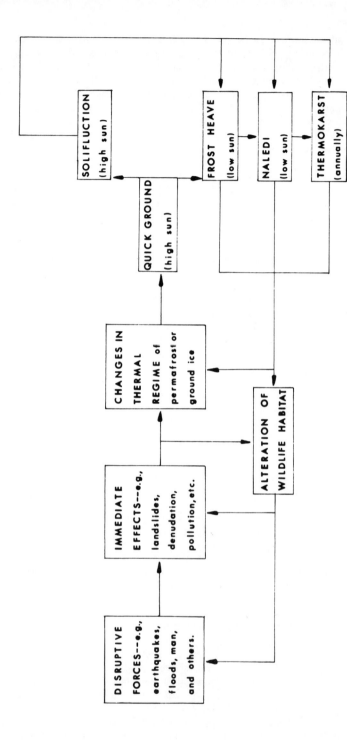

Fig. 5.

region endowed with continuous permafrost may be altered considerably. Moreover, this alteration process, once set in motion, can be perpetual. It is not surprising, then, that major structural damage can be anticipated in the BAM service area, as disruption of the permafrost is no doubt inevitable.

Facing the Problems: Soviet Preplanning

"The economic assimilation of the BAM zone should be accomplished with concern for the unique natural properties of the region. When laying rails, building highways, erecting transmission lines, and felling timber, the permafrost regime should not be disrupted, for this may lead to discontinuous thawing of the soil, catastrophic floods, gullying, and desiccation of the skeletal soils on steep slopes."[34]

Such statements rarely would have been found in Soviet planning journals 25 years ago. At that time, Stalinist bureaucracies were concerned with "transforming" nature, not maintaining it. Since 1960, a new environmental ethic has emerged. Hardly a day goes by without the ideas of conservationists being represented in the Soviet press. However, until now, with the exception of the Lake Baykal controversy, environmentalists in the USSR have not had much influence on truly big projects and especially not on those found in severe, uninhabited climatic regions. For instance, throughout the development of the West Siberian oil and gas fields, little has been written with regard to the environmental impact of that work. This stands in sharp contrast to the concern expressed in the United States over the construction of the Alaska pipeline.

In this sense, the BAM is perhaps the prototype for rational planning of a major project under socialism in any environment, especially an extreme one. Philosophically, under socialism environmental disruption cannot occur because it is resolved through central planning.[79] What abuse remains under that ideology is rationalized as a vestige of capitalism. Unfortunately, too much disruption remains in the USSR for it to be written off so facilely, and most reasonable people there realize it is a symptom of more than just a "decadent" philosophy. The reasons lie with backward technology, meaningless laws, carelessness, and, in the end, lack of concern for the environment.

Not unlike their counterparts in the United States, Soviet industrial officials have been reluctant to assess the potential environmental impact of their economic activities before the latter have gone into operation. In fact, such analyses are not legally binding because in the seemingly endless stream of conservation legislation that has appeared recently in the Soviet Union, there has not been a directive comparable to the National Environmental Policy Act of 1969 by which environmental impact statements were made mandatory in the United States.

The most comprehensive law now in effect in the Soviet Union is the regulation approved by the Central Committee and Council of Ministers in early 1973, "On the Strengthening of Conservation and the Improvement of Natural Resource Use," in which the duties of well over a dozen agencies responsible for decisions affecting the environment were specified. Curiously, the same branches of government that are accountable for achievements in the production sector preside over environmental stewardship as well. The obligations cited by the law are principally remedial in orientation. In other words, once the decision to build an enterprise has been made by higher authority, there is absolutely no question that it shall be built.

There are guidelines within the law, however, which make it clear that the environment should be respected once the project goes into operation.[240] Thus, despite the hazards, there never was any doubt, once the go-ahead was issued, that the BAM would be constructed; but no single comprehensive impact analysis, like the one produced for the Trans-Alaska pipeline project, was required.

As a result, Soviet preplanning traditionally has emphasized extraction or production over ecological considerations. "As a general rule, the man-nature interaction is investigated in the traditional one-sided way—what resources are available for use, where are they located, and how efficient would be their exploitation."[196] Among the few publicized "preplans," the one dealing with the future Sayan territorial-production complex was judged by a leading Siberian economic geographer to be deficient in at least three respects: (1) ecology and dynamics of the natural landscape; (2) work on the use of lands and natural resources; (3) ecology of human life and activity.[195] As an indication of this lack of ecological concern, the same geographer alludes to Kolosovskiy's definition of a territorial-production complex, which is devoid of any reference to the renewal or conservation of natural resources and to optimal living standards.

Preplanning for the BAM has been carried out similarly. Whereas, environmental-impact studies have been authorized simultaneously with the construction and operation of the railway, preplanning has focused, with few exceptions, on the extraction and production of raw materials. Geologists, for example, are charged with creating "a firm ferrous metallurgical base, expanding the copper reserves at Udokan, and developing a raw material base for the lead-zinc industry" in the BAM zone.[205] In order to do this, they have been asked by the authorities to improve their techniques of exploring for fluid fuels, metals and nonmetals. They also have been requested to locate deposits of building materials, new minerals for the chemical industry, and the optimum geologic foundations for structural use.[213] Only in the last case have they been assigned a task that reflects ecological concern. All other responsibilities are exploitive in character.

Articles by geographers and seismologists indicate that much of the needed environmental-impact work has been completed. The efforts of Sochava, Shotskiy, Buks, Alekseyev, Vorob'yev, Prokhorov, and Solonenko indicate that some scientists have dedicated themselves to analyzing and predicting environmental change in the BAM service area.[205] However, one geographer, M. E. Adzhiyev, has been bold enough to suggest that the research, accumulated in many instances since the 1930s, is insufficient to formulate satisfactory predictive models.[136] Another source reveals that "on a number of important issues science is still not ready to provide clear, realistic answers."[139]

The biggest deficiency has been lack of liaison between disciplines. Thus, while the BAM inexorably is extended into the virgin tayga of Pacific Siberia, members of 26 separate institutes, comprising permafrost experts, geographers, geologists, foresters, and nutritionists, who are working on 200 separate problems in six different Siberian cities, are attempting to coordinate their research. Apparently, as happens when this many scientists converge on a given assignment, many studies have been duplicated. To ward off further ambiguity, at least two important colloquia of BAM researchers have convened since January 1975, but again discussions apparently focused on exploitive aspects and not on conservation.[149]

One topic that appears to have been studied exhaustively is earthquakes and faults. Since 1964, V. P. Solonenko, a corresponding member of the Soviet Academy of Sciences and chief of the Seismic Engineering Laboratory in Irkutsk, has compiled a thorough record of seismic disturbances along the BAM route. Having negotiated the entire routeway on foot and by air, Solonenko and his associates are completing a map of seismic regions between Lake Baykal and the Amur River. As a result, the railroad and new settlements within its tributary area can be built in what are theoretically the safest zones. Moreover, because of Solonenko's work, special earthquake-resistant concrete frames for constructing multi-storied structures in areas of high seismicity have been designed by the Irkutsk Civil Construction Design Agency (*Irkutskgrazhdanproyekt*). Such buildings will be lower than ordinary structures and will be raised on proper foundations. Likewise, special reinforced concrete abutments and supports for bridges have been created.[210]

Permafrost research is another area in which Soviet scientists are experienced and perhaps better qualified than any other group of specialists in the world. No doubt, preplanning for this problem has been extensive, but evidently much more remains to be done. Responsibility for studying and making recommendations for construction in permafrost-plagued regions has been delegated to the Permafrost Institute in Yakutsk. On the advice of the institute, engineers are building special retainer walls on steep slopes and are laying appropriate subgrades and ballast as much as 6 feet thick across permafrost zones. Structural foundations consist of mechanically hammered, reinforced concrete pilings in deep boreholes in which perlite is used as insulation. The laying of foundations and the placement of culverts and water pipe through the railway ballast are accomplished in winter and early spring while the permafrost is solid. Trestle bridges of multi-span assemblies are employed over ground-ice zones. In regions of discontinuous or sporadic permafrost, preliminary thawing or wholesale replacement of the ground is achieved before final construction. In every case, care is taken to ensure that the insulating vegetation is disturbed as little as possible.[91]

At various spots along the route, avalanche observation posts are being established. Two such posts were assigned recently to the South Muya Range area and near the site of the Baykal tunnel. Avalanche specialists are being trained by representatives from the Central Asian Hydrometeorological Institute.[238a]

Soviet scientists are making good use of remote sensing in the BAM zone, not only for geological purposes, but also for timber inventories. With such a tool, they can plan more accurately the location of new settlements, green belts, potential agricultural areas, forest fire lanes and breaks, natural protective belts along streams and the railroad itself, and prospective national parks or wildlife preserves. In 1974 and 1975, more than 35 million acres of Far Eastern forests were inventoried in this fashion, a project that will not be finished until 1980.[8]

Regarding urban concentrations, the largest cities in the tributary area of the mainline will be limited to 200,000 persons. Ust'-Kut, Severobaykal'sk, Chara, Tynda, Neryungri, Zeya, Urgal and Amursk are anticipated to attract the greatest number of people.[95]

Acknowledging the potential pollution problem within the BAM zone, Soviet geographers have advised planners to locate the majority of heavy industrial enterprises outside the service area. At Udokan, for instance, they have recommended the establishment of mining and beneficiation activities only. As was mentioned earlier, the smelter and refinery would be situated elsewhere. In association with the making of copper, smelter and refinery gases would be converted to sulfuric acid. It has been suggested that this copper chemical combine be built near the Kruchina titanomagnetite-apatite lode, a very prospective deposit not far from the Trans-Siberian. Thus, sulfuric acid would be utilized to produce phosphate fertilizers, so necessary for the acidic soils of the region.[20a]

Finally, Soviet law requires that all new plants and factories be equipped with the best available water treatment and air pollution abatement technology. The national record for fulfillment of these limits and statutes, so far, has been less than satisfactory, and there is no assurance that they will be followed where the BAM is concerned. Nevertheless, Soviet officials are optimistic.

A critical problem requiring preplanning is food supply. There is no question that agricultural potential in the BAM service area is limited, but the yields on existing arable land can be increased with proper fertilization and management. Especially in the difficult western sector, crops will be restricted to low yields of vegetables and livestock raising. "Therefore, in every city and workers' settlement boiler-heated hothouses should be included in the blueprints."[235a] Despite this recommendation, a town as substantial in plan as Severobaykal'sk was not provided with hothouses.

Reading official reports, it would seem that Soviet authorities are doing everything possible to guarantee protection of the forest in the BAM zone. In late 1974, a Soviet writer, Oleg Volkov, challenged this view through an open letter to the Minister of Wood and Wood-Processing in *Literaturnaya Gazeta*.[252] Long a champion of environmental causes, including leadership in the Lake Baykal controversy, Volkov declared: "It seems to me that the construction of the Baykal-Amur railroad provides grand opportunities for managing the forest industry on a strictly scientific basis, so that the forest will serve as a raw material source for future generations. *I would hope that we have learned from our past mistakes.*" The writer instructed the minister on how his industry should be run, comprising an idealistic, but workable, plan for the BAM. The official replied three months later, assuring Volkov that the timber industrial complexes of the BAM zone would be highly mechanized plants processing virtually all of the felled products, including wastes. The minister said nothing about the possible disruption arising from these activities. As a consequence of this oversight, *Literaturnaya Gazeta* followed with several widely spaced issues that included pros and cons from the public. The argument continues; but if anything is obvious from the exchange, it is the fact that the Soviet people have more than sufficient reason to doubt the Timber Ministry's claim it can conduct a rational felling operation in the BAM zone. Even now, reports emanating from construction sites along the mainline point to "useless clearing of the forest" and "mindless abuse of technology." Most unfortunate of all, the mistakes made during the building of the Tayshet-Lena railway, some 20 to 30 years earlier, are being repeated.[2] Evidently, paraphrasing Volkov's plea, neither the timber industry nor the BAM workers have learned from past errors.

Conclusion

In 1983, provided Soviet workmen can finish it on schedule, the BAM will take its place among the great railroads of the world. It will have made accessible thousands of square miles of heretofore unexploited raw materials. It will play an important role in shaping the future of Pacific Siberia.

Some will argue that the BAM never will pay for itself; that the debts incurred during construction are mere harbingers of exorbitant maintenance and delivery costs; that the promise of foreign trade never will materialize; that the Soviet people never will be attracted to the region in sufficient numbers. Their contentions are well taken. On a strict cost-accounting basis, like the Tennessee Valley Authority or the Columbia Basin project in the United States, the BAM no doubt will be a losing proposition. However, the entire Siberian experience might be viewed in the same way. The fact is, be it for ideological or other reasons, the Soviet regime is determined to develop a new territorial production base in Pacific Siberia. And, in so doing, the leadership is willing to subsidize the project generously.

If the economic risks are great, the societal benefits could be greater. It might be said that it was the manifest destiny of the Soviet people to develop their Pacific seaboard within this century. Raw materials in the heavily populated western third of the USSR are declining both in quality and in quantity. Sooner or later, new raw material bases would have had to have been exploited anyway. In this case, the virgin resources of Pacific Siberia are the key. Because of them, the Soviet Union may maintain self-sufficiency in virtually every strategic mineral, well into the next century. Given the complementary relationship between a mineral-rich USSR and a resource-poor, industrialized West, Soviet authorities will be vested with strong bargaining power by the year 2000. Using this bargaining power peacefully in the realm of foreign commerce and not as a weapon for the spread of international communism, the Soviet Union should become the great industrial power of the 21st century.

For despite the auspicious mineral balance in favor of the USSR, North America still holds a formidable trump card. Now acquiring some measure of population stability and with the finest agricultural endowment on earth, the United States and Canada should continue to produce food surpluses for some time to come. Putting it facetiously, minerals cannot be eaten. The USSR must overcome its agricultural problems or trade surplus minerals for North American food. There is, of course, a third alternative: military conquest of agriculturally productive countries. In light of Soviet overtures toward détente, the last course, it would seem, has been deemed (at least temporarily) unwise, if not suicidal.

Through all of this, the BAM will be a significant factor. Even if expected foreign commerce does not come to fruition, for instance, Japan opts for China instead of the USSR as a major trading partner, the influence of the BAM will be beneficial to Pacific-Siberian industry and services. The standard of living in the BAM service area will rise and, provided the anticipated labor problem of the 1980s and 1990s can be overcome, a new economic region, comprising the southern tier of Pacific Siberia, may be born.

These events will not come to pass without difficulties. Dangers to, and from, the environment abound along the BAM route. As an illustration of the types of problems to be faced, the following example is given as an analog.

In December 1975, following a 50° temperature change in Prudhoe Bay, Alaska, several interconnected oil storage tanks cracked, and 600,000 gallons of petroleum spewed over the countryside.[132] This happened in spite of the unprecedented environmental concern that American oil companies have displayed in Alaska. Soviet efforts in many cases along the BAM reflect no less solicitude for the Siberian environment, but, as the example above indicates, even the most extreme precautions fail to guarantee safety in severe climates like Pacific Siberia and Alaska. Someone once said that wherever man treads, his impress on the environment remains. Nowhere is this statement more true than in periglacial environments.

Soviet planning experts have sworn to surmount these hardships with the least possible damage to the environment, but their record in this regard is dismal. Will they meet this challenge ecologically as well as economically? We shall know the answer within a decade.

Bibliography*

1. "Address: the BAM," *Izvestiya*, 12 July 1975.
2. Adzhiyev, M. E. "Economic-geographic problems of the BAM," *Priroda*, No. 8 (August 1975), pp. 3–11.
3. Akademiya Nauk SSSR, Komissiya po problemam Severa. *Letopis' Severa* (Chronicle of the North), Vol. 2. Moscow: Geografgiz, 1957.
4. Akademiya Nauk SSSR, Sibirskoye otdeleniye. Institut Geografii Sibiri i Dal'nego Vostoka. *Atlas Zabaykal'ya* (Atlas of Transbaykalia). Moscow-Irkutsk: 1967.
5. ———, Limnologicheskiy Institut. *Atlas Baykala* (Atlas of Lake Baykal). Irkutsk-Moscow: 1969.
6. Alekseyev, V. R.; V. V. Vorob'yev; and B. B. Prokhorov. "Problems in the interaction between nature, economy and population in the construction zone of the Baykal-Amur Mainline," *Doklady Instituta Geografii Sibiri i Dal'nego Vostoka*, No. 46 (1975), pp. 13–18.
7. Alpatov, M. "Lines from letters," *Literaturnaya gazeta*, No. 21 (21 May 1975), p. 10.
8. Androshin, A. "How many trees are there in the tayga?," *Pravda*, 13 September 1975.
9. Anuchin, N. "Can economics be 'persuaded'?," *Literaturnaya gazeta*, No. 48 (26 November 1975), p. 11.
10. Bardyshev, O. A.; O. A. Shcherbakov; and L. I. Sal'chenko. "Temporary buildings for repair shops in the BAM region," *Transportnoye stroitel'stvo*, No. 8 (August 1975), pp. 20–22.
11. Baybakov, N. K. "On the state plan for the development of the national economy of the USSR in 1976," *Izvestiya*, 3 December 1975.

*Chiefly articles from Russian and English newspapers and periodicals. The few books included deal with the BAM only in small part. Although books of a scientific nature on the BAM may have been published recently in the USSR, they are not yet available in the United States. In fact, this volume may be the first formal book on the subject in any language.

12. "BAM: The first train is on its way," *Izvestiya*, 25 December 1975.
13. "Build the BAM in exemplary fashion!," *Pravda*, 28 September 1974.
14. "BAM–a national construction project," *Pravda*, 7 August 1974.
15. "BAM welcomes the scientists," *Pravda*, 28 June 1975.
16. "Baykal-Amur Railway will speed up development of Soviet Far East," *Soviet News*, 16 July 1974.
17. "The Baykal-Amur Mainline," *Transportnoye stroitel'stvo*, No. 9 (September 1974), p. 103.
18. Belen'kiy, N. P., and V. S. Maslennikov. "The BAM: Its area of influence and its projected freight flows," *Zheleznodorozhnyy transport*, No. 10 (October 1974), pp. 39–46; translated in *Soviet Geography*, Vol. 16, No. 8 (October 1975).
19. Beloff, Max. *Soviet policy in the Far East, 1944–1951*. London: Oxford University Press, 1953.
20. Belov, V. "BAM: The history of a construction project," *Izvestiya*, 28 December 1975.
20a. Berezovskiy, V. "The contours of a complex," *Izvestiya*, 22 January 1976.
21. "Big deposit of phosphorites has been found in Yakutia," *Soviet News*, 3 June 1975.
22. Bilanenko, V. "A base for the future," *Izvestiya*, 9 July 1975.
23. Biryukov, V. "The Baykal-Amur Mainline: a major national construction project," *Soviet Geography*, Vol. 16, No. 4 (April 1975), pp. 225–230.
24. Bogatko, S. "The Zeya Hydroelectric Station produced its first power," *Pravda*, 28 November 1975.
25. Borodavchenko, I. "Lake Baykal: a new page for its biography," *Literaturnaya gazeta*, No. 49 (4 December 1974), p. 11.
26. Brezhnev, L. "For peace and the happiness of the Soviet people," *Soviet News*, 17 June 1975.
27. ———— "Comrade L. I. Brezhnev's speech," *Pravda*, 16 March 1974.
28. ———— "Comrade L. I. Brezhnev's speech," *Pravda*, 24 April 1974.
29. ———— "On a labor victory!," *Pravda*, 21 May 1975.
30. ———— "On a labor victory!," *Pravda*, 27 December 1975.
31. Brines, Russell. "Look out for those Soviet ships!," *The Christian Science Monitor*, 15 August 1975.
32. Brodov, Ye. Yu., and B. I. Tsvelodub. "Some problems in the design and construction of the subgrade in rock-slope segments of the BAM," *Transportnoye stroitel'stvo*, No. 9 (September 1974), pp. 4–5.
33. Bryukhanenko, Ye. "This is where the builders of Severobaykal'sk will live," *Izvestiya*, 7 October 1975.
34. Bunich, P. "BAM and the development of the economy of the Far East," *Planovoye khozyaystvo*, No. 5 (May 1975), pp. 28–37; translated in *Soviet Geography*, Vol. 16, No. 10 (December 1975).
35. Burnin, V.; A. Gusev; A. Istomin; D. Semenov; and V. Shvidkiy. "Machines are speeding toward idleness," *Izvestiya*, 29 March 1975.
36. Camp, T. R. *Water and its impurities.* New York: Reingold, 1963.
37. Chelnokov, N. D. "The first train has arrived in Tynda," *Transportnoye stroitel'stvo*, No. 8 (August 1975), pp. 3–4.
38. Cheporov, Edgar. "The USSR is a reliable trading partner," *Literatunaya gazeta*, No. 52 (24 December 1975), p. 9.
39. Cherkasov, G. "Is your home far away," *Komsomol'skaya zhizn'*, No. 8 (April 1975), pp. 23–24.

40. Chief Administration of Geodesy and Cartography under the Council of Ministers of the USSR. *The World Atlas.* 2d ed. Moscow: 1967.

41. Chiryayev, G. I. "BAM and Yakutia," *Ekonomicheskaya gazeta*, No. 32 (August 1974), p. 5.

42. ————. "On the verge of a billion," *Sovetskaya Rossiya*, 4 June 1975.

43. Committee of Geological Sciences, National Academy of Sciences. *The earth and human affairs.* San Francisco: Canfield Press, 1972.

44. Connolly, Violet. "The second Trans-Siberian railway," *Asian Affairs*, No. 2 (February 1975), pp. 23–29.

45. "Containers in mass production," *Soviet News*, 14 October 1975.

46. "Container route," *Soviet News*, 29 July 1975.

47. Cowan, Edward. "Soviet said to bar bid by U.S. to buy oil at discount," *The New York Times*, 12 October 1975.

48. Dallin, David J. *Soviet Russia and the Far East.* New Haven: Yale University Press, 1948.

49. Davitaya, F. "A clear-cut program," *Izvestiya*, 19 December 1975.

50. Degtyarev, V. "From the Donbas to the BAM," *Pravda*, 23 May 1975.

51. Dibb, Paul. *Siberia and the Pacific: a study of economic development and trade prospects.* New York: Praeger, 1972.

51a. Dienes, Leslie. "Soviet electric power: problems and trends in resource use," paper presented at the Conference on Soviet Resource Management and the Environment, Seattle, Washington, 6 June 1974.

52. "For those who are building the BAM," *Izvestiya*, 13 August 1975.

53. "For a shockworkers' project," *Izvestiya*, 15 July 1975.

54. D'yakonov, F. "The Far East: problems and prospects," *Ekonomicheskaya gazeta*, No. 5 (January 1975), p. 13.

55. D'yakonova, T. "An uncovering of secrets," *Sovetskaya Rossiya*, 13 December 1975.

56. "Electrification of BAM has started," *Soviet News*, 3 June 1975.

57. Ellis, Harry. "How Soviet grain deal works," *The Christian Science Monitor*, 21 October 1975.

58. Engel'brekht, Uve. "A convincing example," *Izvestiya*, 12 April 1975.

59. Yesaulkov, Yu. "A settlement on the BAM," *Izvestiya*, 29 January 1975.

60. Farafontov, L., and A. Zaytsev. "Rails stretch off into the tayga," *Pravda*, 9 November 1975.

61. Fedin, V. "BAM, a symbol of labor's valor," *Komsomol'skaya zhizn'*, No. 8 (April 1975), pp. 2–8.

62. Feshbach, Murray, and Stephen Rapawy. "Labor constraints in the five-year plan," in U.S. Congress, Joint Economic Committee. *Soviet Economic Prospects for the Seventies.* Washington: U.S. Government Printing Office, 1973, pp. 485–563.

63. Feshbach, Murray. "Manpower in the USSR," paper presented at the Conference on Soviet Resource Management and the Environment, Seattle, Washington, 6 June 1974.

64. Gagina, T.; V. Skalon; and F. Shtil'mark. "Take care of the tayga," *Izvestiya*, 18 December 1974.

65. Galin, A. "BAM–the road to treasures," *Sotsialisticheskaya industriya*, 18 May 1975.

66. Gavrish, V. "A bridge-manufacturing plant," *Izvestiya*, 5 December 1975.

67. Gerasimov, G. "America discovers Siberia," *Literaturnaya gazeta*, No. 46 (12 November 1975), p. 9.

68. Goldman, M. I. "Raw materials, the environment, and foreign trade in the Soviet Union," paper presented at the Conference on Soviet Resource Management and the Environment, Seattle, Washington, 6 June 1974.

69. ———. *The spoils of progress: Environmental pollution in the Soviet Union.* Cambridge: The MIT Press, 1972.

70. Golovanov, A. "BAM—the road into Siberia's future," *Sovetskaya Latviya*, 9 July 1975.

71. Gruliow, Leo. "Ivan working on the railroad," *The Saturday Evening Post*, November 1975, pp. 66–69, 78–81.

72. Gudkov, N. "BAM—a construction project of the young," *Literaturnaya gazeta*, No. 52 (25 December 1974), pp. 10–11.

73. Harris, Chauncy D. "USSR: Resources for heavy industry," *Focus*, No. 6 (February 1969), pp. 1–6.

74. Ibragimova, Z. M. "For a portrait of Siberia's future," *Ekonomika i organizatsiya promyshlennogo proizvodstva*, No. 3 (1975), pp. 23–27.

75. "Important new contract is signed with Japanese firms," *Soviet News*, 29 July 1975.

76. "Important role for Siberian motor road," *Soviet News*, 3 June 1975.

77. Jackson, James O. "Soviets stress quality," *The Houston Post*, 26 December 1975.

78. ———. "Soviets upgrade exports," *The Houston Post*. 1 January 1976.

79. Jackson, W. A. Douglas, ed. *Soviet resource management and the environment.* Columbus, Ohio: American Association for the Advancement of Slavic Studies, 1976.

80. James, Barry. "Russia having difficulty boosting profits in oil," *Houston Chronicle*, 28 September 1976.

81. "Japanese Credits," *Soviet News*, 29 July 1975.

82. "Japan's fishing industry urging rejection of 200-mile limit," *The Houston Post*, 16 November 1975.

83. Jorre, Georges. *The Soviet Union.* London: Longmans, Green, 1961.

84. Karnaukhov, V. "For the BAM workers," *Pravda*, 20 July 1975.

85. Karpinsky, A. "Letter to the Editor: Siberian railroad link." *The New York Times.* 26 August 1950.

86. Katkov, V. "An unfamiliar star is shining," *Komsomol'skaya zhizn'*, No. 8 (April 1975), pp. 10–12.

87. "Every hour, every day, work the shockworker way," *Izvestiya*, 19 August 1975.

88. Kaz'min, Yu. et al. "Rails in the tayga," Part I, *Pravda*, 15 July 1975.

89. ———. "Rails in the tayga," Part II, *Pravda*, 16 July 1975.

90. ———. "Rails in the tayga," Part III, *Pravda*, 18 July 1975.

91. Kedrov, K. "The Baykal-Amur Mainline," *Ekonomicheskaya gazeta*, No. 24 (June 1974), p. 9.

92. Khodachek, V. M. "On the formation of population in regions of the Far North of the USSR (with particular reference to the Aldan mining district)," *Soviet Geography*, Vol. 15, No. 5 (May 1974), pp. 288–298.

93. Khodiy, V. "Power lines for the BAM," *Pravda*, 3 May 1975.

94. Kibal'chich, O. A. "The Baykal-Amur Mainline and the complex development of the economy of the eastern USSR," *Geografiya v shkole*, Vol. 42, No. 5 (September-October 1975), pp. 6–12.

95. ———. "The production-territorial structure of the service zone of the BAM," *Vestnik Moskovskogo Universiteta, seriya geografiya*, No. 4 (July-August 1975), pp. 29–35.

96. Kirby, E. Stuart. *The Soviet Far East.* London: St. Martin's Press, 1971.
97. Krachkovskiy, P. "BAM–construction project of the century," *Novoye Russkoye slovo,* 10 January 1976.
98. Kraft, Joseph. "Japan keys U.S. limits on USSR," *The Houston Post,* 21 December 1975.
99. "Our cooperation strengthens," *Izvestiya,* 7 September 1975.
100. Kryuchkov, V. V. *Krayniy Sever* (The Far North). Moscow: Mysl', 1973.
101. Kurasov, V., and V. Mussalitin. "The scale and reality of our plans," *Izvestiya,* 22 November 1975.
102. Lattimore, Owen. "New road to Asia," *National Geographic Magazine,* December 1944, Map Supplement.
103. Lavrishchev, A. N. *Ekonomicheskaya geografiya SSSR* (Economic Geography of the USSR). Moscow: Ekonomika, 1972.
104. Lebedev, V. "Toward the sun," *Komsomol'skaya zhizn',* No. 8 (April 1975), pp. 2–4.
105. Liverovskiy, Yu. "Both old and young," *Literaturnaya gazeta,* No. 48 (26 November 1975), p. 11.
106. Lomakin, V. "Construction project, settlement, man," *Izvestiya,* 3 January 1976.
107. "Mainlines of 1975," *Izvestiya,* 5 February 1975.
108. "Main movement of population is to the east of the country," *Soviet News,* 3 June 1975.
109. Malakhiyev, M. "Lake-bottom riches," *Izvestiya,* 10 December 1975.
110. ———. "The design of the BAM," *Izvestiya,* 20 May 1975.
111. Mardzhanishvili, A. "Open up those resources!," *Literaturnaya gazeta,* No. 21 (21 May 1975), p. 10.
112. Margolin, A. B. et al., eds. *Dal'niy Vostok* (The Far East). Vol. VII of *Sovetskiy Soyuz,* edited by S. V. Kalesnik et al., 22 vols. Moscow: Mysl', 1971.
113. Medinskiy, V. "Medicine for the tayga," *Pravda,* 16 August 1975.
114. ———. "Parachutes over the tayga," *Pravda,* 28 May 1975.
115. Melik-Pashayeva, A.; A. Ivakhnov; and A. Illarionov. "Nature and man: the inimitable world of the tayga," *Izvestiya,* 20 April 1975.
116. Metreveli, V. "A club for the BAM," *Pravda,* 22 November 1975.
117. Miller, G. Tyler. *Living in the environment.* New York: Wadsworth, 1975.
118. Molchanov, V. "From Baykal to the Amur," *Pravda,* 25 July 1974.
119. Monusov, M. "Siberia 'is off' to America," *Pravda,* 1 August 1975.
120. Morris, Donald. "Congress' foreign policy record appalling," *The Houston Post.* 31 December 1975.
121. "Minerals key to U.S. energy hopes," *The Houston Post.* 9 January 1976.
122. Mote, Victor L. *The geography of air pollution in the USSR,* unpublished Ph.D. dissertation, University of Washington, 1971.
123. Myakinenkov, V. M. "Prospects of the development of production and settlement in the northern Yenisey region," *Soviet Geography,* Vol. 16, No. 7 (September 1975), pp. 578–583.
124. "On the eve of the start," *Izvestiya,* 26 November 1975.
125. *Narodnoye khozyaystvo SSSR v 1972 g* (The economy of the USSR in 1972). Moscow: Statistika, 1973.
126. "Our friend–nature," *Izvestiya,* 5 December 1974.
127. "On the alignment of the BAM," *Transportnoye stroitel'stvo,* No. 10 (October 1974), inside cover.

128. "New Soviet railway to Siberian industrial expansion," *The Austin-American Statesman*, 10 April 1975.
129. Nikiforov, B., and Ye. Bartosh. "What type of locomotive does the BAM need?," *Pravda*, 17 October 1975.
130. Nikitin, N. P.; Ye. D. Prozonov, and B. A. Tutykhin, eds. *Ekonomicheskaya geografiya SSSR* (Economic Geography of the USSR). Moscow: Prosveshcheniye, 1973.
131. Odintsov, M. M., and A. A. Bukharov. "The mineral resources of the zone," *Vestnik Akademii Nauk SSSR*, No. 9 (September 1975), pp. 44–49.
132. "Oil spill biggest in Alaska's history," *The Houston Post*, 19 December 1975.
133. Orlov, B. P. "Tendencies of economic development in Siberia and promotion of the region's role in the national economy," *Soviet Geography*, Vol. 11, No. 1 (January 1970), pp. 1–13.
134. Parks, Michael. "Where the tayga rustled," *Izvestiya*, 12 April 1975.
135. Pastukhov, S., and N. Kamenskiy. "On the construction project of the century," *Pravda*, 22 December 1975.
136. Pavlov, V. I. "BAM–the concern of all Communists," *Ekonomicheskaya gazeta*, No. 6 (February 1975), p. 9.
137. Pavlov, Yu. "The entire country is helping to build the BAM: we won't let it down!," *Komsomol'skaya zhizn'*, No. 8 (April 1975), p. 9.
138. Perevedentsev, V. "Concerning each and every one of us," *Literaturnaya gazeta*, No. 33 (13 August 1975), p. 12.
139. Petrov, G. "The scientific foundation of the BAM," *Pravda*, 30 September 1975.
140. Pinkhenson, D. M. *Ekonomicheskaya geografiya v tsifrakh* (Economic Geography in Figures). Moscow: Prosveshcheniye, 1970.
141. Podgayev, G. "What's it like to live on the BAM," *Izvestiya*, 19 October 1975.
142. Pokshishevskiy, V. V. et al., eds. *Vostochnaya Sibir'* (Eastern Siberia). Vol. VI of *Sovetskiy Soyuz*, edited by S. V. Kalesnik et al., 22 vols. Moscow: Mysl', 1969.
143. Pond, Elizabeth. "Rousing the sleeping giant: the peole who are building Siberia," *The Christian Science Monitor*, 3 June 1975.
144. Potatuyeva, T. V. "Frontage motor roads for building the western segment of the BAM," *Transportnoye stroitel'stvo*, No. 9 (September 1975), pp. 3–4.
145. "Electric power for the BAM," *Pravda*, 27 April 1975.
146. "Ordered by the BAM," *Pravda*, 5 December 1975.
147. Price, Larry W. *The periglacial environment, permafrost, and man.* Washington: Association of American Geographers, 1972.
148. Prigodich, A. "What to read about the BAM," *Stroitel'naya gazeta*, 24 October 1975.
149. "Problems of opening up the BAM," *Sovetskaya Moldaviya*, 20 September 1975.
149a. Prokhorov, B. "Through the mountains into Yakutia," *Izvestiya*, 10 January 1976.
150. ———. "The name of the future town," *Izvestiya*, 30 August 1975.
151. ———. "Truck convoys on the winter road," *Izvestiya*, 22 November 1975.
151a. ———. "Circles over the hill," *Izvestiya*, 15 January 1976.
152. ———. "Store, dining hall, dormitory," *Izvestiya*, 25 November 1975.
153. ———. "The BAM now mixes its own concrete," *Izvestiya*, 18 July 1975.
154. ———. "Rhythms of the route," *Izvestiya*, 18 November 1975.
155. ———. "The bridge is finished!," *Izvestiya*, 27 September 1975.

156. "The Central Committee's draft for the 25th congress: Basic directions for the development of the national economy of the USSR for 1976—1980," *Izvestiya*, 14 December 1975.
157. Pushkar, A. "The second route to the ocean," *Izvestiya*, 23 January 1972.
158. "The river workers' contribution to the builders of the BAM," *Ekonomicheskaya gazeta*, No. 26 (June 1975).
159. "Voyage across the ocean," *Pravda*, 6 July 1975.
160. "Rich natural resources in region of Baykal-Amur Railway," *Soviet News*, 22 July 1975.
161. Romanov, A. "For the BAM workers," *Izvestiya*, 29 July 1975.
162. Rozanov, I. S.; M. L. Sobolev; and M. L. Reks. "Provide the Baykal-Amur Mainline with designs of the highest quality," *Transportnoye stroitel'stvo*, No. 10 (October 1974), pp. 4—5.
163. "Russia No. 1 producer," *The Houston Post*, 9 January 1976.
164. "Next to the Mainline," *Pravda*, 18 August 1975.
165. "Next to the Mainline," *Pravda*, 29 June 1975.
166. Ryashin, Vladimir. "Far Eastern itineraries," *Literaturnaya gazeta*, No. 46 (12 November 1975), p. 2.
167. Sarapas, L. "The route across the Tynda," *Pravda*, 13 November 1975.
168. Schwartz, Harry. *Russia's Soviet economy.* New York: Prentice-Hall, 1954.
168a. Semenov, A. "Siberia's potential," *Izvestiya*, 16 January 1976.
169. Sergeyev, A. "The BAM—a mainline railroad of the first category," *Ekonomicheskaya gazeta*, No. 30 (July 1974), p. 17.
170. Shabad, Theodore. *Basic industrial resources of the USSR.* New York: Columbia University Press, 1969.
171. ———. "Changing resource policies of the USSR," *Focus*, No. 6 (February 1969), pp. 7—8.
172. ———. *Geography of the USSR.* New York: Columbia University Press, 1951.
173. ———. "Letter to the Editor: Trans-Siberian rail link," *The New York Times*, 21 August 1950.
174. ———. "News notes," *Soviet Geography*, Vol. 15, No. 3 (March 1974), pp. 175—177.
175. ———. "News notes," *Soviet Geography*, Vol. 15, No. 9 (November 1974), pp. 587—590.
176. ———. "News notes," *Soviet Geography*, Vol. 16, No. 2 (February 1975), pp. 121—125.
177. ———. "News notes," *Soviet Geography*, Vol. 16, No. 5 (May 1975), pp. 333—346.
178. ———. "News notes," *Soviet Geography*, Vol. 16, No. 8 (October 1975), pp. 547—552.
179. ———. "News notes," *Soviet Geography*, Vol. 16, No. 7 (September 1975), pp. 466—478.
180. ———. "News notes," *Soviet Geography*, Vol. 13, No. 4 (April 1972), pp. 260—262.
181. ———. "Siberia's changing role in Soviet industry," *Proceedings of the Association of American Geographers*, Vol. 6 (1975), pp. 212—215.
182. ———. "Siberian Weekender." New York, 1974 (xeroxed).
183. ———. "Soviet building new Siberian rail line," *The New York Times*, 5 July 1974.
184. Shcheglov, A. "Geologists on the BAM," *Pravda*, 29 October 1975.

185. Shevchenko, Yu. "The climate of the collective," *Komsomol'skaya zhizn'*, No. 8 (April 1975), pp. 25–27.
186. Shinkarev, L. "The BAM–the road of peace," *Izvestiya*, 12 April 1975.
187. ———. "The BAM: the Podymakhins from Podymakhin," *Izvestiya*, 25 August 1975.
188. ———. "The shores of southern Yakutia," Part I, *Izvestiya*, 9 September 1975.
189. ———. "The shores of southern Yakutia," Part II, *Izvestiya*, 16 September 1975.
190. ———. "And a post office," *Izvestiya*, 25 November 1975.
190a. ———. "The people from Ekon'," *Izvestiya*, 8 January 1976.
191. ———. "The bridge across the Lena," *Izvestiya*, 24 September 1975.
191a. ———. "In the forest near Datta," *Izvestiya*, 7 January 1976.
192. ———. "BAM: A base for exploring new riches, road to Siberia's future," *Soviet Life*, September 1975, pp. 20–25.
193. Shlachter, Barry. "Chinese oil export boost predicted," *The Houston Post*, 26 December 1975.
194. Shmyganovskiy, V. "The BAM's gateway to the sea," *Izvestiya*, 27 December 1975.
195. Shotskiy, V. P. "Geographical preplanning studies of economic complexes in the south of Krasnoyarsk Kray," *Soviet Geography*, Vol. 14, No. 9 (November 1973), pp. 572–581.
196. ———. "The tasks and methods of geographical studies for forecasting economic development and resource use," *Soviet Geography*, Vol. 14, No. 9 (November 1973), pp. 572–581.
197. Shtil'mark, F. "How much stone pine is there along the BAM?," *Literaturnaya gazeta*, No. 36 (3 September 1975), p. 10.
198. Shmaylov, Yu. "Upstream along the Vitim," *Pravda*, 29 June 1975.
199. Sidorenko, A. V. "The BAM and the opening up of natural riches," *Ekonomicheskaya gazeta*, No. 36 (September 1974), p. 5.
200. Simurov, A. "The BAM–an All-Union project," *Pravda*, 10 August 1975.
201. Skelton, Max B. "What price Trans-Alaska?," *The Houston Post*, 16 November 1975.
202. Smirnov, B. "From Lithuania's Komsomols," *Komsomol'skaya zhizn'*, No. 8 (April 1975), pp. 16–17.
203. Smith, Hedrick. *The Russians.* New York: Quadrangle Press, 1976.
204. Sobolev, P. "The BAM through the eyes of an engineer," *Stroitel'naya gazeta*, 8 November 1974.
205. Sochava, V. B. "Geographical aspects of the study of the BAM's sphere of influence," *Vestnik Akademii Nauk SSSR*, No. 9 (September 1975), pp. 36–43.
206. ———. "Problems of applied geography in connection with the construction of the Baykal-Amur Mainline," *Izvestiya Vsesoyuznogo Geograficheskogo Obshchestva*, Vol. 107, No. 5 (September-October 1975), pp. 385–396.
207. ———; V. P. Shotskiy; and I. I. Buks. "The route of the Baykal-Amur Mainline and some problems for further study," *Doklady Instituta Geografii Sibiri i Dal'nego Vostoka*, No. 46, (1975), pp. 3–12.
208. Sokolov, A. "This plant supplies bridges for the BAM," *Pravda*, 31 October 1975.
209. ———. "For the builders of the BAM," *Pravda*, 11 September 1975.

210. Solonenko, V. P. "Seismicity of the BAM zone," *Vestnik Akademii Nauk SSSR*, No. 9 (September 1975), pp. 50–59.
211. Solzhenitsyn, Alexander. *The Gulag Archipelago.* Vol. 2. New York: Harper & Row, 1975.
212. "Soviet completes Far East rail link," *The New York Times*, 11 August 1950.
213. SSSR. *Administrativno–territorial'noye deleniye soyuznykh respublik* (USSR. Administrative-Territorial Divisions of the Union Republics). Moscow: Statistika, 1974.
214. Stepanov, T., and L. Shinkarev. "Following up problems on the BAM," *Izvestiya*, 17 September 1975.
215. Stephan, John J. "Russia in the Pacific," *Oceans*, September-October 1975, pp. 60–65.
216. "For the builders of the BAM," *Pravda*, 14 November 1975.
217. "For the builders of the Mainline," *Pravda*, 3 July 1975.
218. "The construction project of the century," *Literaturnaya gazeta*, No. 35 (28 August 1974), p. 10.
219. Suslov, S. P. *Physical geography of Asiatic Russia.* San Francisco: W. H. Freeman & Co., 1961.
220. Svetikov, V. "Help through song," *Pravda*, 14 August 1975.
221. Syrokomskiy, V. "Can the USSR make do without Western aid?," *Soviet News*, 3 June 1975.
222. Tanner, James C. "Russia revives plan to tap gas deposits with aid from U.S. and Japanese banks," *The Wall Street Journal*, 19 November 1975.
223. Taranov, Ye. "Do you want to work here?," *Komsomol'skaya zhizn'*, No. 8 (April 1975), pp. 16–17.
224. Tarasov, G. "To the north of the Trans-Siberian," *Pravda*, 6 May 1975.
225. ———. "Ust'-Ilim," *Soviet Life*, January 1976, pp. 4–9.
226. TASS. "Send geologists to the BAM," *Sovetskaya Rossiya*, 13 August 1975.
227. ———. "Uncaptioned photo," *Izvestiya*, 16 August 1975.
228. ———. "Nakhodka is 25 years old," *Pravda*, 19 October 1975.
229. ———. "The truck convoys are on their way," *Izvestiya*, 15 October 1975.
230. ———. "Uncaptioned photo," *Pravda*, 1 September 1975.
231. ———. "For the Mainline through the tayga," *Pravda*, 30 July 1975.
232. ———. "The western gateway of the BAM," *Pravda*, 7 August 1975.
233. "Landing in the tayga," *Pravda*, 1 June 1975.
234. "The equipment of the BAM," *Izvestiya*, 30 December 1975.
235. Telepko, L. N. *Urovni ekonomicheskogo razvitiya rayonov SSSR* (Economic Development Levels of the Regions of the USSR). Moscow: Ekonomika, 1971.
235a. Tenetov, P. "To the East of Lake Baykal," *Pravda*, 19 January 1976.
236. Timofeyev, N. V. "Our forests should not be locked away in storage," *Literaturnaya gazeta*, No. 10 (5 March 1975), p. 13.
237. Titov, I. "Bridges for Siberia," *Pravda*, 30 August 1975.
238. Troyan, S. "BAM: a settlement by the lake," *Izvestiya*, 14 October 1975.
238a. ———."Unlocking the secrets of avalanches," *Izvestiya*, 20 January 1976.
239. Trushnikova, V. "Along the route of the BAM," *Izvestiya*, 30 July 1975.
240. "On strengthening conservation and the improvement of resource use," *Sobraniye postanovleniy pravitel'stva SSSR*, No. 2 (February 1973), pp. 19–41.
241. Central Statistical Administration USSR. *Chislennost' naseleniya SSSR*

(Numbers of the Population of the USSR). Vol. I of *Itogi vsesoyuznoy perepisi naseleniya 1970 goda.* Moscow: Statistika, 1972.

242. "Yakutia's coal," *Pravda*, 2 June 1975.
243. "Taming the Zeya," *Pravda*, 21 May 1975.
244. "Improve the business of designing," *Izvestiya*, 19 September 1975.
245. U.S. Congress. House Committee on Foreign Affairs. *U.S.-Soviet commercial relations: The interplay of economics, technology, transfer, and diplomacy,* by John P. Hardt and George D. Holliday. Joint Committee Print. Washington: Government Printing Office, 1973.
246. U.S. Congress. Joint Economic Committee. *Soviet economic outlook.* Hearings before the 93d Congress, 1st session, 1973.
247. U.S. Congress. Joint Economic Committee. *Soviet economic prospects for the seventies.* Joint Committee Print. A Compendium of Papers. Washington: Government Printing Office, 1973.
248. U.S. Congress. Senate. Committee on Government Operations. *Russian grain transactions.* S. Rept. 1033, 93d Congress, 2d session, 1974.
249. Ushakov, S. "Construction project of the century," *Komsomol'skaya zhizn',* No. 8 (April 1975), pp. 21–23.
250. "View Siberia in U.S. exhibit," *The Washington Post*, 20 November 1975.
251. "In committees and in groups," *Pravda*, 21 August 1975.
252. Volkov, Oleg. "The farther we go into the forest . . . ," *Literaturnaya gazeta,* No. 49 (4 December 1974), p. 11.
253. Vorob'yev, V. V. "The population dynamics of East Siberia and problems of prediction," *Soviet Geography*, Vol. 16, No. 9 (November 1975), pp. 584–593.
254. Voronin, I. V. et al. "Much is still unclear," *Literaturnaya gazeta*, No. 48 (26 November 1975), p. 11.
255. Voronin, M. I. "The great Siberian road," *Transportnoye stroitel'stvo*, No. 9 (September 1975) pp. 58–62.
256. Voznesenskiy, A. N. et al., eds. *Atlas razvitiya khozyaystva i kul'tury SSSR* (Atlas of Economic and Cultural Development of the USSR). Moscow: 1967.
257. Wohl, Paul. "By the thousands, youths in Russia heed challenge to lay 2,200-mile railroad," *The Christian Science Monitor*, 24 May 1974.
258. "World Oil Briefs," *The Houston Post*, 9 January 1975.
259. Yakobson, V. "Along the route of valor," *Pravda*, 24 May 1975.
260. "Homes are going to the BAM," *Pravda*, 19 May 1975.
261. "On order from the BAM," *Pravda*, 27 May 1975.
262. Zakhar'ko, V. "Come and join us on the BAM," *Izvestiya*, 23 December 1975.
263. Zhuravlev, V. "Land-going pilots," *Sotsialisticheskaya industriya*, 17 September 1975.

Chapter 3

THE BAM: PLANNING ASPECTS

Viktor V. Biryukov

The economic development program envisaged by the directives of the 24th party congress [in 1971] allocated a special place to the productive forces of Siberia and the Far East. The Far East, together with the adjacent regions of Yakutia and Transbaykalia, constitutes one of the largest regions of the Soviet Union, with almost 30 percent of the total territory of the USSR.

The intensive development of the economy of Siberia and the Far East requires especially the construction of additional transport lines along which industrial complexes could arise. The recently adopted Party and Government decree concerning the construction of the Baykal-Amur Mainline (BAM) is of extraordinarily great economic importance. The construction of the line arises from the need for strengthening transport linkages between Transbaykalia and the Far East, on the one hand, and other regions of the Soviet Union, on the other hand, and thus creating favorable conditions for the development of rich natural resources. The construction of the new line will provide a second rail outlet toward the ports of the Pacific Ocean and reduce the length of haul by several hundred kilometers compared with the present Trans-Siberian Railroad.

The BAM line, extending from Ust'-Kut (Lena railroad station) to Komsomol'sk on the Amur over a distance of 3,200 km, will run roughly 200 to 500 km to the north of the Trans-Siberian through sparsely settled areas of Irkutsk Oblast, Buryatia, Chita and Amur oblasts and Khabarovsk Kray.

A number of industrial enterprises are planned in the zone to be served by the BAM, which includes the unusually rich Udokan copper deposit. To the north, in the area of Chul'man and Aldan, are large reserves of coking coal and high-grade iron ore. There are also rich timber resources, including spruce and fir (the best pulp wood species) as well as valuable deposits of asbestos and lead-zinc ores. The construction of the Bam—Tynda—Berkakit railroad is planned concurrently with the BAM project to develop the coking-coal deposits [near Chul'man]. The area is also rich in hydroelectric resources. The Zeya hydroelectric station, the first in the

117

region, placed its first unit into operation in 1975. The productive forces of Siberia and the Far East are expected to develop in the future both through expansion of production in the developed portion of these regions and through development of recently discovered resources.

The construction of the BAM line will greatly stimulate economic changes in the eastern portion of the Soviet Union. "Its construction will make possible the development of rich mineral resources of Siberia and the Far East, such as iron ore, coal, natural gas, copper, lead, tin as well as huge timber resources. The vast energy resources of Siberian rivers will be used on an even greater scale and yield large amounts of cheap electric power" (A. N. Kosygin, "Speech at a voters' rally in the Moscow city election district,", *Pravda*, June 13, 1974). These development projects will give rise to a new territorial production complex, including nonferrous metallurgy, coal mining, timber, woodworking and pulp-and-paper industry as well as consumer goods manufactures.

The expansion of foreign trade with countries of the Pacific basin, including Japan, will give rise to larger oil exports. It has been calculated that the flow of freight to the Far East may reach 100 million metric tons or more a year in the near future.

In connection with the growth of freight traffic, a great deal of work was done during the 9th five-year plan (1971—75) to strengthen the carrying capacity of the Trans-Siberian Railroad and of its connecting links with Pacific ports. Its western segments was being electrified and provided with automatic block signals. The Uglovaya-Nakhodka railroad was double-tracked and an Amur River bridge was completed at Komsomol'sk. The development of air traffic has been easing the long-distance passenger load on the railroads. However, all these measures are still inadequate.

The question of building the BAM was resolved in principle a few years ago, and work began on surveys and designs as well as on construction of the Bam—Tynda spur, which was intended to link the present Trans-Siberian with the BAM at about the middle of the new line. Recently, however, as the future requirements of oil movements to Far Eastern refineries and for export became clearer, the need for construction of the BAM became more urgent.

At first glance, it seemed that the most effective way of easing the load on the Trans-Siberian Railroad would be a construction of a large-diameter oil pipeline from the West Siberian fields to the Far Eastern refineries and Pacific ports. However, careful study of the question by an expert commission of Gosplan USSR, together with the Institute of Complex Transport Problems and with the Transportation and Oil-Gas Industry departments of Gosplan USSR, led to another conclusion. It turned out to be more economical to build a new railroad, with special equipment to carry the entire flow of oil.

If we were to take the combined cost of the BAM and of a pipeline as 100, the cost of just a reinforced railroad together with rolling stock for the transportation of oil, would be as follows:

Investment cost 81 to 93
Operating cost 95 to 107
Total cost 96 to 97

In these estimates, the lower figure refers to the cost of a railroad with newly designed rolling stock and tank-car trains weighing 10,000 tons; the higher figure refers to the use of existing rolling stock and train loads of 6,000 to 7,000 tons.

According to the decision now adopted, West Siberia crude oil will move by pipeline as far east as Tayshet, then over the BAM to Urgal, where it will again be trans-shipped to pipeline via Khabarovsk to Far Eastern refineries and to export terminals. Such a combined pipeline-rail-pipeline system will be more economical that simply a pipeline transport system. The carrying capacity of the BAM will be at least twice as high as the capacity of an ordinary single-track railroad.

With a view to the earliest possible completion of the BAM for the haulage of key commodities such as oil, coal, timber and building materials, the project is to be built at an accelerated rate. The start of work-train traffic over the entire line is scheduled for 1982. In view of the length of the rail line and its location in undeveloped areas with an unusually harsh natural environment, the implementation of this task will require the creation of an industrialized construction base and the use of advanced management techniques and engineering designs.

The new rail line will cut through seven mountain ranges, including the Baykal, North Muya and Udokan ranges. Along the line are a large number of rivers, of which the most important are the Lena, Olekma, Zeya and Selemdzha. Much of the route runs through permafrost, highly seismic areas, inaccessible swamps and rock streams. Earthwork on the road bed will exceed 220 million cubic meters, at least half of it in rocky ground. Four tunnels will be required, including one more than 15 km long. The crossing of rivers and other natural obstacles will require 3,200 artificial structures, including 16 bridges more than 300 meters long, and 120 with a length of 100 to 300 meters. There will be many stations and sidings; at 64 of them, settlements with all essential services will be built to house most of the railroad workers.

Construction is to be speeded and labor-consuming operations are to be reduced by the use of prefabricated building elements made out of lightweight materials. They will include water pipe made out of corrugated iron, *keramzit* [porous clay-filled] panels, and structural elements made of alloyed steels and making use of aluminum.

In view of the specific natural environment of the region, a number of construction problems require special study. Thus the Institute of Physics of the Earth is investigating the microseismic character of the Chara-Tynda segment, and the Permafrost Institute of Yakutsk is drafting recommendations for the construction of artificial structures in permafrost.

Some engineering and economic problems are being handled by design agencies of the Ministry of Transport Construction. One of them is the construction within the short time of eight years of the 15-km tunnel through the North Muya Mountains, including a ventilation system. The point is that the BAM was originally designed for diesel traction, with the crossing of the North Muya Mountains making use of several shorter tunnels and longer trackage. Later a more economical alignment using the single, long tunnel was worked out. It turned out, however, that the removal of exhaust gases from the tunnel would require unusually powerful ventilating equipment and a huge amount of electric power. Now the electrification of the western segment of the BAM (including the North Muya tunnel) is being considered, and this would eliminate the ventilation problem.

The accelerated development of resources along the BAM will depend on strict adherence to construction schedules. For example, the Bam–Tynda–Berkakit spur is to be ready for the start of coal shipments by the end of 1977; along the Ust'-Kut–Nizhneangarsk segment, traffic for timber and other freight is to be open in 1979 as far as the Baykal tunnel, and in 1982 as far as Nizhneangarsk.

An important aspect of the construction project is the provision for future expansion of carrying capacity. The BAM will ultimately have to be double-tracked along the entire length. Therefore some preliminary work (wider road bed, double-tracked bridges) should be done even in the first, single-track stage.

The BAM project will require the provision of an industrial base that will supply the project with building elements, crossties, ballast, *keramzit*, pyrites, asbestos-cement products, chipboard etc. Shimanovsk [on the Trans-Siberian] has been chosen for a complex of construction-materials producers, including a factory for the manufacture of reinforced concrete building elements, a ballast plant with a capacity of 400,000 cubic meters a year, and facilities for the manufacture of *keramzit*. granite facings, sanitary plumbing equipment and electrical goods. The large number of trucks and other equipment on the project are to be kept in good condition by repair facilities, including one at Komsomol'sk for construction equipment, and one yet to be built in Khabarovsk Kray for trucks.

The BAM has been proclaimed a national construction project, and virtually all government agencies are involved in it.

The Iron and Steel Ministry was expected to deliver 5,000 tons of corrugated iron a year starting in 1975, for the installation of water pipe according to specifications given by the State Construction Committee USSR, the Ministry of Railroads and the Ministry of Transport Construction. The use of corrugated iron pipe is a new application, and is expected to help resolve the problem of temperature stresses in water pipe under harsh climatic conditions. Starting in 1975, the Ministry of Transport Construction was also expected to receive 70,000 tons of low-alloy steel sheets annually, including 50,000 tons of thermally improved sheets with guaranteed resilience at temperatures as low as -70°C. The use of such steel is essential in the construction of bridges and overpasses in the zone of low temperatures.

A crucial problem is the provision of electric power both for the construction project and for the industries to be built along the rail line. The Electric Power Ministry was expected to work out a plan in 1974–75 to supply power to the BAM and to the Bam-Tynda-Berkakit spur and to start the construction in 1976 of a 110-kv line from Ust'-Kut to Nizhneangarsk and of a 220-kv double-circuit line from the Ust'-Ilimsk hydroelectric station to [the iron-mining center of] Zheleznogorsk and to Ust'-Kut. In 1975 the ministry was also expected to work out the provision of electric power to the Trans-Siberian Railroad for electrification of the Karymskaya–Skovorodino segment.

Plans have been worked out to supply the project with labor. The Vocational Education Committee USSR and the Council of Ministers RSFSR were expected to provide in their plans of 1975 through 1978 for the training of 13,000 skilled workers for the Ministry of Transport Construction, and the Ministry of Higher Education USSR and the Railroad Ministry were expected to train and assign 4,280 college graduates to the Ministry of Transport Construction in the course of 1975 through 1980. Both the Ministry of Higher Education and the State Committee on Vocational Training were also expected to train and assign 370 specialists with a secondary education (store buyers, bakery and restaurant specialists) as well as 710 service workers (sales personnel, cooks, bakers, etc.) to the BAM project in the course of 1975 through 1977.

Such a major construction project as the BAM required the organized strengthening of construction organizations. The management of construction and the orderly flow of materials and supplies will be supervised: in the Ministry of Transport Construction, by the Main Administration of the Construction of the Baykal-Amur Mainline (Glavbamstroy); in the Ministry of Railroads, by the Administration of Equipment Supply (Transkomplekt) and a corresponding administration within the Main Administration of Capital Construction, and at Tynda Station, by the BAM Construction Directorate. Uninterrupted financing of the BAM project will be assured through local branches of the Construction Bank USSR.

A number of benefits are being granted to the construction organizations and to persons wishing to work on the BAM project. As an exception, 10 percent in excess of the estimated cost will be made available for unforeseen work and expenses on all installations of the BAM and of the Bam-Tynda-Berkakit spur, and 15 percent for temporary structures. In view of the harsh working conditions in the area of the BAM project and of the Bam-Tynda-Berkakit spur, a wage increment of 70 percent will be given to workers engaged in surveys, design, construction, industrial activities, transportation and service agencies during the period of the construction project.

Workers on the BAM project and the Bam-Tynda-Berkakit spur will be entitled to: all the benefits granted to workers in areas equivalent to the Far North, and family members will receive lump-sum payments in the amount established for the Far North. The Construction Bank USSR is authorized to make loans to BAM construction workers of up to 500 rubles per worker, to be repaid within three years. Local municipal authorities are authorized to reserve the housing of skilled workers (Grade 4 and higher) and their family members in their permanent places of residence while they are away working on the BAM project.

The scheduled fulfillment of the BAM project will depend to a large extent on prompt provision of engineering plans, investment funds, materials and supplies as well as manpower. Thousands of employes of more than 30 ministries and agencies are participating in this project of really national scope. Gosplan USSR will be called upon to play a major organizational role. Starting in 1975, the Transport Department and other departments were expected to include in the annual plans a separate item for capital investment in the BAM and the Bam-Tynda-Berkakit spur in the amount provided by party and government decisions. This will require integrated planning of all outlays for production and service establishments and for the construction industry. Gosplan departments concerned with materials allocation must insure that annual plans include a separate item for the provision of materials, supplies, cable, trucks, equipment and other resources to the BAM project in accordance with the planned volumes of work, which are expected to increase sharply from year to year in the early stages of the project.

Responsible tasks also fall upon the Oil-Gas Department, the Transport Department and other departments of Gosplan USSR. They are expected to study proposals from the appropriate ministries regarding the laying of pipelines (together with inlet and outlet terminals) from the Urgal area to consumption and trans-shipment points for the oil to be carried along the BAM line, as well as the construction of a tanker terminal in the Far East, so that these projects will be completed in time to insure the transportation of the required amount of oil for domestic uses and for export.

The Department of Construction and Construction Industry will be charged with supervising the creation of appropriate construction facilities for the BAM project, which will be heavily dependent on the timely completion of such facilities, especially in the initial stage of construction.

The Department of Heavy Machinery and Construction Machinery Manufacture together with the Transport Department will be expected to supervise the Ministry of Heavy Machinery Manufacture in the production and delivery of tank cars in amounts sufficient to insure the adequate carrying capacity of the future rail line.

A matter of special concern will be the provision of housing, medical care and other services to construction workers and the future rail workers.

The BAM project has become a national youth project. The best young people, ready to overcome all hardships, are being commandeered to the project, about which L. I. Brezhnev has said: "The construction of this railroad, cutting through the Siberian landmass with its inexhaustible natural resources, will open the way to the creation of a major new industrial region as settlements and towns, industrial plants and mines rise along the railroad" (L. I. Brezhnev, *Velikiy podvig partii i naroda. Rech' na torzhestvennom zasedanii v Alma-Ate, posvyashchennom 20-letiyu osvoyeniya tseliny* [The Great Achievement of Party and Nation. Speech at a Ceremonial Meeting in Alma-Ata Marking the 20th Anniversary of the Development of the Virgin Lands]. Moscow: Politizdat, 1974, p. 27). The BAM project will continue the chronicle of the labor successes of the Soviet people, begun during the early five-year plans with the construction of the Turkestan-Siberia Railroad, the Dnieper power station and the Magnitogorsk steel plant.

Chapter 4

DESIGN AND CONSTRUCTION
OF THE BAM

N.P. Belen'kiy and V.S. Maslennikov

A glorious new chapter has opened in the history of Soviet rail transportation. Work has begun on the Baykal-Amur Mainline, a project of tremendous significance for the Soviet economy. It bears witness to the steadily growing might of the Soviet Union, with its high economic and scientific-technical potential.

Long-term state planning became the guiding principle of the party and the Soviet state during Lenin's lifetime and found expression in Lenin's brilliant plan for the electrification of Russia, the GOELRO plan. The significance that Lenin attached to the development of rail transportation can be judged from the fact that almost half the appropriations for implementation of the GOELRO plan went into reconstruction, improvement and further development of rail transportation.

One of the super-mainline railroads envisaged by the GOELRO plan was supposed to have a profound impact on the national economy. The GOELRO report stated that this super-mainline was supposed to run from Moscow deep into Siberia, passing through "regions that are extraordinarily rich in natural resources and whose economic accessibility by means of an electrified mainline would create totally new conditions for the future structure of the economy not only in Russia but in world trade." The report went on to say that the creation of new bases for the future economic life of the republic was of a significance that could not yet be assessed with any degree of precision because of the magnitude of the results that would flow from the implementation of the planned measures.

The GOELRO plan envisaged the "construction of a basic transport network made up of routes that would combine low freight transport costs with great carrying capacity." The aim was to put an end to the lag in rail transportation in the eastern regions, which at the time accounted for only 15 percent of the total trackage.

A start in the expansion of the rail network in the eastern part of the USSR was made during the first few five-year plans. Over the last 50 years, the rail net in

123

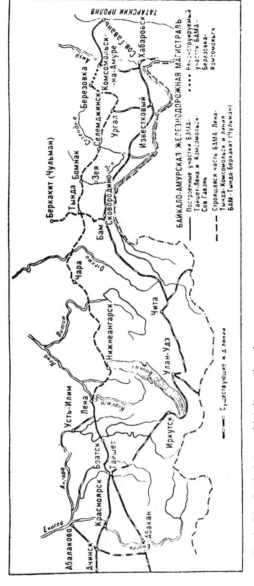

Fig. 1. The Baykal-Amur Mainline railroad

Legend: Existing railroads
Completed BAM segments (Tayshet-Lena and Komsomol'sk-Sovetskaya Gavan')
(dashed line) BAM segment under construction (Lena-Tynda-Komsomol'sk and the north-south connecting line Bam-Tynda-Berkakit [Chul'man])
(dotted line) BAM segment to be rebuilt (Berezovka-Komsomol'sk).

the European part has been expanded by 60 percent, and in the Asian part more than threefold.

Of particular importance in the Asian part has been the construction of the Turkestan-Siberia line, the South Siberian line [Tayshet-Barnaul-Tselinograd-Magnitogorsk] and the Middle Siberian line [Barnaul-Kokchetav-Kustanay]. However, to the east of Tayshet, only one mainline has continued to function as far as the Pacific coast. The time is now at hand to realize Lenin's idea of a railroad through the interior of Siberia and the Far East.

Reference Points of the New Mainline

The problem of the Baykal-Amur Mainline (BAM) already has a 44-year-old history of study, surveys and designs. The idea of building the BAM first arose in 1932. At that time the basic reference points of the proposed railroad took shape. It was to run from the area of Skovorodino north toward Tynda, and then east to Permskoye on the Amur, the site of the present Komsomol'sk. The choice of the future railroad station of Tynda [a settlement then named Tyndinskiy] was dictated by its transport-geographic situation at the intersection of two proposed railroads—the east-west BAM and the north-south railroad to Yakutsk.

Lake Baykal, enclosed within high mountain ranges, represents a gigantic water barrier along the route of the Trans-Siberian Railroad. Upon reaching Tayshet from the west, the Trans-Siberian is forced to veer southeastward to bypass the southern end of the lake. One of the alternative Trans-Siberian routes would have skirted Lake Baykal at its northern end. That is why Tayshet ultimately became the starting point of the new Baykal-Amur Mainline, which bypasses the lake on the north and takes its name from the two major bodies of water in the southern zone of East Siberia and the Far East. The eastern terminus was to be the port of Sovetskaya Gavan' on the Tatar Strait of the Sea of Japan.

Work on the Baykal-Amur Mainline began before World War II with surveys along the route from Tayshet to Sovetskaya Gavan' by the specially created Bamproyekt agency (later renamed Zheldorproyekt). The alignment of the railroad between Tayshet and Ust'-Kut and between Tynda and Sovetskaya Gavan' was determined in 1938–1942. Surveys on the alignment between Ust'-Kut and Tynda were completed in 1944.

At about the same time, construction work began on segments of the mainline and on connecting lines with the Trans-Siberian, continuing with interruptions in the first few years of the war and after the war until 1950. Work was thus completed on the 720-km segment between Tayshet and Lena [a rail station at Ust'-Kut] and on the 468-km segment from Pivan' [opposite Komsomol'sk on the Amur] to Sovetskaya Gavan', and the line between Urgal and Izvestkovaya.

The BAM thus includes both the existing segments Tayshet-Lena and Komsomol'sk-Sovetskaya Gavan', totaling 1188 km, and the intervening 3145-km gap between Lena and Komsomol'sk, to which the present article is devoted (Fig. 1).

The rapid development of productive forces and the opening up of new territories in the eastern regions of the USSR as well as an expansion of foreign trade through its Pacific ports have fostered a rapid growth of freight traffic in the last 15 years. The only railroad now serving the extreme southern portion of East Siberia and the Far East is operating near capacity. Moreover it passes over large distances through regions with unfavorable geographical and engineering-geological conditions that hamper operations. There was thus an urgent need for the development and improvement of interregional transport routes that would link Transbaykalia with the Far East and with other parts of the Soviet Union.

An increase in the economic potential of the Soviet Union, in conjunction with scientific-technical progress, made it possible in 1967 to resume design work on the BAM project in light of improved engineering conditions and devices. The advances made in this area were reflected not only in new survey and design technology and, most important, in improved operating equipment, but also in the expanded study of natural resources and the development of productive forces in the zone that would be served by the BAM.

Along the western and eastern segments of the BAM, large industrial centers and transport nodes had arisen at Komsomol'sk, Bratsk, Sovetskaya Gavan' and Ust'-Kut (with its Lena River port of Osetrovo). Dozens of mineral sites had been discovered between the Lena River and Komsomol'sk; many of them had been explored or were awaiting exploitation. The economic potential of the BAM region had thus greatly increased in the course of 30 years even though the middle segment between Ust'-Kut and Komsomol'sk remained undeveloped.

At the present time, survey and design work on the BAM and the Tynda-Berkakit spur [extending northward to the Chul'man coking-coal deposit] is being handled by several institutes of the Ministry of Transport Construction, the Ministry of Railroads and other agencies under the over-all supervision of the Mosgiprotrans [Moscow Transport Design] agency. The Giprotranstei agency, starting in 1967, has worked out several freight-flow forecasts both for the BAM as a whole and for separate segments as well as for the connecting line between the Bam station [on the Trans-Siberian] and rail junction of Tynda, and between Tynda and Berkakit.

The most recent forecasts project a fundamentally new transport-economic role for the BAM. While earlier designs envisaged basically an important local transport and regulating role, it is now expected, in addition, to play a key function in the Soviet Union's growing foreign trade with the Pacific basin.

Recent surveys have confirmed the earlier route alignment between the Lena River and Komsomol'sk. The line will run through the remote northern portions of Irkutsk Oblast, Buryat ASSR, Chita Oblast, Amur Oblast and Khabarovsk Kray, at a distance of 180 to 500 km north of the Trans-Siberian.

Starting in Irkutsk Oblast at Lena station (serving Ust'-Kut and its port, Osetrovo), the new railroad crosses to the right bank of the Lena River and runs 300 km to the southeast, using valley segments of the Niya and Kirenga rivers and tributaries. After crossing the Baykal Range in a tunnel, the railroad enters the Buryat ASSR and descends to the settlement of Nizhneangarsk, the seat of North Baykal Rayon, at the north end of Lake Baykal. The alignment then follows the broad valley of the Upper Angara River up to the North Muya Range, the divide

126

between the Baykal basin (draining into the Yenisey) and the Vitim River (draining into the Lena). Crossing the range in a 15-km tunnel, the alignment runs along the Muya valley to the Vitim River and then enters Chita Oblast.

Farther east, using the valley of the Syul'ban (a right tributary of the Vitim), the BAM rises to the Chara intermontane basin, passing near the rayon seat of Chara. Then, after having crossed an outlier of the Stanovoy Range, it passes the point where Chita Oblast, Amur Oblast and Yakut ASSR meet, and, continuing along the Khani valley, reaches the Olekma River. After following the Olekma for about 100 km, the BAM crosses the river and runs through the narrow, deep valley of the Nyukzha (a right tributary of the Olekma). It crosses the Lena-Amur divide at about 1650 km and reaches Tynda, the seat of Dzheltulak Rayon and a major future rail junction.

This is the area where the BAM and the Trans-Siberian come closest to each other, and that is why construction on the entire project began with the 176-km connecting line between Bam and Tynda. The line (opened in 1975) made it possible to unfold construction on the BAM line both west and east from Tynda. At the same time, the connecting line also represents the initial segment of the future Yakutsk railroad, which was to be completed as far as Berkakit, in the Chul'man coking-coal district, by the end of 1977. This represented an acceleration of the original construction schedule, which called for Berkakit to be reached in 1979.

From Tynda, the BAM continues southeastward, almost parallel to the Trans-Siberian, first along the Gilyuy River and then across the gently rolling, swampy Zeya-Bureya plain. The construction of the Zeya hydroelectric dam above the town of Zeya has formed a reservoir that the BAM will skirt on the north, crossing the Zeya River at Zeysk, a new town. About 100 km after crossing the Selemdzha River, the rail line enters Khabarovsk Kray and in the area of the [coal-mining] settlement of Chegdomyn joins the existing spur from Izvestkovaya [on the Trans-Siberian] to Urgal.

The construction of the BAM will give rise to the Urgal railroad node in this area. To the east the BAM will cross the Bureya Range through a tunnel and then, sharply changing direction from southeast to northeast, follow the valley of the Amgun' River to Berezovka, the terminus of an existing lumber railroad from Komsomol'sk. This segment will have to be rebuilt as part of the BAM project. After completion of the bridge across the Amur at Komsomol'sk, there will be a direct rail link to Sovetskaya Gavan' and the railroad ferry to Sakhalin.

Characteristics of the Area Served by the Railroad

The territory gravitating toward the BAM encompasses all or parts of 21 rayons in the above-mentioned autonomous republics, oblasts and kray, with a combined area of 1.1 to 1.2 million km^2 and a population, at the present time, of 250,000. It should be noted that this area will gradually expand with the development of local feeder routes from the railroad. However, in the initial period, when such feeder routes will still be lacking, the area of gravitation will be limited to the river valleys immediately adjacent to the alignment of the BAM. At points of intersection with major rivers, the Kirenga, Vitim, Olekma, Zeya, Selemdzha; in the Baykal zone, and at points of intersection with motor roads, the zone of gravitation will be much wider.

127

Its southern limit will be affected by the service zone of the Trans-Siberian, and will run at 60 to 160 km south of the BAM, and up to 200 km to the south within the Buryat ASSR. As for the northern limit of the BAM service zone, it may be regarded as running 200 to 400 km from the alignment. It must be borne in mind that the construction of such a major railroad parallel to the Trans-Siberian will cut heavily into the latter's service zone. The BAM will take over most of the transport-economic linkages of regions north of Lat. 55° N that now gravitate toward the Trans-Siberian.

In physical-geographic terms, the region to be served by the BAM is a mountain-tayga zone with widespread permafrost, waterlogged areas known locally as *mar'* and, in the Baykal region, seismic phenomena. In terms of geographical setting, especially the complexities of landforms, seismicity, and the presence of explored mineral sites, the entire region can be divided at the Olekma River into western and eastern portions.

The western portion is a typical mountain region, encompassing the Middle Siberian tableland, the North Baykal upland and the Stanovoy Range. A characteristic landform feature is the alternation of dissected plateaus and uplands, rising to 500-700 meters, and higher mountain ranges. Landform dissection is particularly pronounced to the east of Lake Baykal within the North Baykal upland, where the Baykal, North Muya, Kolar, Udokan and other ranges rise to 2000-2600 meters. Between these ranges, a chain of intermontane basins, up to 200 km long by 50 km wide, extends from Lake Baykal to the Olekma River.

This area contains one of the most active inner continental earthquake zones, with possible intensities ranging up to 9 points. Roughly 1,000 km of the BAM runs through this seismically active zone.

The relief of the eastern portion of the BAM service zone consists of low mountains and large waterlogged depressions, with higher, short mountain ranges found in a few areas. In the extreme east, the zone borders on the rolling Lower Amur lowland along the Amur River.

The drainage net of the BAM zone is well developed and belongs to the Yenisey (Baykal), Lena and Amur basins. Its configuration reflects the alignment of landforms: all the major rivers—Lena, Kirenga, Vitim, Olekma, Zeya, Selemdzha, Bureya, Amgun'—flow either north or south; only a few valley segments can be used by the east-west BAM alignment, and generally tend to intersect the rail line. Altogether the BAM has to cross more than 3,000 watercourses along its route. The Vitim, Olekma, Zeya and Selemdzha are endowed with hydroelectric potential. The first major hydroelectric station in the entire region—the Zeya station—began generating power in 1975. The small Mamakan hydro station has been in operation for some years on the Mama River in the Bodaybo district.

The climate of the zone is highly continental. The mean annual temperature ranges between −1° and −4°C; the minimum drops to −58°, and the maximum rises to +36°. Mean annual precipitation increases from west to east, with 380 mm at Nizhneangarsk and 520 mm at Komsomol'sk. The generally cold and snowless winters last seven months in intermontane basins and eight to nine months in mountain country, with many sunny days and light winds. Summers are short and humid. The climate is somewhat more moderate in the mountain basins, and in some cases permits the cultivation of crops, especially in the Muya valley.

Intensive physical weathering, the occurrence of permafrost and the high seismicity in the western portion of the BAM zone account for a widespread distribution of a variety of physical geological phenomena: the *mar'* areas, ground ice, thermokarst, river icings, frost heaves, rockslides and placer deposits, landslips and mudflows. There is an avalanche danger in the Baykal, North and South Muya ranges.

The construction and operation of the BAM will be accompanied by environmental impact studies and the search for effective ways of controlling unfavorable natural phenomena along the route. Work on these problems will be done, in particular, by a permafrost research station to be established in the BAM zone.

The BAM zone is among the Soviet Union's poorly studied and underdeveloped northern regions with a huge resource potential. The opening up of such regions, the development of industry and capital construction, especially of transport routes, is fraught with difficulties because of the harsh environment, sparse population and difficulties of access. In physical conditions for human activities, the entire BAM zone is equivalent to the Far North.

So far resource development has been quite limited in the zone between the Lena River and Komsomol'sk. Only a few resources are being exploited, and both economic activity and human settlement tend to be scattered in isolated sites. The present activities are mining and lumbering.

Gold is being mined in Bodaybo Rayon of Irkutsk Oblast and in Baunt Rayon of Buryat ASSR, in northern Chita Oblast, and in the upper reaches of the Zeya, Selemdzha and Bureya rivers; mica in the Mama-Chuya district, and coal in the Bureya, Selemdzha and Chul'man districts.

Lumbering operations are under way on the Kirenga and Upper Angara rivers, in the Zeya and Selemdzha districts and in the Bureya basin. The Urgal lumbering district ships about 800,000 m³ of timber a year. About the same amount is being shipped out of the sector served by the Komsomol'sk-Berezovka lumber railroad. Total timber shipments in the BAM zone run nearly 2.5 million m³ a year.

Agriculture is of subordinate significance, consisting of animal husbandry (cattle, reindeer) and some crops of potatoes and vegetables in the valleys of the Lena, Kirenga and Amur rivers, around Bodaybo and Nizhneangarsk. Fur trapping is significant in the mountain tayga.

Geological prospecting and exploration are becoming an increasingly significant economic activity in the region.

Transport routes have been limited thus far to virtually non-navigable rivers and seasonal roads. Rivers like the Kirenga, the Upper Angara, the Vitim, the Zeya (above Zeysk) and the Selemdzha have had no guaranteed depths even for shallow-draft vessels. The Vitim still makes use of the *karbas*, a boxlike vessel that is floated once downstream with cargo and is then dismantled. The only usable water routes are the Lena River and Lake Baykal, which carry goods destined for the Mama-Chuya and Bodaybo districts and the north shore of the lake. Most of the transport linkages of Baunt Rayon in Buryat ASSR and northern Chita Oblast are assured by winter roads, which handle, for example, 85 percent of all the freight moving into Baunt Rayon.

The transport situation is somewhat better in the eastern portion of the BAM zone. This region is served mainly by north-south feeder roads of the Trans-Siberian, with virtually no east-west communications.

The Aldan-Yakutsk highway runs north from Bol'shoy Never rail station [on the Trans-Siberian] through the town of Tynda and handles most economic linkages of the Aldan-Chul'man district; another road leads along the Selemdzha to the gold placers in the river's upper reaches. The settlement of Chegdomyn [in the Urgal coal-mining district] and the city of Komsomol'sk have rail connections with the Trans-Siberian.

Future economic development in the BAM zone will focus mainly on mineral resources. A number of nonferrous and rare metal deposits have already been discovered, including gold, copper, nickel, tin, zinc and molybdenum. There are also large deposits of coal, iron and manganese ores, mica, asbestos and building materials.

The most detailed exploration has been done in the mica and gold deposits of the Vitim River basin, the Udokan copper deposit, the Orekitkan and Katuginskoye molybdenum deposits, the Barvinskoye and Lugovskoye lead-zinc deposits, the Molodezhnyy chrysotile asbestos site and a number of coal and iron deposits. The Udokan copper site lies in Kalar Rayon of northern Chita Oblast in the immediate vicinity of the BAM route. It has an unusually high metal content, and is one of the largest deposits in terms of reserves. The copper-bearing sandstones cover a wide area and can be worked in open pits. The high tenor of the ores and favorable engineering and economic parameters of copper extraction will provide the basis for the construction of a large mining and concentrating complex.

The Orekitkan molybdenum site lies in Baunt Rayon of Buryat ASSR. The Barvinskoye and Lugovskoye lead-zinc deposits lie in the Baykal Range of Irkutsk Oblast. These deposits are significant because of large reserves of lead and zinc and associated metals. The Molodezhnyy chrysotile asbestos site has been explored on the northern slopes of the South Muya Range, 30 km from the future Taksimo rail station.

The BAM and its Tynda-Berkakit spur will provide favorable conditions for the development of the rich coal and iron-ore deposits of southern Yakutia. Coal reserves here have been estimated at 15 billion tons, including 5 billion tons of recoverable reserves; the predicted iron-ore reserves are almost 8 billion tons. Coal mining is also to be expanded in the Bureya (Urgal) basin for local use.

The expansion of geological prospecting in the BAM zone has already yielded a number of highly promising mineral indications. The construction of the railroad will help speed up the exploration of these sites and the start of extraction, and foster an expansion of the entire geological exploration effort in the BAM zone. There is also no doubt that the appearance of the BAM will prompt a review of the order of priorities of various mineral development projects. Such factors as remoteness and inaccessibility will henceforth have a less significant impact on the prospects of resource development.

The BAM also runs through forests covering an area of 20 million hectares. Mature timber stands have been estimated at 1.4 billion m^3. Timber of particularly high quality is found in the Kirenga River basin of Irkutsk Oblast, in the Selemdzha basin of Amur Oblast, and in the Amgun' basin of Khabarovsk Kray.

The dominant forest formation over most of the BAM zone is larch forest. In area and in timber reserves, larch is the most important tree species in the entire tayga zone east of Lake Baykal. The most productive larch forests are found in floodplains, on well drained river terraces, and on gentle hillslopes. A high specific weight, good physical-mechanical properties, rot resistance and durability provide a wide market for larch in the Soviet economy.

The timber industry is expected to become one of the key economic activities in the BAM zone, with wood chemicals and pulp and paper ultimately rounding out the wood-industry cycle. Several dozen large lumbering operations are to be established along the BAM alignment, with timber to be hauled 100 to 200 miles over motor roads to processing and loading points on the railroad. Initially more than 6 million m^3 of timber is to be shipped each year out of the BAM zone. A large part of this timber will move over the BAM and the Trans-Siberian to Pacific ports.

The construction of the BAM will have a fundamental impact on the whole transport pattern in the region. The railroad will give rise to a network of local transport routes. Present connections will be altered and new connections will be shaped; large freight-generating and freight-receiving stations will appear, and the role of seasonal means of transportation will sharply decline.

The BAM will provide conditions for the settling of sparsely populated regions of East Siberia and the Far East and stimulate the growth of the material and cultural well-being of the local population. The railroad will foster expansion of the agricultural and engineering uses of the large land resources and the construction of new centers of population, especially in favorable physical-geographic locations—the valleys of the Kirenga, Upper Angara, Vitim, Zeya, Selemdzha and Amgun' rivers, and the Muya and Chara intermontane basins; recreation areas will develop in the Baykal lake basin. The north shore of Lake Baykal, with its picturesque scenery and mineral springs, is expected to become a resort zone. At the same time the BAM, while passing for nearly 350 km through the Baykal lake basin, is also expected to foster conservation and optimal use of the natural riches of that unique body of water.

The opening up of new territory and the development of productive forces in the BAM zone will require extensive transport construction within the region and in adjoining territories, and the proposed railroad will play a key role as a pioneering support base. In this connection, work should already now be started on an integral plan of economic development and location in the BAM zone over the long term with a view to implementing the basic provisions of such a development program as soon as operations on the new railroad begin.

Freight Traffic

Most of the freight movements on the BAM (70 to 75 percent of the ton-kilometers) will be made up of West Siberian crude oil for the Far East. It will move by pipeline as far as Tayshet for trans-shipment to tank-car unit trains going as far as Urgal. There the crude oil will again be pumped into a pipeline for movement to Far Eastern refineries and seaports.

Such a transport arrangement has been shown to be more economical under the conditions of the BAM project than an all-pipeline route, both because of the high cost of pipeline construction in the region, approaching the cost of a single-track railroad, and the advantages offered by a railroad as a more universal form of transportation.

The second most important commodity in BAM freight operations will be timber (10 to 18 percent). Local freight movements will consist of building materials, steel, refined oil products, coal, machinery and industrial equipment, and consumer goods. Local freight traffic is expected to be significant in the following segments and stations: Lena (Ust'-Kut)–Nizhneangarsk; Vitim; Chara; Tynda; Zeysk-Fevral'sk; the Urgal railroad junction, and the Berezovka-Komsomol'sk segment. Special mention needs to be made of the Berkakit station, which will have the largest volume of car loadings in the BAM zone because of its shipments of coal.

The BAM railroad falls into two sections in its interaction with the present rail net and the magnitude of freight traffic: a western section between Lena and Tynda, and an eastern section between Tynda and Komsomol'sk.

By providing a second connection with the ports of the Pacific coast and reducing the length of haul, the eastern section of the BAM will have significant advantages over the present Trans-Siberian in linking the Komsomol'sk–Sovetskaya Gavan' district, Sakhalin, Kamchatka, the Okhotsk coast and Magadan Oblast with all regions of the Soviet Union situated to the west of Tayshet as well as with southern Yakutia. The combined length of haul by rail and sea from Tayshet to the ports of southern Sakhalin, Kamchatka and Chukotka will be 1,000 km or more shorter by the BAM than by the Trans-Siberian, with the savings in rail distance alone being 450 km. However, the interregional freight traffic of those regions is still quite small, and therefore such transit movements over the BAM will tend to be limited in the initial period.

The western section of the BAM, moreover, will reduce the length of haul by almost 160 km between Tayshet and the southern regions of Amur Oblast and Khabarovsk and Maritime krays. The western section will thus be able to handle substantial additional freight movements to the Far East if necessary.

The BAM not only will be of great local significance, but will play a highly important role as a transit route. The above-mentioned interaction with the present Trans-Siberian will produce heavy freight traffic between Lena and Tynda; somewhat lower freight movements between Tynda and Urgal, and the lowest traffic volume in the east between Urgal and Komsomol'sk. In general eastbound movements will be far greater than westbound freight. The busiest transit junction will be Tynda, with heavy coal traffic from southern Yakutia intersecting the eastbound flows of crude oil, timber and other commodities.

The design and construction of the BAM follow the norms of railroads of the first category, equipped with advanced traction and operating equipment with a view to future expansion of the line's carrying capacity, especially in the western section between Lena and Tynda. The BAM is scheduled to go into full regular operation in 1983; partial traffic will open on segments as they are completed.

As a result of the construction of the BAM, Eastern Siberia and the Far East will acquire an east-west transport route running parallel to the Trans-Siberian and fostering the accelerated economic development of the eastern regions.

Chapter 5

ECONOMIC IMPACT OF THE BAM

Pavel G. Bunich

In implementing the program of construction of the material and technical foundations of communism, the party's Central Committee and the Soviet Government are consistently following a course of accelerating scientific-technical progress, developing the nation's productive forces on a growing scale and enhancing the efficacy of social production. A special role in the implementation of this course belongs to the development of resources in Siberia and the Far East and to construction of the Baykal-Amur Mainline, which is of extraordinarily great economic significance. In terms of the inputs of materials and labor, the scale of construction work, its economic and socio-political significance, and its impact on the nation's economic development, the BAM is really a grandiose project.

The BAM and the Overcoming of the Transport Barrier on the Development of the Far East

The length of the railroad from Ust'-Kut to Komsomol'sk is 3,145 kilometers, and if the completed sections between Tayshet and Ust'-Kut (680 km) and between Komsomol'sk and Sovetskaya Gavan' (450 km) are added, the overall length of the rail line to the Pacific coast is 4,275 km. True, the segment between Komsomol'sk and Sovetskaya Gavan' is already connected to the present Trans-Siberian, but as long as there is no special outlet for the BAM to the coast, this segment will also handle traffic from the BAM.

The portion of the BAM that runs through the Far East economic region, from Tynda to Komsomol'sk, accounts for 46 percent of the total length to be built, 41 percent of the earth-moving work, 38 percent of the engineering structures, 48 percent of the large bridges and 41 percent of the cost of productive construction. About one-third of the alignment runs through plains and two-thirds through mountains. If the Amur Oblast segment to the west of Tynda is included, the share of the eastern portion of the line would be even greater.

Construction will require large outlays for both productive and nonproductive facilities. A total of 222 million cubic meters of earth will have to be moved. There will be 3,200 engineering structures, including 136 bridges of more than 100 meters each (of which 16 bridges will be more than 300 meters each). The line will traverse seven mountain ranges and four tunnels with a combined length of 25.3 km, one of which, the North Muya tunnel, will be 15 km long. The laying of track in the permafrost zone will pose particular problems.

Freight traffic in an eastbound direction will initially amount to 35 million tons a year, including 25 million tons of crude oil (for greater detail on the engineering aspects of the BAM, see the other contributions in the present volume.

The width of the zone served by the BAM will vary from place to place. It will depend mainly on the efficacy of development of new areas and the expansion of existing areas. On the average, the tributary zone would extend 150 to 200 km to the north and about the same distance to the south, which along the entire BAM would represent an area of 1.0 to 1.5 million km^2, or 5 to 8 percent of the Soviet Union. Development projects within that zone may ultimately rival Magnitogorsk, the Kuznetsk Basin, Bratsk and Tyumen' is magnitude.

The BAM is expected to have a major impact on the further development of the Far Eastern economy. This is evident from research data and from the initial calculations of design institutes that provided convincing grounds for the need for the BAM project. The next job will be to study the tributary region from the point of view of the development of the economy and an inventory of resources, without which optimal sites for industrial establishments and cities cannot be picked. This will require more work by geological agencies, industrial research institutes and design agencies with a view to selecting optimal alternatives. The research establishments of the Academy of Sciences, including its Far Eastern Research Center, are involved in this effort. Detailed investigations are still ahead of us, but some general conclusions can already be stated.

Transportation has thus far been one of the limiting factors in the development of the Far East. In view of its huge area, relatively limited local demand and the scarcity of rail lines, the mean length of haul in the Far East has been about 10 to 11 times greater than the Soviet average [the mean length of haul on all forms of transport in the USSR was about 180 km in 1973; the mean length of haul in the Far East would thus be 1,800 to 2,000 km—Editor]. The transport component of the cost of goods in the region exceeds the Soviet average by 40 to 50 percent. That is basically why this economic region, with 6.2 million m^2, or one-third of the Soviet Union, is also the least populous region. The mean population density is one person per km^2. The Far East accounts for 2.4 percent of the Soviet Union's population, and an even smaller portion of the aggregate product—2.3 percent.

And yet the region is extraordinarily rich in resources, which in view of the gradual depletion of resources or the lower efficacy of resource use in the western regions would seem to call for a regrouping of productive forces in favor of the Far East.

Where is the development of new parts of the Far East supposed to begin? G. M. Krzhizhanovskiy used to say quite aptly that the main problem in the development of these areas is the struggle against space. The key to enhancing the economic role of the region is the development of transport routes that would provide access to undeveloped areas. The BAM is a concrete step in that direction. It will help open up new areas that will thus be able to sell their product and participate in the social division of labor. Rail "tentacles" will penetrate into coal deposits (Chul'man and Zeya-Selemdzha areas) and iron deposits (Aldan area). The first of these lines is already being built (Tynda-Berkakit [Chul'man] almost 400 km long). Ultimately the BAM may serve as the base for the construction of rail lines to Yakutsk, to Udskoye and, in the distant future, to Magadan. Such a rail line would reduce the distance to Pacific ports by several hundred kilometers, thus lowering freight costs.

In connection with the construction of the BAM, the carrying capacity of the line from Komsomol'sk to Sovetskaya Gavan' will evidently have to be increased. Otherwise it would be unable to carry the freight flow of two transcontinental lines at once [the Trans-Siberian and the BAM]. Other alternatives should be investigated, including the construction of a separate outlet for the BAM to the coast.

The BAM will also help stimulate the development of other forms of transport. A system of motor roads will be needed to carry goods over short distances. They might run north and south from the BAM, possibly to the Trans-Siberian. Over the long term one may have to consider the construction of east-west motor roads to make fuller use of motor transport.

The new rail line also enhances the potential of river transport, both on large and small streams. Air-cushion vehicles might be used on the smallest rivers. The possibility of combined river-sea freight movements has already been demonstrated, so that part of the freight on reaching Komsomol'sk via the BAM might be transferred to river-going ships going down the Amur River to Sakhalin, Magadan and the Okhotsk coast.

The railroad will also affect sea-going transport by creating a need for supertankers, large ore and timber carriers, and container ships, and requiring the reconstruction of ports and the construction of new ports, especially oil terminals. The construction of the rail line will be combined with pipelines. [Editor's note: The plan is to transport West Siberian crude oil by pipeline as far east as Tayshet, then by tank-car unit trains to Urgal, and then again by pipeline to Pacific ports.]

The construction of the BAM will require the building of airfields both along the western and the eastern segments, and the provision of helicopter pads.

The construction of the new transcontinental line will thus help alleviate the transport constraint on regional development and make it possible to initiate the production of transport-intensive commodities. Such a trend would also be fostered by the fact that westbound movements along the BAM are expected to be below capacity.

New Trends in the Development of Industry in the Far East

The construction of the rail line will help develop a large energy potential. Predicted coal reserves in southern Yakutia are estimated at 40 billion tons. The coal, mainly high-grade coking coal, lies near the surface and can be strip-mined. The Neryungri deposit, 40 kilometers southwest of Chul'man, has been explored in detail, with commercially accessible reserves of 486.7 million tons, including 349.7 million tons of coking coal. The capacity of the proposed strip mine is 12 million tons a year. Mining is scheduled to begin in 1978 after the mine is reached by the Bam—Tynda—Berkakit railroad. The Bureya coal deposit in Amur Oblast is also of interest.

The BAM will help open up oil and gas resources in the Lena-Vilyuy province. Predicted gas reserves have been estimated at 12 trillion cubic meters. There are also prospects for such resources in southern Yakutia.

The great navigable streams in the BAM zone—the Zeya, Gilyuy, Selemdzha, Bureya and Amgun'—have a hydroelectric potential. Some of these sites are soon to be used (for example, the Zeya site), others are to be built in the near future (the Neryungri station [Editor's note: This appears to be an error. The Neryungri station is to be a coal-fired station using local coal.] The hydro stations, aside from generating electric power, would also help regulate the sudden changes of streamflow that are characteristic of the permafrost zone, where rainwater and spring meltwater run off straight into river channels with little infiltration.

As a result, the Far East will not only cease to be an energy-short region, but in fact will begin to attract energy-intensive industries (chemicals, metallurgical, including aluminum). And it is not only a matter of increases in the supply of energy, but the local availability of cheap energy resources, particularly coal and gas, which would help reduce the costs of production in the Far East. This would be an effective way of eliminating the gap between the presence of huge energy resources and the growing need for energy in the West, where fuels are becoming increasingly short.

The Far East was long regarded as a steel-consuming region. The Amurstal' steel plant, which uses scrap, has been inadequate to meet regional needs. This situation is expected to change over the long term. The elimination of the transport and energy constraints, combined with the presence of rich iron-ore and coking-coal resources and rising demand both within the region and in nearby foreign areas, will make it possible to establish a new Soviet iron and steel base in the Far East. The requirements for regional needs and for export are estimated at 9 million tons of pig iron, 10 million tons of crude steel and 9 million tons of rolled products. This would have to be the capacity of an integrated iron and steel plant. It would help expand the development of machine-building, construction and other steel-consuming industries in the marketing zone of such a new plant.

The large iron ore resources are found in the Tayezhnoye, Pionerskoye and Sivagli deposits of the Aldan iron-ore district, 80 to 100 km north of the Chul'man coal deposit. The predictive ore resources are estimated at 2.5 to 3 billion tons. Other ore deposits in the Chara-Tokko and Olekma-Amga deposits, 150 to 400 km to the west and northwest of Chul'man, are said to have predictive reserves of at least 10 billion tons, and even larger ones are being mentioned. The confirmed ore reserves in the Aldan district are 1.5 billion tons.

The economics of iron and steel production should be quite favorable in view of the proximity of coal and ore, the presence of the Zeya hydro station and others, the availability of other ingredients needed by an iron and steel plant, and the relatively low cost of building materials. Several alternative plant sites need to be investigated with a view of selecting the optimal location in terms of the cost of end-products at market destinations. The iron and steel complex should be so located as to be in the center of the principal market zone.

The construction of the BAM will also improve prospects for the chemical industry. The newly available energy and transport facilities, combined with a growing regional need for fertilizers required for the use of low-productivity soils that are common in the Far East and in the BAM zone, would suggest the need for investment in a phosphatic fertilizer industry based on the Seligdar apatites in the central Aldan district, estimated at several billion tons of reserves. The production of phosphorus concentrates might be possible in the Uda-Selemdzha area, in the north of Khabarovsk Kray.

Energy plus Yakutian gas will furnish the basis for a number of chemical industries. Some types of coking coal can also be used for coke gas, ammonia and other coke chemicals. A integrated chemical complex might yield urea, lavsan [the Soviet polyester fiber], formaldehyde, etc. Peat, which is available in huge amounts in the BAM zone, might be used for making tars, paraffin, anthracene and other chemical products. Wood processing also yields chemical byproducts.

One of the basic reasons for the economic underdevelopment of the Far East has been an uneven distribution of productive forces. This aspect, which is inevitable in pioneering stages of development, led to increased transport costs of hauling building materials to remote areas that had no local supplies, raised the cost of industrial construction because of the need of providing infrastructure, such as roads, hospitals and social community centers, and led to a duplication of foundry, repair and tooling services, which also increased costs. All these features of Far Eastern development will be alleviated and ultimately eliminated by the construction of the BAM, thus raising the efficacy of development and thus accelerating regional growth.

Investment will be particularly effective in the multipurpose use of natural resources through deep processing to the manufacture of end-products. This applies to the use of all coproducts in the mining of nonferrous metals, the reduction of wood waste in logging, the enrichment of ores, the development of the final stages of the pulp and paper industry, the use of waste products, etc.

The concentration of production along the alignment and in the zone of influence of the BAM (combined with a rapidly growing Siberian economy and the expansion of foreign trade with countries of the Pacific and Indian oceans) will create a substantial regional demand for manufactured products. As a result there will be accelerated development of machine-building (with feedback stimulation of iron and steel production), light industry, glass, printing and some food-processing industries, which in turn will help overcome the uneven distribution of productive forces and foster Far Eastern specialization increasingly in manufacturing industries. Over the long term, the region's production structure will approach that of the highly developed regions of the Soviet Union.

Accelerated Development of Traditional Industries of
the Soviet Far East

In addition to fostering the appearance of new economic activities, the BAM will also accelerate the growth of the traditional industries of the Far East. The construction of the BAM and associated transport routes will stimulate the development of nonferrous metallurgy. There are good prospects for a rise of gold production in Amur Oblast, especially from lode deposits. To the northwest of Komsomol'sk are the large Badzhal and Komsomol'sk tin deposits, where a concentrating complex yielding some of the cheapest tin in the Soviet Union will be expanded and a new tin smelter is being built.

Adjoining the Far Eastern region are the copper, sulfur and silver reserves of Udokan in Chita Oblast. There are also large deposits of molybdenum, tungsten, mercury, bauxites, rare and disseminated elements, and phlogopite mica.

The new railroad will also stimulate development of forest industries. The construction of the BAM will help open up 40 million hectares of Siberian and Far Eastern tayga with timber reserves of roughly 2 billion cubic meters. Over the long term, the area may yield 5 to 6 million cubic meters of wood a year (including spruce and fir).

The rates of growth of the industry will depend on the introduction of technology for converting deciduous and low-grade wood into chips for use in the manufacture of particle board and pulp and for export. One of the possible end-products of this type of material is paper. The USSR now makes 14 percent of its paper from this material, but this is far from being the limit, especially in the case of newsprint, which the developed countries make out of low-grade wood up to 22 to 24 percent of total output. This share is to be virtually doubled by the year 2000.

The fishery industry, one of the oldest in the Far East, will also expand as a number of fish-rich streams are made accessible, fish hatcheries are created around hydroelectric stations, the limiting impact of inadequate rail transportation on the unloading of fish-laden vessels is eliminated and the length of haul for fishery products is reduced (fishing vessels might, for example, unload in the Sakhalin port of Kholmsk, from where the processed fish might move by rail ferry to the mainland [at Sovetskaya Gavan'], which would be cheaper than transporting them through the ports of Maritime Kray).

A special comment needs to be made about the future of agriculture. The expansion of industry, transportation, construction and housing will tend to draw more people into the Far East, espcially into the BAM zone, and thus increase the demand for farm products.

Along the BAM alignment there are some areas suitable for farming; others have infertile brown bog soils, large swamps and extensive permafrost. A large part of the zone is mountainous. Areas along the BAM are affected by large diurnal and seasonal temperature ranges and a short frost-free period. Areas suitable for agriculture tend to be scattered, at great distances from settlements and deprived of good transport links with processing centers and markets.

Priority should be given to the local processing of perishable produce, such as fresh meat, dietetic eggs, fresh milk, vegetables and fruits. This requires the construction of poultry and dairy farms in the BAM zone together with meat-packing plants and milk plants as well as the cultivation of vegetables both in open fields (cabbage, potatoes) and in spring-winter greenhouses (a wide range of vegetables). Feed grains need to be cultivated for livestock herds. The expansion of agriculture will also require some land reclamation and the use of fertilizer.

Shortages of farm produce that are to be expected in the early stages should be overcome through a redistribution of produce within the Far East and imports from Siberia and other parts of the country.

The construction of the BAM may also help stimulate other forest activities and the raising of reindeer.

The BAM and Foreign Trade

The BAM will play a key role in expanding foreign trade with the countries of the Pacific basin and the Indian Ocean. These include both highly developed countries and developing countries that are rapidly shaping their national economies. Many of them are interested in expanding trade with the USSR. The USSR, in turn, wants to expand trade with foreign countries. This expansion has proceeded at a particularly rapid rate in recent years, and will be further stimulated by the BAM.

The rail project will be important, in particular, for hauling wood products and South Yakutian coking coals to Japan and for implementing plans for the joint development of the Yakutian gas fields. The Japanese Export-Import Bank has extended to the Soviet Union a credit of $1.05-billion for the purchase of equipment, ships, building materials and consumer goods in Japan. The credit is to be repaid by Soviet deliveries of wood products, coal and gas. Total exports to Japan will, of course, be much greater. For example, compared with a Japanese credit of $450-million for the development of the coking coal deposit, total coal exports will be worth $4-billion. An export-oriented wood-processing complex is planned for the Tynda area.

The USSR and Japan have also concluded an agreement for the exploration and extraction of oil or gas on the continental shelf around Sakhalin. Under the accord, Japan will finance geological exploration over a 10-year period, extending a commercial credit of $100-million for the first five years. If, after that period, the two parties decide to continue the exploration program, Japan will extend an additional credit of $100-million, for the purchase of offshore drilling rigs, special-purpose vessels and other equipment needed for the exploration program. The credit would be repaid with deliveries of oil or gas from the jointly developed deposits.

Prospects are also good for an expansion of foreign trade between the USSR and Australia. The Soviet Union is now supplying chemicals, wood, textiles, nonferrous metals, machines, machine tools, fish and other goods, and is buying wool, manufactured goods, sugar and meat.

Aside from handling export goods, the BAM will also carry Soviet imports as well as goods moving in transit through the Soviet Union to Europe. This transit flow from Japan to Western Europe amounted to 50,000 containers of 20 to 30 tons in 1974. The container flow is expected to expand after completion of the BAM.

The railroad's impact on the development of ocean-going transport, shipbuilding, ship repair, foreign trade, offshore extraction of oil and gas, fisheries, the creation of seaside resorts, and an expansion of ocean cruises represent the BAM's contribution to economic development of oceanic activities, which in our view will be an important trend in the future.

Integrated Approach to the Construction of the BAM

The accelerated construction of the BAM will require smooth coordination of the work of many ministries, agencies and industrial establishments. It will involve construction agencies, suppliers of building materials and transport equipment, transport agencies, electric power suppliers, vocational training, retailing organizations, and research institutes. In an effort to insure smooth coordination, BAM construction activities figure separately in the government's economic plan starting in 1975. In addition, the contributions to the project by individual ministries are planned as part of their activities. So far the BAM program includes only its transport aspect, and it would be desirable in the future to extend the program planning to all economic activities that will be generated by the new railroad.

Within the BAM, viewed as a big system, we can distinguish several subsystems, such as the Aldan-Chul'man coal and steel complex, the Komsomol'sk industrial complex and, over the long term, the Uda-Selemdzha industrial district. A programmed planning of these complexes should be designed to foster the development of electric power, transport, auxiliary activities, infrastructure, etc., for all economic activities combined, and not for each activity separately. This would insure the highest degree of synthesis between spatial and sectoral planning, financing and management and insure economic benefits deriving from agglomeration, a better and balanced coordination of all types of supplies, a unity of material and financial allocations and integrated decision-making for all operational problems.

The development of the BAM zone will require a large amount of labor. In view of the fact that the developed portions of the Far East have long suffered from a shortage of labor, there is no point in counting on a redistribution of labor resources within the region; additional labor will have to be brought in from other parts of the country.

This can be achieved only by providing superior living conditions in the zone of future industrial development, including comfortable housing, a high level of services and the provision of high-quality foods and consumer goods so that the purchasing power of the population can be satisfied.

Workers associated with the BAM project will be entitled to a regional wage increment of 70 percent for the duration of the construction work as well as benefits established for the Far North and equivalent areas. They will also receive the maximum lump-sum payment for resettlement. The Construction Bank has been

142

authorized to grant resettlement credits of 500 rubles per worker, to be repaid within three years. This is the only way to attract hundreds of thousands of new workers to the project. Labor turnover has been very costly for the Soviet economy. It tends to reduce labor discipline and the productivity of labor, and results in a waste of travel payments. The outlays set aside for attracting labor to the BAM zone will be greater than those used for the southern portion of the Far East, and certainly greater than in other parts of the Soviet Union.

With a view of reducing labor requirements, it would be economically justified to introduce a maximum of labor-saving technology in the BAM project. This will, of course, raise the cost of construction and operation of new factories, mines and state farms, especially since more skilled labor will have to be employed. But the number of "physical" units will be reduced, and that is the most important thing in saving on infrastructure outlays. The point is not simply to provide the worker with more machines. This is justified only for some kinds of equipment. One might, for example, seek to increase the number of machine tools, trucks, ocean-going and river vessels that are in short supply. But once full mechanization has been achieved, there is no point in installing new machine tools similar to existing older equipment. There would be no available factory space nor unused labor. A more general principle would be to design special-purpose technology that would minimize labor inputs. The additional energy requirements involved in such an approach could be met by expanding and unifying the fuels and energy system, which in turn would also help achieve labor economies.

The proposed development of new industries both for the domestic market and for export as well as all the auxiliary activities and housing will require a large volume of construction, the creation of new construction agencies and expansion of the production of building materials and the manufacture of construction equipment. Otherwise, construction will become expensive and the rates of construction will be slowed down, making it again a bottleneck in economic development.

The building materials industry is already provided with an adequate resource base. Along the BAM alignment are deposits of limestone, for use in the cement industry; perlite and vermiculite, used as porous fillers; building stone and facing materials.

Economic development in the BAM zone must seek to preserve the natural environment. An effort must be made to prevent railroads, motor roads, power transmission lines and logging operations from disturbing the permafrost, which may cause melting of the frozen ground, flooding and gullying in the case of loams, or desiccation in the case of the skeletal soils of hillslopes. Bare rocks on hillslopes have a natural tendency to generate rock streams and mudflows, likely to cause great damage to the economy and population. Building-material quarries and other open-cut mines that violate the "rules" of the permafrost may be subject to seasonal flooding.

In the forest industry, potential logging areas will have to be carefully selected to insure reforestation and preserve the nature-conservation functions of forests. Conifers often grow along riverbank ridges that help contain spring floods and should therefore be preserved. Logging in such areas may cause riverbank erosion,

143

increase the turbidity of the water, and disturb fisheries and the entire river regime. The vegetation cover also needs to be preserved on hillslopes, along roads and cultivated fields, around cities and towns (if only to save heating costs), and in recreation zones.

Fisheries also require special treatment in the area. Fishes tend to reproduce slowly in the cold, so that provisions must be made for annual fishing quotas, the most favored spawning areas, and artificial fostering of the natural fertility of waterbodies.

Chemical plants, iron and steel mills, pulp and paper mills, electric power stations and other industrial establishments use a great deal of water and generate wastewater. This wastewater poses a particular threat in the BAM zone both because self-purification processes tend to be slowed by the low water temperature, and because biological waste treatment techniques are not effective in winter. Special waste treatment methods are therefore required in the Far East if the resources of large and small streams are to be preserved. An effort must also be made to preserve spawning areas in the building of bridges over small rivers.

Climatic peculiarities and the prevailing direction of winds must be considered in siting industrial establishments and population centers with a view of reducing their negative impact. Seismic activity must also be borne in mind in the selection of construction sites. Nature reserves, protected areas and experimental plots for ecological studies must be set aside in the zone for long-term studies of the impact of reclamation on waterlogged soils and the selection of crop varieties adapted to northern conditions.

The BAM can rightly be regarded as a nationwide project. Thousands of people from all walks of life are expected to participate. The success of the project will depend on the coordination of activities among ministries and agencies, planning and design institutes and the organization of widespread socialist emulation among construction workers, the employes of survey, research and design agencies and among industrial establishments for timely fulfillment of orders for the BAM project.

Chapter 6

THE BAM AND ITS ECONOMIC
GEOGRAPHY

Oleg A. Kibal'chich

Along with such major spatial development problems as resource development in the West Siberian plain, the development of power-intensive industries in the Angara-Yenisey region, and land reclamation and the transformation of agriculture and rural settlement in the Nonchernozem zone of the RSFSR, the present stage of construction of the material and technical basis of communism in the Soviet Union also requires a decided upsurge of economic development east of Lake Baykal and provision for increasing volumes of freight hauls in that region.

The principal means of resolving this problem is the construction of the Baykal-Amur Mainline from Ust'-Kut (on the Lena River) to Komsomol'sk (on the Amur). Speaking in 1974 at the 17th congress of the Komsomol [Young Communist League], L. I. Brezhnev said: "The Baykal-Amur Mainline will cut through the age-old tayga, passing through areas with huge resources that must be placed at the disposal of the Motherland. A great new industrial district of the Soviet Union will be created there together with new cities and settlements."

This is not the first time that rail transport, with its reliability and huge freight-carrying potential, will be used as a means of bringing disparate territories closer together and thus making use of the benefits offered by a geographical division of labor. The first attempt at such economic maneuverability was the creation of the Urals-Kuznetsk combine, which linked the cheap iron ore of Magnitogorsk and the coking coal of the Kuznetsk Basin by means of a modernized Trans-Siberian Railroad. Then followed the Turkestan-Siberia Railroad, the Pechora mainline, the rail lines in the virgin lands of Kazakhstan, and the Lena railroad. Each of these helped to develop new resource areas and to expand the economically active zone of the Soviet Union.

Now the turn of the Baykal-Amur Mainline is at hand. There has long been a need for that railroad. Surveys have been conducted along its alignment since the 1930s. Construction on some segments of the line began on the eve of the Great

145

Patriotic War [World War II]. But the realization of this "construction project of the century" has become possible only at the present time, when the economic power of the Soviet state has been significantly enhanced and it is able to muster the billions of rubles of investment in the BAM while attending to other important problems of development of a communist society.

The new transport outlet from the inland areas of the USSR to the Pacific coast will make possible an increase in Soviet exports, particularly to Japan, whose economy has been traditionally dependent on large imports of raw materials, fuels and semifinished goods.

A second, no less important and even more grandiose objective of the BAM is to accelerate the economic development of huge areas of East Siberia and Far East. This applies, in particular, to resource use in an area about one-twentieth of the Soviet Union that adjoins the railroad. The economic potential created in this area by the new rail line will ultimately serve as a bridgehead for further advance into the Northeast of the USSR with additional resources of raw materials, fuels and hydroelectric energy.

The BAM construction program is essentially designed to improve transportation in the region between Tayshet, in the west, and Sovetskaya Gavan' in the east. Much of the work is to be done during the new, 10th five-year plan [1976–80]. The BAM mainline between Lena Station (at Ust'-Kut) and Komsomol'sk on the Amur is to be built in 1974–1983; the connecting line Bam–Tynda–Berkakit in 1974–1977, and the present Lena Railroad, from Tayshet through Bratsk to Ust'-Kut, is to be double-tracked in 1974–1982. In addition, steps are to be taken to increase the carrying capacity of the Trans-Siberian Railroad between Tayshet and Khabarovsk and of the rail line between Komsomol'sk and Sovetskaya Gavan' (Fig. 1).

This transport system also includes the rail ferry between Vanino (at Sovetskaya Gavan') and the Sakhalin port of Kholmsk. The length of haul from Tayshet to the ports on Sakhalin, Kamchatka, the Okhotsk coast and Chukotka over the BAM will be almost 1,000 kilometers shorter than over the present Trans-Siberian.

The most important and most difficult task in this entire project will be the construction of the single-track BAM mainline, 3,150 km long. It will run 180 to 300 km north of the Trans-Siberian, mainly through inaccessible portions of the Stanovoy uplands (with elevations of up to 3,000 meters) and across outliers of the Stanovoy mountain range that will complicate the laying of the roadbed.

Construction will he hampered not only by mountains and foothills, but by the entire set of environmental conditions, including a harsh climate, permafrost, landslides, ground ice, an abundance of rivers and swamps as well as a high level of seismicity.

The area through which the railroad will be laid has a highly varied environment. High mountain ranges alternate with intermontane basins, which are deeply incised and almost totally closed in, causing temperature inversions in winter, stagnation of cold air and the threat of smog. Slope stability is also unusual in the area. The firmest slopes occur in the upper portions of average declivity, while the

146

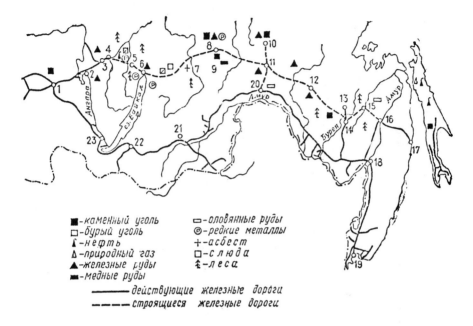

Fig. 1. Map of the Baykal-Amur Mainline project.

Legend: bituminous coal tin ore
brown coal rare metals
petroleum asbestos
natural gas mica
iron ore timber
copper ore

railroads in operation
railroads under construction

Numbers key:

1–Tayshet	9–Udokan	17–Sovetskaya Gavan'
2–Bratsk	10–Berkakit	18–Khabarovsk
3–Ust'-Kut	11–Tynda	19–Vladivostok
4–Lena	12–Nora	20–Bam
5–Kunerma	13–Chegdomyn	21–Chita
6–Nizhneangarsk	14–Urgal	22–Ulan-Ude
7–Molodezhnyy	15–Berezovka	23–Irkutsk
8–Chara	16–Komsomol'sk	

gentle lower portions consist of unconsolidated material. This makes it difficult to lay the roadbed along basin bottoms. Landslides are common all along the BAM alignment.

Up to 2,000 earth tremors are recorded each year in the BAM zone, which is one of the seismically most active segments of the earth's surface. Earthquakes of up to 9 or 10 points [on the Mercalli scale] may be recorded. One such tremor occurred in June 1957 in the North Muya mountain range, not far from the BAM alignment.

The relationship between the condition of the permafrost and the magnitude of earthquakes is a highly complex one, but scholars have observed that destruction of the permafrost tends to increase the threat of seismic events. Therefore construction techniques along the BAM route should be so designed as to preserve the permafrost. Both the preservation of permafrost and the provision of earthquake protection measures will have the effect of raising construction costs.

The BAM will cross seven major mountain ranges (Baykal, North Muya, Kodar, Udokan, Dusse-Alin' and others) and more than 3,000 streams, including such major rivers as the Lena, Kirenga, Upper Angara, Vitim, Olekma, Nyukzha, Gilyuy, Zeya, Selemdzha, Bureya, Amgun'. More than 3,000 engineering structures will be required to overcome mountain ranges, gorges, river valleys and swamps; they will include four tunnels (through the Baykal, North Muya, Kodar and Dusse-Alin' ranges) and 140 major bridges.

The most difficult construction segment will be the mountainous western portion of the BAM between Ust'-Kut and Tynda, where twice as many engineering structures will be required per kilometer as in the eastern portion. To the east of Tynda, gentler landforms prevail, with the relatively low outliers of the Stanovoy mountain range passing into the Lower Amur plain.

The rate of construction of the Trans-Siberian east of Lake Baykal at the end of the 19th century was 0.6 kilometer a day. The planned rate of construction of the BAM will be 2.5 times greater.

It should be remembered that the Trans-Siberian was built under more favorable environmental conditions and through a more highly populated territory. The proposed rates of construction along the BAM are to be achieved by means of large-capacity construction equipment and the use of advanced technology. Bridges, for example, will be assembled from prefabricated lightweight sections, including corrugated iron pipe. This will insure a rapid rate of construction and a high degree of strength in the completed structures.

The acceleration of construction will be made possible by the fact that work can be done simultaneously in several areas: From Ust'-Kut and from Komsomol'sk as well as both east and west from Tynda.

The BAM is being designed as a first-class rail line, using a heavy-duty track that can be easily maintained despite intensive use.

Over a distance of 350 km the railroad will pass through the drainage basin of Lake Baykal. Everything possible is to be done to disturb the natural condition of this unique waterbody and riparian areas as little as possible.

148

The latest advances in railroad engineering are to be used in the BAM project. The western segment from Ust'-Kut to Nizhneangarsk, which is closest to the great Bratsk and Ust'-Ilimsk hydro stations, is to be electrified, and the rest of the railroad will be using diesel traction. [Editor's note: The electrified segment will actually extend beyond Nizhneangarsk as far as the east portal of the North Muya tunnel.] Traffic will be handled by high-speed unit trains and automatic controls. Signals and switches will be watched by dispatchers to insure complete traffic safety. Electric engines and diesel engines are to be equipped with automatic signals. This will enable locomotive drivers to operate even under conditions of poor visibility.

The Bam-Tynda line, 180 km long, was completed in 1975 between the Trans-Siberian and the future BAM railroad. This connecting line is being extended northward toward Berkakit and the Chul'man coal basin [at Neryungri] over a distance of 270 km that will require a great deal of earthwork. The line will have to cross the Stanovoy mountain range through a tunnel, and the entire 450-km line is ultimately to be electrified.

The second railroad to the Pacific coast and the spur from southern Yakutia will thus meet all the requirements of modern railroad engineering. The entire rail system will serve as a powerful stimulus in the economic development of the eastern regions and foster a greater geographical division of labor between those regions and the Soviet Union's foreign trade partners.

This transport net will provide the basis for a long-term development program in the eastern regions of the USSR.

The natural resources of the area to be served by the BAM are huge. Foremost in diversity, reserves and importance for the national economy are mineral resources.

Copper is one of the key metals of today. It is required in ever growing amounts by electrical engineering industries. The Soviet Union's largest copper deposit with a relatively high metal content in the ore has been discovered and explored in the northern part of Chita Oblast, in the Udokan area. This discovery and the preparation of the deposit for commercial development have been an important achievement of Soviet geologists. In terms of reserves, Udokan alone is the equal of the copper reserves at Dzhezkazgan. But near Udokan are still three other large deposits—Syul'ban, Unkur and Krasnoye. Large copper-nickel deposits have also been identified.

In recent years attention has been focused on the coal basin in the southern portion of the Aldan plateau, with total reserves of more than 40 billion metric tons. In addition to steam coals, the basin contains high-grade coking coal. It is the only major coking-coal deposit east of the Yenisey River, and is suitable for strip mining. The thickness of the coal seam in the Neryungri deposit is more than 50 meters, and it contains more than 500 million tons of high-calory coal.

Near the coking-coal deposits lies the large Aldan iron-ore province, with reserves estimated at 20 billion tons. The best known deposit is Tayezhnoye, whose ores have a mean metal content of 42 percent. A large portion of the deposit can be mined by open-pit methods. Several deposits of relatively rich magnetite ores have also been explored in the Aldan district—Pionerskoye, Sivagli and Desovskoye. In the northern portion of Chita Oblast, in the immediate vicinity of the BAM alignment, geologists have discovered large reserves of iron quartzites of the Krivoy Rog type. Ore reserves in these two districts are sufficient for a major iron and steel complex in the Far East.

In northern Buryatia, 25 kilometers from the BAM route, is the Molodezhnyy asbestos deposit, which was explored in the 1960s. In total reserves it is up to the level of the world-famous Thetford Mines and Black Lake area in Canada, and in reserves of textile-grade long-staple fibers, the Buryat deposit has no equal in the world.

In Transbaykalia and in Khabarovsk Kray, geologists have also identified significant deposits of nickel, tin, tungsten, molybdenum, lead, zinc, mercury, mica, nephelite, apatite and a wide range of building materials. Prospecting for oil and natural gas is under way. The Yarakta oil and gas deposit in the interfluve between the Lena River and the Lower Tunguska is already known. A number of mineral springs have also been identified along the BAM route, ranging in type from Narzan and Matsesta waters to Karlovy Vary waters. They can be put into commercial use with relative ease.

Over a substantial distance the BAM will traverse the zone of the Siberian and Far Eastern tayga. The forest area in the BAM zone covers 20 million hectares, with timber reserves estimated at 4 billion cubic meters, including almost 2.5 billion cubic meters of mature and overmature tree stands. The best commercial timber occurs in the basins of the upper Lena, the Kirenga, Selemdzha, Amgun' and lower Amur. Permafrost areas (northern Buryatia, the northern portion of Chita Oblast and the northwest part of Amur Oblast) are covered with low growths of larch. They can also be used, but by means of chemical rather than mechanical processing technology.

Water resources also represent a major asset in the new development area. Of particular value are the pure freshwater reserves of Lake Baykal, the world's largest natural reservoir.

Some of the larger streams, such as the Lena, Kirenga, Vitim, Olekma, Zeya, Bureya and Amur, offer a potential for large hydroelectric stations. The first station, on the Zeya River is under construction in Amur Oblast. [Its first 215,000-kw unit was placed in operation in November 1975—Editor.] Engineering surveys are under way along the Vitim River and its tributaries. A whole series of large hydro stations is contemplated here. Calculations also suggest that a high level of economic benefit can be derived from the construction of hydro plants on the Bureya River.

The natural resources of the region that will be traversed by the BAM are so significant, and the need for them in the Soviet economy is so great, that economic development of the region will assume broad scope in future five-year plans, requiring large capital investments.

What will be the priority projects to be financed by these funds?

One of the principal tasks will be to generate mutually beneficial foreign trade through the Far East. Income from foreign economic relations, especially with Japan, will enable us to recoup the billions of rubles of investment that will be needed for resource development in the eastern regions of the USSR. Compensation deals in some cases will make it possible for us to develop resource sites along the BAM with imported, modern, highly productive technology and then pay for the technology with the resulting product.

Under an agreement signed in 1974, the USSR will have to ship more than 100 million tons of South Yakutian coking coal to Japan over a 20-year period. In the past Japan has been importing coking coal from the Kuznetsk Basin, at a rate of roughly 3 million tons a year. Shipments of South Yakutian coal will start in 1983 with 3.2 million tons a year and gradually increase to 5.5 million tons a year. Steam coals are also to be shipped from South Yakutia to Japan. Another accord with Japan calls for the delivery of 17.5 million cubic meters of log timber and 900,000 cubic meters of sawnwood over a five-year period.

For the development of the South Yakutian coal mine, the Soviet Union will import Japanese machinery and equipment, including machines adapted to extremely low winter temperatures. Large amounts of Japanese road-building equipment, transport equipment, logging and woodworking machinery are also expected to be delivered. All this technology will be purchased by the Soviet Union with Japanese credits.

There has long been discussion of the development of a new iron and steel complex east of Lake Baykal. The economic development associated with the construction of the BAM is now likely to increase the demand of iron and steel products for the construction of new rail lines, oil and gas pipelines, etc.

The presence in southern Yakutia of coking coal and iron ore within less than 100 kilometers of each other would seem to offer a good basis for the construction of an integrated iron and steel plant in the Chul'man area. However, the mountainous terrain and the harsh climate of the area pose serious problems in the operation of such a complex. Moreover, experience shows that iron and steel plants tend to attract additional industries such as coke-based chemicals, fertilizers, metalworking, etc., for which there are no favorable conditions in the Chul'man area. Thought should therefore be given to moving the second and third stages of the iron and steel cycle out of southern Yakutia into Amur Oblast or Khabarovsk Kray (into the Komsomol'sk area). On the other hand, it is possible that technological progress will help replace the blast-furnace technology with new techniques, such as direct conversion, making the site selection for an iron and steel complex in the Far East more flexible.

An important resource use in the BAM zone will be the mining of nonferrous and rare metals, especially the copper ores of Udokan and nearby deposits. The copper sulfide ores in the area can be mined by open-pit methods. Large-capacity excavating equipment and dump trucks are to be used for transporting the ore.

Only mining and concentrating facilities are to be located on the actual deposit in the Chara area. The Udokan copper concentrate is to be converted into blister copper and electrolytic copper in areas supplied with cheap electrical energy. Such a power-intensive industry is best combined with chemical production since the large amount of sulfuric acid obtained as a by-product of copper smelting is not easily transportable. There are suggestions that such a copper refining complex might be located at Tayshet, Lesosibirsk or Minusinsk.

Mining and concentrating complexes are also likely to develop in the northern portion of the Buryat ASSR where nonferrous and rare metals have been identified, particularly the Kholodnaya lead and zinc deposit. There are also important prospects for the further development of tin mining in the Komsomol'sk area (Solnechnyy and other deposits).

The general course of development of the forest products industry in the basins of the upper Lena, the Kirenga, Selemdzha, Amgun' and lower Amur will call for the construction of large and medium-size processing complexes that will yield a complete range of wood products, from sawnwood, plywood and prefabricated housing sections to woodpulp, paper, paperboard, yeast, chipboard and fiberboard. The largest logging enterprises and processing establishments are to be created in the areas of Ust'-Kut, Tayura, Kazachinskoye, Tynda, Zeya and in the upper reaches of the Vitim and the Selemdzha. Pulp and paper mills are being planned for Kazachinskoye, Kirensk, Svobodnyy and for Amursk (where the first stage is already operating).

Economic calculations suggest that the investment needed for development of the wood products industry in the BAM zone will be about equal to the combined investment in the iron, steel and nonferrous industries of the zone. The development of the timber lands in the area will transform it into a major Soviet producing area of a wide range of wood products.

A major role in the economic development of the entire region east of Lake Baykal will be played by electric power. The shortage of labor will tend to encourage high levels of mechanization and automation in all production processes, thus raising the electric power requirements per worker.

In the early stages of development of the BAM zone, power will be supplied largely by the Ust'-Ilimsk hydro station, which will transmit power to the east as far as the Udokan industrial node.

In the eastern segment of the BAM, the principal power source will be the Zeya hydroelectric station, where the first generating turbine unit was placed in operation in 1975. Future projects include the Mok hydro station of one million kw on the Vitim River as well as thermal stations based on Kansk-Achinsk, Kharanor, South Yakutian and Bureya coals. The design for the Neryungri thermal power station in the Chul'man area calls for a capacity of 600,000 kw in the first stage. Several heat and power stations will also be required for the technological needs of the wood-products complexes.

A key problem in the development of the BAM zone will be the expansion of crop production to provide food products to the growing population. Many parts of the BAM zone lack sufficient heat for the maturation of crops, and the growing season is only 40 to 90 days (with a minimum of 110 days needed for stable crop cultivation).

The task will be to use local pastures in stream valleys for the production of fresh milk, to raise early potatoes and vegetables wherever possible in open ground, and to produce other vegetables in hotbeds and greenhouses. Long-haul chicken feed might also be used for local egg and poultry production (broiler chickens). However most of the food will still have to be produced in adjacent areas of East Siberia and the Far East, within 500 to 600 km of the BAM. Those will be the basic supply areas for potatoes, milk and meat as well as feed for the dairy cattle. Cost estimates suggest that bread grains and feed grains will have to be hauled from southern areas of Western Siberia, and some vegetables from as far away as Central Asia.

Development designs in the BAM zone call for the creation not just of individual industrial establishments or groups of establishments, but integrated territorial-production complexes and groups of populated places conforming to modern concepts of spatial economic development. Ultimately there will be about a dozen medium-size complexes. So far only the rough outlines of the future complexes can be discerned since design studies are just beginning.

The development of the *Upper Lena* complex, covering the mountain tayga of Irkutsk Oblast along the upper reaches of the Lena and the Kirenga, should begin with the use of the large coniferous forest reserves in the area. The next stage might be associated with the development of oil and gas resources that have long been predicted in this area. Large hydro stations on the Lena and the Kirenga may provide the basis for power-intensive industries, including petrochemicals and salt-based chemicals.

The *North Baykal* complex, within northern Buryatia, on the other hand, should begin with the development of mining centers (asbestos, nonferrous and rare metals), to be joined at a later stage by wood-products industries. The construction of the Mok hydro station would greatly strengthen the electric power base of the complex.

The *Bodaybo* complex in the extreme northeast of Irkutsk Oblast (the Patoma upland) is already taking shape both as a mining district with a predominance of nonferrous metallurgy [gold] and mica mining. Also predominantly mining-oriented will be the *North Chita* complex, where the first project will be the development of the Udokan copper deposit.

A more complex structure is likely to arise in the *South Yakutian* complex. In addition to existing nonferrous metallurgy [gold] and mica mining, the complex may ultimately include a set of pyrometallurgical industries (coking coal, iron ore, refractories and iron and steel smelting). Over the next few years, coking coal will be the first resource to achieve commercial development. Electric power production will be based on local coals.

The *West Amur* complex, covering the western portion of Amur Oblast, should develop as a forest products area, with a predominance of sawmilling (the Zeya complex). There may also be some mining of nonferrous metals. Tynda and Zeya should become steel-fabricating and machine-manufacturing centers. The amelioration of agricultural land would help increase the local food supply. The main power generating base of the area will be the Zeya hydro station, with an ultimate capacity of 1.3 million kw.

The *Selemdzha-Urgal* complex will take shape in the eastern portion of Amur Oblast and the western part of Khabarovsk Kray. Here there are prospects for the expansion of logging operations and wood processing (sawmilling, plywood), and the mining of coal, iron ore, nonferrous and rare metals. The hydro potential of the Bureya River is also likely to be developed.

The *Lower Amur* complex is the most highly developed area in the BAM zone, with its center at Komsomol'sk, a city of 246,000. This complex is taking shape in the western portion of Khabarovsk Kray on the basis of both local and long-haul resources. The complex includes a number of interrelated activities: mechanical and chemical processing of wood, including the production of viscose fiber and fabrics; the mining of nonferrous metals (gold, tin); steel production [using scrap and long-haul pig iron—Editor]; transportation and hoisting equipment; and the production of vegetables, potatoes and fresh milk. Future activities that may be added include the processing of Tyumen' oil and Vilyuy natural gas, and the production of mineral fertilizer. Power generation will be largely coal-based, thus limiting the expansion of power-intensive petrochemical and nonferrous industries.

A broad industrial belt with an optimal system of settlement is thus likely to arise on both sides of the BAM over the next 20 to 30 years. It will include a number of cities (Ust'-Kut, Severobaykal'sk, Chara, Tynda, Neryungri, Zeya, Urgal and Amursk) with populations of up to 200,000, several dozen large workers' settlements and a host of rail-station settlements. All these populated places should fit harmoniously into the system of territorial production complexes rising in the new industrial region of the Soviet Union.

Bibliography

Anikin, N. I. *Stroyka veka* [The Construction Project of the Century]. Moscow: Transport, 1974.
"BAM, the concern of all Communists," *Ekonomicheskaya gazeta*, 1975, No. 6.
Biryukov, V. "The BAM, a major national economic construction project," *Planovoye khozyaystvo*, 1964, No. 10 [*Soviet Geography*, April 1975].
Degtyar', A. *BAM—nachalo* [BAM, the Beginning]. Moscow: Molodaya gvardiya, 1974.
Sobolev, Yu. A. "The BAM, a construction project of the entire nation," *Znaniya—narodu*, 1974, No. 11.
Tarasov, G. L. "The BAM, a transport and industrial complex," *Promyshlennyy transport*, 1974, No. 11.
Shinkarev, L. "The great blueprint of Siberia," *Novyy mir*, 1975, No. 1.
———. *Baykalo-Amurskaya magistral'* [The Baykal-Amur Mainline]. Moscow: Sovetskaya Rossiya, 1975.

Chapter 7

REGION-SHAPING FUNCTIONS
OF THE BAM

Oleg A. Kibal'chich

N. N. Kolosovskiy once said that "the investigation of transportation lines is the job of specialized transport institutes, but at the same time, transportation networks and the system of network hauls are to a large extent geographical problems closely linked to the overall system of economic regionalization of productive forces" (Reference 6). The two aspects are equally important in the case of BAM. Elsewhere we called attention to the large unit investment required by the project and to its unusually distant payoff (5), both of which, however, can be reduced and overcome through more appropriate engineering designs and the haulage of more valuable commodities (say, for export) as well as suitable development of adjacent territories.

The character of the interaction between the BAM as a pioneering transportation route and the future economy of these territories has been discussed from various points of view in the literature. Some authors have sought to portray the BAM as a decisive region-shaping factor at the upper level of economic regionalization (3, 8). Such an approach, however, tends to ignore the fact that the pioneering function of the BAM will be less significant than its role as a specialized transport route for hard-currency-earning export goods. Moreover, those authors tend to reduce the highly intricate process of region-formation and complex-formation (2) to the infrastructure aspect, which is admittedly an important factor, but certainly not the only factor in the formation of regional territorial-production complexes.

It would be appropriate, however, to envisage the zone of influence of the BAM as representing a new industrial area of the Soviet Union (11) with a "truncated" chain of technological production linkages, a high level of electric power supply per worker, rigorous conditions for the provision of specialized manpower to production enterprises, etc. It must be remembered that an industrial regionalization does not coincide with a general economic regionalization of a territory.

It needs to be borne in mind that the system of basic economic regions east of the Yenisey River still has not been adequately studied so that we find a wide variety of approaches to allocating particular middle-level regional structures to basic economic regions. Two approaches are the most common. One, based on the work of N. N. Kolosovskiy (7) and endorsed by the present author, is to distinguish the following regions:

Yenisey (Middle Siberia);
East Siberia (including Irkutsk and Chita oblasts, Buryat ASSR);
Yakutia;
Far East.

The other point of view, advocated particularly by V. A. Krotov (9), would provide for the following divisions:

Angara-Yenisey (including Krasnoyarsk Kray, Tuva ASSR, Irkutsk Oblast);
Transbaykalia (Buryat ASSR and Chita Oblast);
Amur Valley (Amur Oblast and Khabarovsk Kray);
Pacific;
Northeast.

(Without going into a detailed examination of the two proposed regional networks, we want to draw attention to a key aspect that would be significant in the future location of energy-intensive manufacturing activities based on mineral and forest resources along the BAM, but located outside the BAM zone as part of the process of "truncation" of production linkages. The two regional proposals differ, in particular, in the idea of delimiting a combined Angara-Yenisey economic region. Incidentally, the idea that the Angara-Yenisey energy-oriented industrial complex represents the basis for the East Siberian economic region and thus does not allow for a separation of Krasnoyarsk Kray and Irkutsk Oblast is quite widespread in the economic and economic-geographic literature. At first glance, the potential resources of the two areas would indeed appear to have a great deal in common [cheap hydroelectric resources, large lignite reserves, huge timber resources as well as raw materials for energy-intensive industries]. These requisites would seem to favor similar structures of cheap electric power generation, the refining of light metals, chemical industry, oil refining and petrochemicals, and wood processing. If we were to be logical to the end, we would have to admit that such similarities would actually not have an integrating impact bringing the two areas closer together, but would in fact drive them apart. Closer examination suggests, however, that there are significant differences between the two areas, providing an objective basis for the development of each in a separate economic region. The availability of cheap fuel resources in Krasnoyarsk Kray [lignite of the Kansk-Achinsk Basin—Editor] favors primarily the fuel-intensive industries based both on local and long-haul (crude oil) resources, while Irkutsk Oblast, with its vast cheap hydroelectric potential, would appear to favor mainly the development of power-intensive industries.)

At any rate, it is worth noting that neither regional proposal views the BAM zone as a single economic region; one proposed regional system divides it among the East Siberian, Yakutian and Far Eastern regions, and the other among the Angara-Yenisey, Transbaykal, Amur and Northeast regions.

156

It seems to us that it is precisely this economic-geographic situation of the BAM zone, at the juncture of several economic regions, that is its most characteristic feature, calling for more than one type of approach to the problem of economic location within the railroad zone. The BAM zone can be visualized as an arena of interaction for regions performing different functions within the nationwide division of labor.

Three basic types of interactions may be distinguished: (1) with East Siberia; (2) with the Northeast; (3) with the Far East.

The first type of interaction, between East Siberia and the BAM zone, may be viewed as a "bridgehead" function. The economic growth of the Cis-Baykal region, especially through the generation of cheap hydroelectric power and the development of power-intensive industries, has provided a "bridgehead" for further economic advance into the resource areas of Transbaykalia. Buryat ASSR and Chita Oblast, with large resources of heavy and rare metals and the absence of a cheap fuel base, operate in a different economic setting than Irkutsk Oblast. It would therefore seem tempting to develop the economy of these three major civil divisions within a single complex, based largely on the hydroelectric potential of the Cis-Baykal region. (It should be borne in mind that the large-scale transmission of electric power from Irkutsk Oblast westward to Krasnoyarsk Kray will not be rational over the long term because it would run counter to eastward movements of Kansk-Achinsk steam coals. It will therefore become all the more essential to transmit surplus power from Cis-Baykalia to Transbaykalia.)

In the first stage of development, the transport linkages within such an Irkutsk-Transbaykal complex would be insured by a rail transport ring (to be completed by the BAM project) linking Irkutsk with Chita and Bam Station along the Trans-Siberian Railroad; the Bam-Tynda connecting line; the Tynda-Chara—Ust'-Kut segment of the BAM; and through Bratsk and Tayshet back to Irkutsk. Such a rail ring would serve the main interregional and transit flows and would be bisected by the Lake Baykal diameter, with its limited shipping potential. Over the longer term, there will evidently be need for a more effective rail cross-connection than the Baykal shipping route, either within Buryat ASSR (say, along the east shore of the lake or along the route Mogzon—Sosnovo-Ozerskoye—Bagdarin toward the BAM) or within Chita Oblast (say, along the route of the present winter road from Mogocha to Chara). All these north-south routes would pose great engineering problems, but the internal logic of development of the East Siberian territorial production complex will ultimately require that one of them be built. (We might note, incidentally, that the Yenisey regional complex, too, is gradually giving rise to a ring-shaped transport system, once envisaged by V. D. Guseva [4] and conforming to the pattern of economic linkages within the complex: the railroad ring would run from Achinsk north to Abalakovo [the new timber city of Lesosibirsk—Editor], then east toward Boguchany, then southward back to the Trans-Siberian at Nizhnyaya Poyma [Reshoty Station], then to Tayshet, and back to the west via the South Siberian through Abakan to Achinsk. Within this rail ring are two intersecting diameters—the Trans-Siberian Railroad segment Achinsk-Krasnoyarsk-Tayshet, and the north-south Yenisey water route.) The two-stage sequence of transport development within the Irkutsk-Transbaykal complex would correspond to two stages of economic development: the first based on the economic potential already functioning in Irkutsk Oblast, and the second involving greater participation of the southern areas of Transbaykalia in the development of the western segment of the BAM zone.

The interaction between the BAM zone and the Northeast has thus far not been region-shaping and has been largely in one direction. The existing transport routes [both the Lena River route from Ust'-Kut northeastward into Yakutia and the motor road from Never Station on the Trans-Siberian northward into Yakutia—Editor] have served predominantly as supply routes for the Northeast, carrying machinery and industrial equipment, liquid fuels, food and consumer goods into the vast area of the Yakut ASSR. The reverse aspect of the interaction, in the form of the outflow of goods, has been extremely weak. This situation is likely to change significantly in the future. The construction of the north-south rail line from Bam Station on the Trans-Siberian through Tynda to Berkakit, the railhead for the Chul'man coking-coal basin, and its probable northward extention through Tommot to Yakutsk would provide a basis for closer interaction between central and southern Yakutia and the BAM zone; for the foreseeable future, this north-south interaction will not be as great as the east-west interaction, which has traditionally played a far more significant role in the BAM zone. At the very least, however, the extension of the railroad into southern and central Yakutia will foster the development of a local complex within the territory.

The linkages between the southern portion of the Far East and the BAM zone, as has already been suggested in the literature (10), will be affected by the unique economic-geographic situation of the area, primarily its maritime aspect, which is also likely to extend to the eastern segment of the BAM zone. In view of the developed transport network in the southern portion of the Far East (1) and its export orientation, the interaction between this area and the BAM zone should be designed to foster the extraction of resources, beneficiation and primary processing in the BAM zone (Amur Oblast and Khabarovsk Kray), with further processing and preparation for export located in the maritime area. Such an interaction will be promoted by a transport system consisting of the railroad ring (Bam Station—Tynda—Urgal—Komsomol'sk—Volochayevka—Bam Station), with the north-south bisecting line between Izvestkovaya on the Trans-Siberian and Urgal on the BAM, and two outlets to the coast: one to the east (from Komsomol'sk to Vanino and Sovetskaya Gavan'; the other to the south (from Khabarovsk through Ussuriysk to Vladivostok and Nakhodka-Vostochnyy).

The BAM zone, being thus located at the juncture of three major regional structures, will also comprise three geographically distinctive groupings of middle-ranking complexes:

(1) Upper Lena, North Baykal and North Chita subregions within the East Siberian region;

(2) South Yakutian subregion within the Northeast region;

(3) West Amur, Selemdzha-Urgal and Lower Amur subregions within the Far Eastern region.

It must be stressed that all these middle-ranking structures, except for the Lower Amur, are in the initial stages of formation, and can therefore be outlined at the present time only in very general terms.

The *Upper Lena Subregion* encompasses the mountain-tayga rayons of Irkutsk Oblast along the upper course of the Lena River and the Kirenga River as well as the Lower Tunguska (a reserve area for future development). The subregion is rich in forest resources, with timber reserves in the billions of cubic meters. There are also encouraging prospects for oil and gas-condensate finds (11). The resource base thus suggests two basic production chains in the future complex: wood industry and petrochemicals. Design institutes have suggested the establishment of several major timber complexes along the BAM. Ultimately there may also be development of hydroelectric potential along the Kirenga (the Shorokhovo hydro site) and the Lena (the Upper Lena hydro site), but priority needs to be given to thermal heat and power stations for the timber industry (using either Kansk-Achinsk or South Yakutian steam coals).

The *North Baykal Subregion* encompasses the northern half of Buryat ASSR, which offers serious obstacles to economic development because of its mountainous character. The area offers a wide range of mineral resources for commercial development: copper-nickel sulfide ores (Chaya and Dovyren deposits), polymetallic ores (Kholodnaya deposit), chrysolite asbestos (Molodezhnyy deposit), molybdenum, tungsten, graphite, rare metals and nephrite. The subregion is relatively well forested, with a predominance of low-grade larch. Future activities will evidently be associated with the extraction of minerals that are particularly valuable or are short in the Soviet economy, for example, the textile-grade asbestos, with a ready export market, as well as the processing of wood resources (for example, the proposed Vitim timber complex). The Muya basin is suitable for the production of vegetables and fresh milk. The development of the Mok hydro site on the Vitim River may ultimately be cost-effective, but initially both the Upper Lena and North Baykal subregions will be supplied with power from the Ust'-Ilimsk hydroelectric station.

The *North Chita Subregion* will take shape on the right bank of the Vitim River within the northern portion of Chita Oblast. The area poses physical development problems because of mountainous terrain, high seismicity, permafrost and harsh climate. This is the area where copper deposits have been discovered (Udokan and others). The ores in the group of deposits are of high grade and include both sulfates and Noril'sk-type [copper-nickel sulfide] ores requiring different processing technologies. The Udokan deposit, which contains sulfur and various coproducts, will be given priority in development. In view of the harsh physical environment and the relatively high cost of electric power, the local processing of the ore would be limited to extraction and beneficiation, with subsequent refining stages located in areas with cheap electric power (Tayshet or the Yenisey subregion).

The *South Yakutian Subregion* is situated in the basin of the middle Olekma and upper Aldan rivers within the Yakut ASSR. It has mountainous relief and harsh climate. The basis for the future territorial production complex will be the large reserves of South Yakutian coking coal and iron ore (including magnetite). There is a controversial proposal for developing an integrated iron and steel plant in the Chul'man area. Coking coal resources are to be developed for export (the Neryungri strip mine), with steam-grade coals to be used in a minehead thermal power station. Present mica mining is to be expanded in the subregion.

The *West Amur Subregion* covers the western part of Amur Oblast, which is relatively favorable for economic development. The main power source will be the Zeya hydroelectric station, with a designed capacity of 1.3 million kw. Forest

159

resources, with timber reserves of 1.5 billion cubic meters, will serve as the basis for the development of wood-based industry, mainly sawmilling. A major Zeya wood-processing complex is planned. Thus far, pine stands have supplied most of the wood, but, in the future, larch is also expected to be used. Nonferrous metal-ore extraction is another prospect, together with some metalworking and machine manufacture (at Tynda and Zeya). Land reclamation would help increase the local food supply (grains, potatoes, milk and meat).

The *Selemdzha-Urgal Subregion* includes the northeast portion of Amur Oblast (upper reaches of the Selemdzha and Nora rivers) and the western portion of Khabarovsk Kray (upper Bureya River), with a predominance of high elevations (Turan and Bureya mountains). Forests of larch and broadleaf species may support further expansion of logging and wood-processing activities (sawmilling and plywood). The subregion includes the Gar' iron-ore deposit, which may find some commercial use. The Bureya hydro station now under construction will serve as the main source of power supply.

The *Lower Amur Subregion* has been taking shape in the eastern portion of Khabarovsk Kray. Its center, the city of Komsomol'sk, has a population of 246,000. The area is generally favorable for economic development. The structure of the territorial production complex is somewhat intricate, being based both on local and on long-haul resources. Timber reserves of 1.5 billion cubic meters (larch, spruce, broadleaf species) can support a series of wood-based industries, including mechanical and chemical processing and the production of viscose fiber and fabric (the Amursk complex and others). There is also a group of mining activities associated with the extraction of valuable nonferrous metals in short supply in the national economy [particularly tin—Editor]. The future extraction of phosphate rock may provide the basis for a fertilizer industry. The subregion also contains a series of metalworking industries, including a nonintegrated steel plant and the manufacture of transportation and hoisting equipment and electrical engineering goods. An oil refinery in the area now uses Sakhalin crude oil, and may ultimately use Tyumen' oil as well as Vilyuy natural gas (for the production of nitrogenous fertilizers). There are limited prospects for agriculture in the subregion. Greater fertilizer use and land reclamation may help expand the production of vegetables, potatoes and fresh milk. The energy supply of the area is based on the relatively expensive Bureya and Raychikhinsk steam coals so that the development of energy-intensive industry is unlikely. This is true particularly of nonferrous metals refining and petrochemicals.

Bibliography

1. Aleksandrov, Yu. K.; V. V. Kistanov; A. S. Epshteyn. "A quantitative approach to designing a system of economic regions of the USSR," *Izv. AN SSSR, ser. geogr.*, 1974, No. 2 [*Soviet Geography*, November 1974].
2. Belousov, I. I. "Factors in the formation of economic regions," in the book *Geografiya otrasley i rayonov SSSR i zarubezhnykh stran* [Geography of Economic Activities and Regions of the USSR and Foreign Countries]. Moscow Branch of the Geographical Society USSR, 1974.
3. Biryukov, V. "The Baykal-Amur Mainline: a major national construction project," *Planovoye khozyaystvo*, 1974, No. 10 [*Soviet Geography*, April 1975].

4. Guseva, V. D. "Some aspects of the design of the Yenisey regional production complex," *Voprosy geografii*, No. 65, 1964.

5. Kibal'chich, O. A. "Economic and economic-geographic issues of the scientific-technical revolution," in the book *Osobennosti razmeshcheniya khozyaystva v usloviyakh nauchno-tekhnicheskoy revolyutsii* [Peculiarities of Economic Location under the Conditions of Scientific-Technical Revolution]. Moscow Branch of Geographical Society USSR, 1974.

6. Kolosovskiy, N. N. *Osnovy ekonomicheskogo rayonirovaniya* [Fundamentals of Economic Regionalization]. Moscow: Geografgiz, 1958.

7. ————. *Teoriya ekonomicheskogo rayonirovaniya* [Economic Regionalization Theory]. Moscow: Mysl', 1969.

8. Kotov, V., and I. Prostyakov. "Urgent problems in the drafting of the 10th five-year plan," *Planovoye khozyaystvo*, 1974, No. 10.

9. Krotov, V. A. "Economic regionalization of Siberia and the Far East," in the book *Ekonomicheskiye problemy razvitiya Sibiri* [Economic Problems of Siberian Development]. Novosibirsk, 1974.

10. Mayergoyz, I. M. "The unique economic-geographic situation of the Soviet Far East and some problems of using it over the long term," *Vestnik MGU, ser. geogr.*, 1974, No. 4 [*Soviet Geography*, September 1975].

11. Tarasov, G. L. "BAM—a transportation and industrial complex," *Promyshlennyy transport*, 1974, No. 11.

Chapter 8

THE BAM:
PROBLEMS IN APPLIED GEOGRAPHY

Viktor B. Sochava

The construction of the BAM, now under way, is a bold and truly grandiose project. Its implementation requires a great deal of geographical information, both with respect to the zone to be served directly by the railroad and, on a smaller scale and in a different context, with respect to the entire area that will fall within the BAM's economic-geographic zone of influence over the long term.

This brief article has the modest purpose of drawing geographers' attention to those basic problems for which information needs to be collected. At the same time, we would like to stress the most effective and constructive form of such information, namely geographical prediction.

Spatial problems need to be resolved on several levels in connection with the BAM. Of particular importance is the use of geographical information for checking the validity of adopted engineering decisions by inspection [14] or expert appraisal [17]. Such expert appraisals are required for all engineering designs in the BAM zone and should involve the systematic participation of geographers. The experience of the Geographical Society in such practical problems goes back to the end of the 19th century. We might recall the consultation work done by P. P. Semenov-Tyan-Shanskiy, V. L. Komarov and other geographers in the construction of the Trans-Siberian Railroad and its various segments.

Let us first distinguish the immediate service zone and the broader zone of economic-geographic influence of the BAM.

The Service Zone. This zone should include all the rayons [minor civil divisions] that either are crossed by the BAM or are situated in its immediate vicinity. Within the six administrative-economic subdivisions (Irkutsk, Chita and Amur Oblasts, Buryat ASSR, Yakut ASSR and Khabarovsk Kray), there are 43 such rayons. Their combined area is 1.6 million square kilometers; and the width of the zone is 400 to 500 km.

163

The zone has a highly varied environment. It belongs to three physical oblasts (Middle Siberia, Baykal-Dzhugdzhur and Amur-Sakhalin), which, in turn, break down into 26 natural provinces. The diversity of natural conditions is suggested by the physical regionalization of East Siberia [11] and the Far East [13] performed by the Institute of Geography in Irkutsk in the 1960s. This regionalization should now be revised for the BAM project in light of new data. There is a need for identifying homogeneous natural areas within the BAM zone and characterizing them in quantitative terms. Such a revision should make use of a wide range of thematic physical maps, which would be analyzed quantitatively by means of computers.

For general orientation it may be useful to divide the immediate BAM zone into three portions corresponding to the three physical-geographic oblasts: Middle Siberia, Baykal-Dzhugdzhur and Amur-Sakhalin (Fig. 1).

The BAM's Future Economic-Geographic Zone of Influence. This zone can be interpreted in very broad terms, but we will limit ourselves to those spatial industrial and agro-industrial systems that will be organically linked to the BAM. In the south the zone of influence, from Krasnoyarsk to Khabarovsk, would have to extend to the Trans-Siberian, and even farther south since some of the industrial establishments based on raw materials and concentrates from the BAM zone will have to be built in more southerly areas. This is justified by savings in investment, especially in infrastructure, and particularly by more favorable living conditions. The latter aspect deserves particular attention.

The second aspect that determines the linkages between the BAM and adjacent areas is the provision of food for the BAM zone. The Middle Siberian segments and parts of the Amur-Sakhalin segment offer relatively favorable conditions for agriculture. In the west, this is for the most part cultivated land, and in the east, undeveloped virgin land in the southern tayga and partly in mixed broadleaf-needle forest. The BAM will provide prospects for developing the southern tayga and the upper and middle Amur valley farther south. These areas, together with the Zeya-Bureya lowland, would also fall within the BAM's zone of influence. Transverse railroads linking the BAM with the Trans-Siberian, such as Bam—Tynda—Berkakit; Izvestkovaya-Urgal and Volochayevka-Komsomol'sk, will help foster economic linkages between the Amur valley and the BAM zone. To the south of the Yankan-Tukuringra range, as far as the Amur [12], there are large areas of south tayga land with spruce and pine, as well as some birch, that could be converted to cropland without much difficulty. Farm production from these lands might be shipped westward along the Bam-Tynda line, and through Berkakit to the north for the South Yakutian territorial production complex (especially the Chul'man industrial node, now in process of development).

The Amur portion of the zone of influence also offers new prospects for forestry development. The gentle slopes of the east-west ranges in the Yankan-Tukuringra-Dzhagdy system might be afforested at least in their lower third, yielding highly productive timberlands. Connections with the BAM might be handled through Urgal and Tynda, and with the Trans-Siberian through Izvestkovaya and Bam station. The resolution of this problem, especially its geographical aspects, should begin to be given consideration, especially in connection with the amelioration of waterlogged land and measures designed to raise the productivity of

164

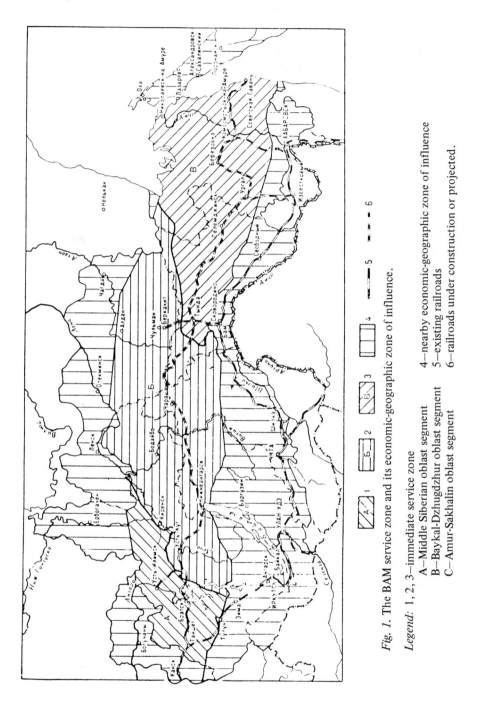

Fig. 1. The BAM service zone and its economic-geographic zone of influence.

Legend: 1, 2, 3—immediate service zone

    A—Middle Siberian oblast segment

    B—Baykal-Dzhugdzhur oblast segment

    C—Amur-Sakhalin oblast segment

4—nearby economic-geographic zone of influence

5—existing railroads

6—railroads under construction or projected.

forest plantings in the Amur mountain tayga. The provisional boundaries of the BAM's zone of economic-geographic influence appear in Fig. 1.

Intermontane Basins and Problems of Development in the BAM Zone. The BAM segment that is most difficult and varied in environmental terms extends from the Lena River to the upper reaches of the Tynda River within the Baykal-Dzhugdzhur physical oblast. Of the six natural provinces to be traversed by the railroad, three contain bare-topped mountains rising to 2,500—2,900 meters or more. The most inaccessible portions of the rail line are to be overcome by means of tunnels (the Baykal and North Muya tunnels in the west, and the Dusse-Alin' tunnel in the east).

The highest portions of the Baykal-Dzhugdzhur oblast also contain clearly defined rift valleys of the Baykal type. They will play a key role fostering settlement in some portions of the railroad; the largest are the Upper Angara valley, the Muya valley and the Upper Chara valley [1, 8, 10].

The relief, soils and surface waters of these intermontane basins favor settlement and the development of private garden plots. The climate of the basins is continental, with cold air masses accumulating in winter, and heating of the air during the brief growing season, with moisture shortages in some places.

The Muya basin drew settlers as early as the 19th century. The Upper Angara basin was one of the potential settlement areas envisaged during the government-sponsored settlement of Siberia in the late 19th and early 20th centuries. The Upper Chara basin served in recent years as the base of operations for the exploration and prospective development of the Udokan copper ore deposit. A comparative study of soils in all three basins has been performed by V. A. Kuz'min [8]. The physical conditions and agricultural potential of the Upper Chara basin have been described by V. S. Mikheyev [10] and by Yu. P. Mikhaylov [9].

The use of the basins for settlement would be a significant development. Geographical research is required to establish the limits of such use and optimal techniques. The scientific principles for developing the mountain tayga basins represent one of the timely problems in the applied geography of East Siberia to which the attention of geographers needs to be drawn. One point that needs to be borne in mind in connection with the use of the intermontane basins is the limited natural ventilation; this leads to the stagnation of cold air in winter and may result in heavy air pollution from industrial emissions.

Therefore an effort must be made to keep air-polluting industrial activities out of the valley bottoms, which happen to provide optimal space for built-up areas and garden plots. This can be done by moving most industries outside the BAM service zone and by locating the essential minimum of industries on the edges of steep-walled valleys, where conditions for air-mass stagnation are generally absent. The whole matter needs to be investigated at an early stage before preparation of the plan for the location of industry in the BAM service zone and the economic-geographic zone of influence.

There is also a danger of overestimating the farm potential of the Baykal-Dzhugdzhur intermontane basins in view of their limited heat supply, the short duration of the growing season, occasional waterlogging and other factors. In the Upper Chara basin, in particular, farming for the Udokan copper mining project will have to be limited to private vegetable gardens and the raising of dairy cattle for dietary needs and for children's institutions. The Muya and Upper Angara basins offer better prospects for crops and livestock, but even so the over-all farm potential is negligible since the combined area of the three basins is only 10,500 km^2 (including useless land).

Particular attention needs to be given to intermontane basins of the Amur-Sakhalin oblast. These basins display temperature inversions all year round; their valley bottoms are cold not only in winter, but in summer; they tend to be waterlogged and often turn into swampy depressions. Conditions are more favorable on alluvial cones at the bottom of the slopes bordering these basins, and that is where settlement and agriculture are concentrated.

Basins of the Amur type at the latitude of the BAM and in tayga regions to the south require reclamation of the moisture and heat regimes of soils. Optimal farming sites are found on slopes.

Avalanches, Ground Ice and Snow Drifting. Ground ice and avalanches represent a serious negative factor in the Baykal-Dzhugdzhur segment of the BAM. Both have posed a problem in the construction and operation of railroads in many parts of the Soviet Union as well as abroad. However the BAM in its middle segment, from the Lena River to the upper reaches of the Tynda, lies in particularly adverse physical-geographic conditions. According to V. R. Alekseyev [2] and other sources, ground ice cover in the Baykal-Dzhugdzhur segment ranges from 1 to 3 percent; the area of some ground-ice fields reaches 4 to 5 km^2, with a length of up to 50 km and a thickness of 7 to 8 meters [3]. At higher elevations, avalanche foci reach a density of five or six per km^2, and avalanches reach a volume of 600,000 m^3 or more. Under such conditions, a clear picture of local ground ice and avalanche conditions in the Baykal-Stanovoy uplands is needed before control measures can be attempted. This requires repeated aerial photography in winter at various stages of ground-ice and avalanche development.

Snow drifting poses a serious threat in the eastern segment of the railroad. It is well known that the lower reaches of the Amur, like Sakhalin, receive a substantial portion of their precipitation in the form of snow; however this problem has not been investigated at the topological [local] level, which is particularly relevant for snow and avalanche control along the BAM.

In general, on the basis of past experience with ground-ice and avalanche control, there is a need for the following types of investigations:

(1) the geographical distribution of avalanches and ground ice; regional patterns of development and any data relating to snow cover in the Lower Amur region;

(2) techniques for evaluating avalanche and ground-ice danger on the basis of aerial and ground observations;

(3) mapping of these phenomena together with the principal causative factors.

Accumulations of snow giving rise to avalanches and drifts are closely related to the winter monsoon from the Pacific; it manifests itself at low elevations as far inland as Urgal, and at higher elevations farther west toward Lake Baykal. The Pacific monsoon has not been adequately studied, especially at the latitude of the BAM. Detailed investigation should be a basic task for geographical and dynamic climatology.

At the same time, work should begin on ground-ice and avalanche studies from the point of view of the dynamics of development and possible preventive measures. This will require snow-cover studies, investigations of the conditions of snow crystallization and its various causative factors, a task to be assigned to geographical field stations along the BAM with staffs of snow-cover experts.

These field stations will yield research results only after some time. An immediate problem is the organization of an avalanche service that would seek to predict possible danger periods so that avalanches might be artificially released by bombardment or blasting. In some cases, avalanches may have to be controlled by engineering structures.

All the operations should be based on geographical information being collected by Siberian geographers. This work needs to be expanded and accelerated.

Cartographic Program. Thematic maps of varying content are needed both for the immediate service zone of the BAM and for its future zone of economic-geographic influence. The particular themes of maps will, of course, differ in the two areas [16].

Of particular significance for the BAM zone are so-called correlation maps, showing not only the spatial distribution of a particular phenomenon, but its relationship to major factors. An example might be a map of homogeneous vegetation areas together with certain heat parameters, dryness indices, etc. Such maps are needed not only for an understanding of the present situation, but for prediction in cases where a particular factor may change through time. Such a series of thematic correlation maps might include one showing the relationship between plant cover and heat supply, with isolines representing temperature sums (the sum of temperatures for the period in which the daily mean is above 10°C). This index may be somewhat arbitrary for mountain landscapes, but it will reflect the general situation. The temperature sum, in turn, corresponds to a certain dryness index, to a limited range of biomass productivity and a particular vegetation invariant (in this case, the native vegetation together with all its variable states).

Similar thematic maps need to be compiled for other phenomena to reflect the relevant relationships. Such an approach, judging from the French experience in thematic mapping, is particularly promising in the case of socio-economic maps.

The above-mentioned vegetation map would clearly reflect the heat supply in various segments of the BAM zone. Areas with a moderate heat supply (temperature sums of 1600 to 2000°C) would include part of the Middle Siberian segment (the Angara and Lena river basins) and a large area in the Amur basin. In the Amur-Sakhalin segment, plateaus and high plains with an adequate heat supply represent potential agricultural land, with potential timberland in low mountain areas. A high spontaneous phytomass productivity (7.5 tons per hectare) occurs only on the left bank of the Amur near Komsomol'sk, and to the south.

The implementation of practical measures will, of course, also require correlation maps at larger scales; these will require additional field work on climate and vegetation by Siberian geographers.

An important aid for the resolution of BAM problems will be the Landscape Map of Eastern Siberia, which will include the East Siberian portion of the BAM (without the Far East) and will provide information on a wide range of natural conditions.

All the maps in the BAM program should be so designed that a comparison of two or more maps will yield additional engineering, economic and resource information not shown on any one map alone. This will require comparability of both maps and legends.

We want to stress, in particular, the need for predictive maps showing potential environmental modification under the impact of human activity and resource use as well as maps suggesting the spatial organization of production over the long term [15].

Natural Regimes and Geographical Experimentation. One of the problems in the BAM zone will be optimization of the natural environment for human life and working conditions and an increase in the productivity of forest and pasture and in the fertility of cropland. All this calls for accurate information on natural regimes under various local conditions. Furthermore, environmental modification in the course of development, starting with the actual construction of the railroad, calls for an understanding of the resulting dynamic processes. Natural regimes and the dynamics of natural phenomena lie at the basis of rational prediction.

Siberian geographers have long been aware of this, and the Institute of Geography in Irkutsk has been operating geographical field stations in various parts of Siberia, some of them continuously for 12 years [17]. However these stations do not reflect natural conditions in the BAM zone and we face the need for setting up additional stations there.

The operation of such field stations requires both funds and personnel. University departments of geography and nature conservation can play a useful role in training people.

Wherever possible, experimental field work and long-term field observations should be combined with nature conservation in specially designated test sites and reserves. Natural regimes should also be studied within the two state nature reserves along the BAM—the Barguzin and Zeya reserves.

Priority in setting up a new geographical field station should evidently be given to the Upper Chara basin, where population is likely to grow, agriculture may be expanded and the environment is faced with the greatest threat from mining activities.

The program of activities of such a field station is a highly complex issue that requires separate discussion; we only want to stress that such a program must conform to modern requirements for geographical experimentation and be implemented by trained geographers of different specialties. The work of the various disciplines would be integrated by the technique of so-called complex ordination [17].

The Problem of Population Growth. The principal population components will be: (1) railroad personnel settled along the BAM and its connecting lines; (2) population in mining districts; (3) population in lumbering areas.

The BAM will have a total of 200 stations and sidings, including divisional stations and freight yards with open and covered loading areas. Provision will be made for all the usual facilities associated with the operation of a railroad. All this will require a large labor force, representing together with their families tens of thousands of people. They are to be accommodated in properly built settlements with services, cultural and medical facilities.

The population involved directly in the operation of the railroad should, of course, be as stable as possible, and this might be achieved in two possible ways: (1) the settling of construction workers who have proved themselves over the years and have adapted to local conditions; (2) the transfer to the BAM of railroad workers from the Trans-Baykal segment of the Trans-Siberian, where environmental conditions are somewhat similar to those along the BAM. This problem should be studied at an early stage with the participation of population geographers.

Another approach will be required in providing a labor force for the new mining districts. The most difficult problem will be the development of the Udokan copper deposit and the South Yakutian coal and iron ore deposits, where large industrial centers with populations of tens of thousands are to be built.

The Udokan mine and concentrator will require about 6,000 workers, or a population of 20,000, together with families. There is, first of all, the problem of an optimal site for this facility so that air and water pollution by industrial wastes can be minimized. The project site should provide optimal living conditions, and this may require locating it at some distance from the actual raw-material source. It is easier to move raw material to an industrial establishment some distance away than to protect a sensitive natural environment against deterioration from industrial wastes. We therefore welcome the proposed siting of the copper-chemical plant based on Udokan ore outside the immediate BAM railroad zone.

The peopling the new lumbering areas should begin in more or less productive timberlands situated near transport lines. There will be a need for lumbering settlements, railroad settlements and other types of populated places associated with forest industries. Lumbering settlements tend to be widely scattered and mobile. They usually deplete timberlands over a period of 10 to 20 years, and the lumbering operations then move on to new areas. This form of settlement, which is customary in Siberian forest industries, will be cominant in the BAM zone in the early stages.

However, if we take a long-term view, there will also be a need for permanent forest-industry settlements serving areas in which lumbering operations would be adjusted to natural growth rates. Such permanent settlement, which is more rational than the other approach, may be feasible in the western segment of the BAM zone as well as in Amur Oblast and Khabarovsk Kray.

Another population group that merits attention is the one engaged in hunting and reindeer raising. It would be in the interests of the BAM project and of the entire zone to stimulate the rate of natural increase within this population group and to improve its living and working conditions. Hunters' and reindeer herders' settlements in the immediate vicinity of the BAM should be moved deeper into the hinterland of the respective rayons. Such a resettlement program should be carried out in close consultation with population geographers and an effort should be made to render it as painless as possible.

A great deal of work will have to be done in the entire field of population geography, including the population pattern of present settlements, the mapping of functional types of places and so forth [4, 5]. Particular attention needs to be given to settlement patterns within individual collective and state farms, the arrangement of populated places, types of land, industrial establishments and so on.

The Hunting Economy and Reindeer Herding. The BAM is envisioned as a transport artery of the first category, with a high level of technology and automatic traffic controls as well as modern facilities covering all aspects of railroad operation. Many industrial establishments in the outer zone of economic-geographic influence are also being designed on an advanced technical level.

Under such conditions, it may sound odd for us to be concerned with the age-old activities of the Siberian aborigenes, hunting and reindeer herding, which in the view of some are bound to decline in any event.

As a matter of fact, disregard for the significance of the hunting and reindeer economy in the East Siberian and Amur tayga may have highly undesirable consequences.

Furs have been and will continue to be a key Soviet export item, and have also been in increasingly short supply on the domestic market. The basis of the hunting and trapping economy in the western and central portions of the BAM zone are sable, squirrel and muskrat and, among ungulates, the musk deer, roe deer, reindeer, red deer and elk. The removal of the huge BAM zone from the fur-trapping economy and the extermination of ungulates in the area cannot be tolerated. The development of the tayga must be accompanied by a strict hunting regime and the protection of hunting grounds. These should be not only strictly protected, but improved wherever possible. To preserve game animals is not enough; game resources should be further enriched. Poaching and the violation of hunting regulations in the BAM zone must be absolutely prohibited [6].

To be specific, we might cite the following example: In the Upper Angara country, where a segment of the BAM is already under construction, animals have had a virtually undisturbed haven along the Kichera River and on two tributaries of the Upper Angara, the Katera and the Churo. Natural spawning grounds insured the reproduction of the North Baykal schools of the omul [a whitefish]. Water fowl nest in the area, including ducks, swans, cranes and geese. The area is now being invaded by people, not all of whom are able to respect the tayga and its denizens. The problem of nature conservation and enforcement of hunting rules therefore becomes particularly timely.

Sport hunting and fishing will have to be regulated around the principal settlements along the BAM. This applies particularly to the settlements of Kunerma, Severobaykal'sk, Chara, Tynda, Zeysk, Urgal and Berezovka, and other places that are likely to grow in population. Around such places, in keeping with the way of life of the East Siberian tayga, there will be great demand for hunting and fishing both as a form of recreation and as a sport.

These pressures will soon overcome the natural capacity of the environment for reproduction and will necessitate measures to maintain animal numbers at a given level.

The Soviet Union does not have much experience in regulating sport hunting and fishing, and might well use foreign experience in this respect. It seems to me that the BAM zone with its proposed high level of economic development might well serve as a testing ground for preserving animal populations not only for commercial hunting purposes, but also for recreational and sport purposes.

A particular effort should be made to maintain reindeer numbers. Reindeer have been virtually irreplaceable as pack animals for geological and survey parties in the BAM zone; helicopters can perform such a role only to some extent. It is therefore crucial that reindeer herds be strengthened and that the number of pack animals be increased. The particular type of reindeer economy would, of course, have to conform to the new conditions in the BAM zone.

It must be remembered that historically reindeer have been used as pack animals throughout the BAM zone, from the North Baykal country to the basin of the Tumnin River, which flows to the Tatar Strait.

Protection of the Environment, Resources and Natural Monuments. Environmental pollution may result from industrial activity and from failure to observe lumbering regulations. Industry in the BAM zone is being created from scratch; the structure of industrial establishments and their technology, including waste and emission treatment systems, are still in the design stage. In view of the specific conditions of the BAM zone, industrial designs should be subjected to particularly careful geographical appraisal. Such an appraisal cannot be left to the design institutes themselves; it requires special forms of organization within the BAM zone as a whole.

As for conservation measures, these should be provided for as part of the resource development plan and its technology.

Forest conservation is cause for the greatest concern. Care will have to be taken to preserve forest stands for water and soil conservation, and this applies to most of the forests in the Baykal-Dzhugdzhur segment of the BAM. As for the technology needed in mountain lumbering operations, this is already available. The problem is to observe existing regulations.

One organizational problem is in order at this point. Care must be taken not to "decentralize" lumbering operations because decentralization makes supervision more difficult. It might be useful to establish a unified Administration for Timber and Forest Products Industries in the BAM zone, with responsibility both for lumbering and for forest conservation.

172

Industrial establishments are the principal water polluters. If most of these will be located outside the intermontane basins, half the battle will be won. A second source of pollution are the household wastes of settlements, which, as it happens, are to be located in the intermontane basins. In this case, rules of sanitation will have to be enforced, providing for treatment facilities, including biological techniques.

No regulations will protect the environment against damage from unforeseen, but more or less probable causes, such as forest fires. The most modern techniques will have to be used in this case. A firefighting service equipped with reconnaissance planes will be required in the entire BAM zone, with particular attention to areas around construction sites.

The development of the BAM zone will inevitably result in modification of the original environment. Yet any measures aiming at optimization of the environment will have to be based on the existing structure and regime of the indigenous landscape. Hence there will be a need for preserving some undisturbed areas for control purposes. The issue has already been raised in the Scientific Council on Tayga Development (Siberian Division of the Academy of Sciences USSR) with respect to all of Siberia and the Far East. At that time, only two control sites were proposed for the BAM zone—in the Chul'man area and in the Tukuringra mountain range. This is clearly inadequate in light of the BAM project, and we should work out a more detailed plan for a whole network of control sites, with particular emphasis on the Baykal-Dzhugdzhur segment of the railroad, an area of high mountains and the timberline, with Far Eastern spruce, Erman's birch, alpine meadows and associated facies. A total of 36 small glaciers with a highly distinctive regime have already been identified. All these geosystems must be preserved as natural monuments. Sometime in the future, when comfortable passenger trains will travel along the BAM, this area might well be turned into a natural park of worldwide significance.

The ranges of the Stanovoy upland are continental Alpine mountains with distinctive forms of glaciation and landforms that reflect "live tectonics" and a distinctive Quaternary history. In many respects they might be regarded as antipodes of the European Alps. The fauna and flora of these uplands contain species that are highly unusual both in ecology and in their geographical linkages.

This "museum of nature" and, at the same time, a laboratory for field work will be easily accessible for investigators and tourists from several stations along the Baykal-Amur Mainline.

Geographical Prediction and Expert Appraisal. The need for geographical prediction in the opening up of new areas is now beyond question. Any measure involving the construction of the BAM and the opening up of adjacent areas inevitably involves environmental modification that needs to be anticipated. The predictive element should be part of any engineering design, and the role of geographical expert appraisals is to insure that this rule is implemented.

In addition, as construction proceeds, there is need for forecasts of possible avalanche danger, of the deformation of the subsoil as a result of permafrost processes and other natural processes related to particular types of construction or human impacts on the environment. Even though almost every engineering design is accompanied by a special-purpose prediction, this is still inadequate.

173

The natural environment tends to change as an entity, as a system of blocks subjected to human impact. A geographical forecast is supposed to provide an integral picture of the geographical systems of the future in light of all the possible changes that can be predicted within the study period [15].

Geographical prediction in this sense (providing a picture of the geosystems of the future) has now become the principal task of Siberian and Far Eastern geographers. At the present time we can offer only preliminary, incomplete forecasts since we do not know the totality of factors that man is likely to introduce into the environment in the course of the construction of the BAM and the development of the BAM zone.

A report on geographical prediction would, of course, consist of textual material and of illustrations, but the basic predictive documents will be maps of future geosystems and explanatory thematic maps.

Geographical prediction and the mapping of the BAM zone thus need to be merged into a single study program for geography research centers.

Almost everything in the BAM zone is being created from scratch. Prognostication thus assumes particular significance since all the positive recommendations of such a forecast are likely to be implemented in the course of development. As for negative aspects, there is still time to prevent them.

The various problems we have examined here relate to the field of applied geography; some of them may seem to be commonplace in economic management. However, all of them require a sound geographical approach, based on the concept of geosystems. Geosystems theory, including its Siberian and Far Eastern aspects, should therefore be further expanded both in research centers and in university departments. The importance of the systems concept in geography has probably never been so clear as it has now become. We are always acutely aware of this when we deal with geographers' potential contributions to the resolution of major economic development problems.

Bibliography

1. Aleksandrova, T. D., and V. S. Preobrazhenskiy. *Landshafty malykh kotlovin gornoy taygi* [Landscapes of Small Intermontane Basins in the Mountain Tayga]. Moscow-Leningrad, 1964.
2. Alekseyev, V. R. "Ground ice in Siberia and the Far East," in *Sib. geogr. sb.*, No. 8. Novosibirsk, 1974.
3. ———— and A. T. Naprasnikov. "Estimates of the avalanche danger in the Udokan Mountains of northern Transbaykalia," in *Sib. geogr. sb.*, No. 7. Leningrad, 1971.
4. *Geograficheskiye aspekty osvoyeniya tayezhnykh territoriy Sibiri* [Geographical Aspects of the Development of Siberia's Tayga Areas]. Irkutsk, 1966.
5. *Geografiya naseleniya Vostochnoy Sibiri* [Population Geography of Eastern Siberia]. Moscow, 1962.
6. Danilov, D. N. *Novoye v okhotnich'yem khozyaystve* [New Trends in the Hunting and Trapping Economy]. Moscow, 1972.
7. Kosmachev, K. P. "Problems of economic-geographic expert appraisal of the data base of the spatial organization of production," *Dokl. Inst. geogr. Sib. i DV.*, No. 45, 1974.

8. Kuz'min, V. A. "The soil resources of intermontane basins in the Stanovoy upland," in *Zemel'nyye resursy Sibiri* [Siberia's Land Resources]. Novosibirsk, 1974.

9. Mikhaylov, Yu. P. "An appraisal of the environment of the Chara basin for purposes of truck-produce farming," in *Geograficheskiye aspekty. . .*, op. cit.

10. Mikheyev, V. S. *Verkhne-Charskaya kotlovina. Opyt topologicheskogo izucheniya landshafta* [The Upper Chara Basin; a Landscape Study at the Topological Level]. Novosibirsk, 1974.

11. Ryashin, V. A. and V. S. Mikheyev. "Physical-geographic regionalization of new development areas (with particular reference to the south of East Siberia)," *Dokl. Inst. geogr. Sib. i DV.*, No. 21, 1969.

12. Sochava, V. B. "Zonal features of plant cover in the area between the Tukuringra Mountains and the Amur River," *Bot. zhurn.*, Vol. 42, No. 2, 1957.

13. ————. *Prirodnoye rayonirovaniye Dal'nego Vostoka* [Natural Regionalization of the Far East]. Irkutsk, 1962.

14. ————. "Searching for new forms of organization of applied geography work," in *Prikladnaya geografiya* [Applied Geography], conference proceedings. Irkutsk, 1966.

15. ————. "Prognostication, a key research area in modern geography," *Dokl. Inst. geogr., Sib. i DV.*, No. 43, 1974.

16. ————; V. P. Shotskiy and I. I. Buks. "The BAM alignment and some problems for further investigation," *Dokl. Inst. geogr., Sib. i DV.*, No. 46, 1975.

17. *Topologicheskiye aspekty ucheniya o geosistemakh* [Topological Aspects of Geosystems Theory]. Novosibirsk, 1974.

18. Chernoyarova, A. A. *Muyskaya dolina (priroda, lyudi, khozyaystvo)* [The Muya Valley; Environments, People and Economy]. Ulan-Ude, 1966.

Appendix

PRINCIPAL PLACES ALONG THE BAM

Place*	Urban Status	Year	1976 Population	Economic Function
Tayshet—Ust'-Kut segment[1]				
Tayshet	city	1938	35,000	transport
Oktyabr'skiy (Sosnovyye Rodniki)	settlement	1955		timber
Chunskiy (Chuna)	settlement	1955		timber
Vikhorevka	settlement city	1957 1966	19,000	
Chekanovskiy (Anzeba)	settlement	1960		aluminum
Bratsk	settlement city	1953 1955	195,000	hydropower woodpulp
Osinovka (Gidrostroitel')	settlement	1960		
Vidim	settlement	1963		

*Rail station name in parentheses.
[1] Completed in 1954.

177

Place*	Urban Status	Year	1976 Population	Economic Function
Tayshet–Ust'-Kut segment (cont'd)				
Shestakovo (Zatoplyayemaya)	settlement	1956		
Zheleznogorsk-Ilimskiy (Korshunikha)	settlement city	1958 1965	27,000	iron-ore mining
Khrebtovaya	settlement	1967		RR junction
Ust'-Kut	settlement city	1943 1954	38,000	
Osetrovo (Lena)	settlement (inc. into Ust'-Kut, 1954)	1938		Lena River port
Ust'-Kut–Komsomol'sk segment[2]				
Zvezdnyy (Tayura)	settlement	1974	5,000	
Niya				
Nebel'				
Magistral'nyy (Kirenga)	settlement	1975	4,500	Kirenga River port
Ul'kan	settlement	1976		
Kunerma				
(Baykal Range tunnel)				
Severobaykal'sk (Nizhneangarsk I)	settlement	1975		Lake Baykal port
Nizhneangarsk (Nizhneangarsk II)	settlement	1938		
Kichera				
Chencha (Angoya)				

*Rail station name in parentheses.
[2] Under construction 1974–83.

Place*	Urban Status	Year	1976 Population	Economic Function
Ust'-Kut–Komsomol'sk segment (cont'd)				
Uoyan	settlement	1976		
Yanchukan				
(North Muya tunnel)				
Muyakan				
Lapro				
Taksimo				base for Molodezhnyy asbestos development
Vitim				Vitim River crossing
Kuanda				
Syul'ban				
Leprindo				
Chara				base for Udokan copper development
Ikab'ya				
Khani				
Vel'betkan				
Olekma				
Ust'-Nyukzha				
Dyugabul'				
Chil'chi				
Lopcha				
Larba				
Khorogochi				
(Lena-Amur divide)				

*Rail station name in parentheses.

Place*	Urban Status	Year	1976 Population	Economic Function
Ust'-Kut−Komsomol'sk segment (cont'd)				
Kuvykta				
Tynda	settlement city	1941 1975	30,000	RR center
Sivachkan				RR junction
Dzhalingra				
Marevaya				
Dipkun				
Tutaul				
Baralus				
Zeysk				Zeya River port
Izhak				
Tungala				
Dugda				
Meunchik				
Fevral'sk				Selemdzha River crossing
Fed'kin Klyuch				
Eterkan				
Alonka				
Ust'-Urgal (Urgal II)				RR junction
Urgal (Urgal II)	settlement	1974		RR junction
Soloni				
(Dusse-Alin' tunnel)				

*Rail station name in parentheses.

Place*	Urban Status	Year	1976 Population	Economic Function

Ust'-Kut–Komsomol'sk segment (cont'd)

Place*	Urban Status	Year	1976 Population	Economic Function
Suluk				
Gerbi				
Dzhamku				
Amgun'				
Berezovka				lumbering
Duki				
Evoron				
Gorin				
Khurmuli				
Komsomol'sk	city	1932	246,000	Amur River port RR junction multifunctional manufacturing

Komsomol'sk–Sovetskaya Gavan' segment[3]

Place*	Urban Status	Year	1976 Population	Economic Function
Pivan	settlement	1954		
Gurskoye (Khungari until 1972)	Settlement	1949		
Vysokogornyy	settlement	1949		
Vanino	settlement	1958	15,000	Pacific port
Oktyabr'skiy (Sovetskaya Gavan'- Sortirovochnaya)	settlement	1959		RR yards
Sovetskaya Gavan'	city	1941	31,000	shipyards fish processing sawmilling

*Rail station name in parentheses.
[3]Completed 1945.

Place*	Urban Status	Year	1976 Population	Economic Function
Little BAM; Bam-Tynda;[4] *Tynda-Berkakit*[5]				
Bam				RR junction on Trans-Siberian
Murtygit				
Yankan				
Belen'kaya				timber center
Tynda	settlement city	1941 1975	30,000	BAM RR center
Sivachkan				RR junction
Mogot				
Nagornyy	settlement	1941		
Zolotinka				
Berkakit	settlement	1977		
Neryungri	settlement city	1972 1975	11,000	coking-coal mine

*Rail station name in parentheses.
[4] Completed 1975.
[5] Due in 1977.

INDEX

185

187